BASIC TEXTS IN COUNSELLING
AND PSYCHOTHERAPY

Series editor: Stephen Frosh

This series introduces readers to the theory and practice of counselling and psychotherapy across a wide range of topic areas. The books appeal to anyone wishing to use counselling and psychotherapeutic skills and are particularly relevant to workers in health, education, social work and related settings. The books are unusual in being rooted in psychodynamic and systemic ideas, yet being written at an accessible, readable and introductory level. Each text offers theoretical background and guidance for practice, with creative use of clinical examples.

Published

Jenny Altschuler
WORKING WITH CHRONIC ILLNESS

Bill Barnes, Sheila Ernst and Keith Hyde
AN INTRODUCTION TO GROUPWORK

Stephen Briggs
WORKING WITH ADOLESCENTS AND YOUNG ADULTS 2nd Edition

Alex Coren
SHORT-TERM PSYCHOTHERAPY 2nd Edition

Jim Crawley and Jan Grant
COUPLE THERAPY

Emilia Dowling and Gill Gorell Barnes
WORKING WITH CHILDREN AND PARENTS THROUGH SEPARATION AND DIVORCE

Loretta Franklin
AN INTRODUCTION TO WORKPLACE COUNSELLING

Gill Gorell Barnes
FAMILY THERAPY IN CHANGING TIMES 2nd Edition

Fran Hedges
AN INTRODUCTION TO SYSTEMATIC THERAPY WITH INDIVIDUALS

Sally Hodges
COUNSELLING ADULTS WITH LEARNING DISABILITIES

Linda Hopper
COUNSELLING AND PSYCHOTHERAPY WITH CHILDREN AND ADOLESCENTS

Sue Kegerreis
PSYCHODYNAMIC COUNSELLING WITH CHILDREN AND YOUNG PEOPLE

Ravi Rana
COUNSELLING STUDENTS

Tricia Scott
INTEGRATIVE PSYCHOTHERAPY IN HEALTHCARE

Geraldine Shipton
WORKING WITH EATING DISORDERS

Laurence Spurling
AN INTRODUCTION TO PSYCHODYNAMIC COUNSELLING 2nd Edition

Paul Terry
COUNSELLING AND PSYCHOTHERAPY WITH OLDER PEOPLE 2nd Edition

Jan Wiener and Mannie Sher
COUNSELLING AND PSYCHOTHERAPY IN PRIMARY HEALTH CARE

Shula Wilson
DISABILITY, COUNSELLING AND PSYCHOTHERAPY

Steven Walker
CULTURALLY COMPETENT THERAPY

Jessica Yakeley
WORKING WITH VIOLENCE

Invitation to authors

The Series Editor welcomes proposals for new books within the Basic Texts in Counselling and Psychotherapy series. These should be sent to Stephen Frosh at the School of Psychology, Birkbeck College, Malet Street, London, WC1E 7HX (e-mail s.frosh@bbk.ac.uk)

Basic Texts in Counselling and Psychotherapy
Series Standing Order ISBN 0–333–69330–2
(*outside North America only*)

You can receive future titles in this series as they are published by placing a standing order. Please contact your bookseller or, in case of difficulty, write to us at the address below with your name and address, the title of the series and the ISBN quoted above.

Customer Services Department, Macmillan Distribution Ltd, Houndmills, Basingstoke, Hampshire RG21 6XS, England

WORKING WITH VIOLENCE

A Contemporary Psychoanalytic Approach

JESSICA YAKELEY

First published 2010 by
PALGRAVE MACMILLAN

Palgrave Macmillan in the UK is an imprint of Macmillan Publishers Limited,
registered in England, company number 785998, of Houndmills, Basingstoke,
Hampshire RG21 6XS.

Palgrave Macmillan in the US is a division of St Martin's Press LLC,
175 Fifth Avenue, New York, NY 10010.

Palgrave Macmillan is the global academic imprint of the above companies
and has companies and representatives throughout the world.

Palgrave® and Macmillan® are registered trademarks in the United States,
the United Kingdom, Europe and other countries.

ISBN-13: 978–0–230–20363–1

This book is printed on paper suitable for recycling and made from fully
managed and sustained forest sources. Logging, pulping and manufacturing
processes are expected to conform to the environmental regulations of the
country of origin.

A catalogue record for this book is available from the British Library.

A catalog record for this book is available from the Library of Congress.

10   9   8   7   6   5   4   3   2   1
19 18 17 16 15 14 13 12 11 10

Printed and bound in Great Britain by
CPI Antony Rowe, Chippenham and Eastbourne

CONTENTS

Foreword by Stanley Ruszczynski   viii

Acknowledgements   xi

Introduction   1

1 **Violence: Psychoanalytic Perspectives**   7
   A psychoanalytic history of aggression   8
   Definitions of violence   10
   Different forms of violence   11
   Attachment, trauma and loss   13
   Mentalization   14
   The internal object world, the role of the father
      and superego   16
   The role of phantasy   19
   Defence mechanisms and defensive systems   20
   The external setting and situational factors   22
   Towards a multi-dimensional framework   24
   Summary   25

2 **Violence, Mental Illness and Personality Disorder**   26
   Diagnostic classifications   27
   Personality disorder   29
   Psychosis   33
   Summary   39

3 **Psychopathy**   41
   Historical conceptions of psychopathy   41
   Definitions of psychopathy and the Hare
      Psychopathy Checklist   43

Developmental origins and the internal world
   of the psychopath 44
Personality organisation 45
Failures of internalisation 45
Internal object relations and the grandiose self 46
The psychopathic superego 48
Countertransference reactions 50
Psychopathic violence 51
Psychopathic breakdown and the fallacy
   of dual diagnosis 52
Summary 54

4 **Violence, Sexuality and Perversion** 56

Definitions of perversion 57
Polymorphous perversion 59
Perversion as a defence against castration anxiety 60
The erotic form of hatred 62
A defence against generational and sexual
   difference – the facts of life 65
Summary 67

5 **Violent Women** 68

Violence against the body 69
Infanticide 74
Munchausen's Syndrome by Proxy 77
Domestic violence 80
Summary 82

6 **Violence and Society, Race and Culture** 84

Group violence 84
Racism and violence 87
Dehumanisation, genocide and terrorism 93
Summary 96

7 **A Psychoanalytic Approach to Risk Assessment** 97

Models of risk 98
Subjectivity 100
Violence as communication 101
Countertransference 102
Transference and the index offence 106

Towards a psychoanalytic risk formulation
   and framework 110
Summary 113

8 **Working in Medium and High Security Settings**   **114**
Containment 114
The sick and fragmented institution 116
Treating the institution 118
Working in prisons 123
Summary 125

9 **Individual Psychoanalytic Psychotherapy for
Violent Patients**   **127**
Assessing the violent patient 129
The setting 134
Engaging the patient 135
Transference and countertransference 140
Mourning and working through 145
Summary 149

10 **Group-Analytic Psychotherapy for Violence**   **150**
Selection for group-analytic psychotherapy 151
The group process 153
The setting, group 'rules' and boundaries 155
Transference and defence 157
Endings and beginnings 161
Summary 163

11 **Working with the Wider Professional Network**   **164**
Confidentiality 165
Multi-Agency Public Protection Arrangements 168
Working with the courts 172
Summary 176

Glossary 178

References 189

Index 204

FOREWORD

The issue of violence in its various guises predominates in many of our contemporary discussions, debates and concerns. In the social domain, there are fears about violence in the streets, especially, most recently, among young people engaged in gun and knife crime. In the political domain, we feel threatened by terrorism and loss of life in military conflict. And in both the mental health services and the criminal justice system, there are major concerns about how to manage, contain and offer appropriate treatment to the anti-social patient or offender, whether he or she is delinquent, criminal or violent, or acting on cruel or harmful sexual impulses.

It is a matter of debate as to whether objectively there is more violence in our contemporary world than in the past. What appears to be indisputable is our general sense that we now live in a world where, both in our local communities and on the international stage, violence seems to be more widespread. It is almost certainly the case that the more we know about violence and abuse, whatever its actual prevalence, the more violated, abused and disturbed we feel. For one of the results of violence is to produce fear and a sense of violation. Terrorists, of course, often act from this very position, but it is no less true, though usually less conscious, in other perpetrators of violent and anti-social behaviour.

Acts of violence, whether carried out physically on another's body, perpetrated through emotional abuse or directed at the self, such as in self harming or suicidal behaviour, inevitably have an impact not only on the victim but also on those who read or hear about them in the media, or witness them directly. Clearly, there are times when such acts of violence are extremely disturbing and even defy us to dwell on them. The emotional impact often arouses very difficult feelings in us – whether of fear, anger or vengeful hatred. It is hard not to think that the provocation of very frightened and disturbing feelings in someone else is not somehow central to the violent act. These feelings inevitably poison the mind of the victim but also of those who come to know about the violation. There is then a danger that the object of our fear, hatred and vengefulness is demonised to the detriment of their essential humanity. We find it difficult to think properly about the perpetrator, possible causes of the violence, its meaning and ways in which it might best be responded to. Acts of violence can then more often lead to counter-acts of vengeance, retaliation and punishment, leading to the marginalisation of the perpetrator.

However, in the context of our apparently increasingly violent world, there has been, both in the mental health services and in the criminal justice system, an attempt to respond differently to patients and violent offenders. In the not too distant past, there used to be a rather simplistic differentiation between 'the mad' and 'the bad'. 'The mad' were dealt with by psychiatric services and 'the bad' were left to be contained and/or punished by the criminal justice system. Though with some clear ambivalence – the prison population has risen dramatically in recent years and many psychiatric hospitals and asylums were closed before proper alternatives were put in place – there is now an attempt in both the mental health and criminal justice systems to think differently about the perpetrators of violence and of other anti-social acts. Rather than simply respond with punishment or control, there is a concerted effort to design services which try to offer not just some constraint, punishment and risk management but actual treatment which might result in certain patients and offenders becoming less likely in the future to behave in an anti-social way. Inherent in this development is the important requirement of establishing sophisticated measures of risk and dangerousness.

It is vital to develop some understanding about violence and other anti-social acts in order to design and implement these services. This statement alone implies that the violent act may come to be understood as having a meaning and purpose which can perhaps come to be known. It is likely that this purpose and meaning is not consciously known to the perpetrator and has been expressed in a distorted way through the anti-social action. Much delinquent, criminal, violent and sexually abusive activity is consciously and unconsciously driven by hatred, vulnerability and fear and also by a – sometimes conscious and sometimes unconscious – conviction that the best way to avoid being abused and violated is to create an abused and violated other in the person of their victim.

In this invaluable book, the author traces how psychoanalysis as a theory of the development of the mind has increasingly offered

ways of thinking about violence and, as a result, ways of offering treatment to the perpetrators of violence. I am not suggesting
that psychoanalytic theory has all the answers: something which is
enacted is always likely to defy anything approaching full understanding; equally, something as complex as violence is unlikely to be
understood by just one theoretical framework.

Perhaps the fundamental value of the psychoanalytic approach
is that it holds fast to the idea that the violent act has a meaning
which may never come to be known fully, and at the same time
appreciates that a curiosity and concern about that possible meaning might begin to change the relationship between the perpetrator
and his or her actions. The clinical practitioner, who is able to adopt
a stance of curiosity, interest and enquiry, may, in their thoughtfulness and reflection, offer the kernel of an alternative behaviour for
the perpetrator of violence. Taking such a stance requires a theoretical structure which this text provides in a thoughtful, concise and
helpful way. Jessica Yakeley is realistic enough in her exposition to
be clear that, in the attempt to offer reflection and understanding of
violence, the issue of risk and assessment of dangerousness is crucial.

Getting the balance right between the care offered in the thoughtful clinical stance and the control inherent in the assessment and
appropriate management of risk offers some perpetrators of violent
and other anti-social acts a robust framework within which they can
perhaps begin to move away from violent actions towards the beginning of reflection and the painful understanding of some reasons
why they are compelled to create fear, pain and rage in their victims.

Stanley Ruszczynski
Director, Portman Clinic
Tavistock and Portman NHS Foundation Trust

ACKNOWLEDGEMENTS

The source of many of the ideas in the book comes from the experience of working with patients at the Portman Clinic and what I have learnt and continue to learn from my colleagues there, who offer a wealth of clinical experience and inspiration for this fascinating and challenging work. I am grateful to Don Campbell, Richard Davies, Sira Dermen, Rob Hale, Dorothy Lloyd-Owen, Estela Welldon and many others for their collective wisdom accumulated over many years, and to my present colleagues, particularly Stephen Blumenthal, Judy Freedman, Carine Minne, Stan Ruszczynski and Heather Wood, whose ideas I expand in this book. I am also grateful to my psychoanalytic colleagues with whom I trained and who continue to provide fora in which psychoanalytic work and ideas can be explored and extended to the applied psychoanalytic field of forensic psychotherapy. I would also like to acknowledge the patients I have worked with and whose cases I have supervised, who formed the basis for some of the clinical examples in the book. All case material is disguised and fictionalised in order to preserve confidentiality and anonymity.

I would like to thank Karnac Books for their kind permission to reproduce verbatim two case examples I had written in *Lectures on Violence, Perversion, and Delinquency*, edited by David Morgan and Stanley Ruszczynski, Karnac Books, 2007 (pages 72–75).

Finally, I could not have written this book without Richard, whose patience, support and advice are unsurpassed.

INTRODUCTION

In the last two decades the mental health field has spawned a proliferation of publications and books about the risk of violence: how
to assess and manage such risk, the links between mental illness and
violence and the debate as to whether mental health workers should
be involved in risk prediction at all. But while much has been written about the prediction and prevention of violence, less attention
has been paid to the treatment of violent behaviour. Furthermore,
much of the literature is written from a medical perspective, focusing
on the small proportion of individuals whose violence is associated
with mental illness and can be treated with medication or short-term
behavioural treatments. Yet many mental health workers in forensic
and non-forensic settings, as well as professionals from other disciplines such as probation, police and social services, work closely with
violent individuals who may not be formally mentally ill, but clearly
in need of help.

In contrast to these burgeoning writings on dangerousness in the
wider mental health arena, within the discipline of psychoanalysis
little has been written about violence until very recently, despite an
extensive and rich psychoanalytic literature on the nature of aggression and destructiveness. This deficit may be partly explained by
the fact that although psychoanalysts and psychotherapists may be
familiar with murderousness and violent fantasies in the patients
they see in their clinical practice, few actually see patients who act
on these fantasies to become violent, violence being one of the criteria
that most would see as a contraindication to such therapy.

This traditional psychotherapeutic playing field has shifted significantly in the last two decades with the creation of the discipline of
forensic psychotherapy, which is concerned with the psychoanalytic
understanding of offenders and their treatment with psychoanalytically informed therapies. Although this book may be viewed as
an addition to this rapidly evolving field, it is not solely aimed at
the readership of psychoanalytically minded psychotherapists and
counsellors, but hopes to introduce psychoanalytic thinking as a way

of understanding violence to many other professionals, including psychiatrists, psychiatric nurses, prison, police and probation officers, social workers and the managers and planners of mental health services, who have contact with violent individuals or groups of people, but who may have little, if any, knowledge of psychoanalysis. I have therefore not assumed the reader to have a prior knowledge of psychoanalytic theory, and have tried to explain the psychoanalytic concepts and terminology as they are introduced in the text. I have also compiled a glossary of the psychoanalytic terms and ideas used in the book, which the reader can refer to if something is not clear. Moreover, it should be emphasised that the psychoanalytic viewpoint expressed in this book aims to complement and enhance, rather than replace, the predominant theories of violence from other disciplines traditionally concerned with this topic, such as criminology, sociology and forensic psychiatry.

One of the central tenets of the arguments put forward in this book is that violence is not a senseless, incomprehensible act, but is, by contrast, a communication that is meaningful, although the meaning may not be obvious, or conscious, to either perpetrator or victim. A psychoanalytic understanding of violence promotes the exploration of its meanings and significance, focusing specifically on the unconscious meanings, which are not immediately available to the conscious mind. Thus, violence can be thought of as a communication rather than solely as a dangerous act to be condemned and eliminated, and what is communicated in the violent act may be intimately related to the life and history of the violent individual involved. Violence and other acts of criminality in the external world can be understood in relation to the inner world of the mind of the offender, his conscious and unconscious wishes, fantasies and his representations of relationships in his mind. Psychoanalysis can help us decipher the offender's mind, not by subjecting all violent individuals to psychoanalytic treatment, but by using psychoanalytic theories and concepts to understand the development of the person and why he feels compelled to use violence in his relationships with others rather than accessing less aggressive modes of relating.

This book is predominantly concerned with violence in adults, and does not specifically address the presentation or treatment of violence in children and adolescents in any detail, as this is a specialised field in itself. However, all violent adults have been children, often troubled children, who have been neglected or abused, and understanding their childhood and adolescent experiences and development is a pre-requisite to understanding their adult violent behaviour. This emphasis on a developmental approach is present throughout the book, and is discussed in detail, along with examining the predictive precursors of adult violence in childhood, in the chapters relating to violence, personality disorder and psychopathy. It should also be emphasised that this book is not primarily concerned with self-harm and suicide, obviously both violent acts against the body, but focuses on violence enacted against the external world and other people, rather than against the self (although this may also be occurring in fantasy).

The book is divided into two parts. The first half introduces contemporary psychoanalytic theories of violence and explores these in relation to mental illness, personality, sexuality, gender, society, race and culture. These theories are also discussed in relation to some of the main ideas from the related disciplines of criminology, sociology and psychiatry, which provide the context into which these psychoanalytic ideas about violence can be integrated. The second half of the book focuses on how these psychoanalytic theories can be used in practice with violent individuals or offenders in different settings, with particular attention given to the assessment, individual and group treatment of the violent patient.

Chapter 1 provides a historical overview of the psychoanalytic understanding of aggression and violence, and introduces key writers and concepts on these subjects. Although this chapter may appear at first sight rather dry and theoretical, the ideas that are introduced here in theory will hopefully become more meaningful and alive as the book progresses, highlighted by the clinical examples and vignettes used throughout the following chapters. All clinical examples are based on real cases, but have been disguised and details changed to protect the confidentiality of the individuals, professionals or institutions involved.

Chapters 2 and 3 explore the links between violent behaviour, mental illness and personality disorder, looking at psychopathy in depth as an extreme example of a disorder of character in which there is abnormal development and expression of aggression. In these chapters I highlight some of the limitations of current psychiatric diagnostic classifications in their attempts to categorize illnesses and disorders on the basis of observable symptoms and behaviours, rather than looking at underlying personality dynamics. However, in the following chapters on women and sexuality, and in discussing clinical material throughout the book, I retain the current psychiatric diagnoses that I have been criticising, not only because this is what most medical and non-medical readers who work in health services will be familiar with, but perhaps also because it reflects a tension in myself between conflicting identities of psychiatrist and psychoanalyst.

Chapters 4 and 5 examine violence in relation to sexuality and gender. These are highly charged subjects that are difficult to talk about without appearing critical or offensive to people who may engage in unusual sexual practices that are consensual and not illegal. For this reason, I give some space to defining the term 'perversion', a word that has pejorative connotations, but, I will argue, remains useful as a concept in psychoanalytic thinking. I will explore how all of sexuality contains elements of aggression, and how in perversions, activities that appear to be predominantly sexual in nature may conceal underlying hostility and fears of intimacy. Similarly, discussions of violence and gender may be simplified and misunderstood, and provoke accusations of sexism. Although most would accept that men are more likely to be violent than women, it appears more difficult to accept that a minority of women are also violent to others, and moreover are more likely to direct their aggression at their partners or children. For many, deliberately harming one's own children seems unthinkable, which may explain the prevailing attitude in society today that mothers are incapable of such crimes, particularly when they are of a sexual nature. In the rare and extreme cases where there is indisputable proof that maternal abuse has occurred, public reaction is one of moral outrage with the urge to swiftly attribute blame, which is often then located in the professionals involved, for failure to detect or protect the child victim. Such an emotional response, while understandable, impedes our ability to think and try to explore the complex motivations, conscious and unconscious, that might contribute to a mother being violent to her own child, or a woman remaining in a violent relationship with her partner. This is not about blaming mothers or abused women, but aims to elucidate the underlying conflicts that govern destructive behaviour, the awareness of which may enable the woman (or man) to discover agency and choose more healthy solutions and ways of relating.

Chapter 6 addresses socialized violence, looking at some of the reasons why individuals who would not normally indulge in violent behaviour do so under the sway of the group. This brief chapter only skims the surface of a huge topic that has claimed the attention of historians, sociologists and politicians to name but a few, but aims to add a psychoanalytic perspective to understanding the group processes involved in socially sanctioned acts of violence, including the mass violence of warfare, genocide and torture, and focuses on issues of race and ethnicity which underscores much of such group violence. I link recent writings by contemporary psychoanalysts on racism in the consulting room to thinking about how racist attitudes or 'racist states of mind', based on fear of the 'other', become amplified in the group to justify harming or killing others who are perceived as different and therefore dangerous.

The second half of the book looks at how some of these ideas may be encountered in clinical practice. Chapter 7 shows how psychoanalytic thinking can make the process of risk assessment, which many consider a necessary, but tedious exercise, more meaningful. Chapter 8 looks at the dynamics of the institutions in which violent patients and offenders are housed and examines how the pathology of antisocial individuals gets played out and reflected by the institution, which may then warrant treatment itself. Chapters 9 and 10 address the topics of specific psychoanalytically based assessment, individual and group treatments for violent patients, while remaining mindful of the institution, or setting, in which such interventions are taking place. In contrast to non-forensic settings where the relationship between patient and therapist can be conducted in private, forensic psychotherapy always involves a triangular relationship between offender/patient, psychotherapist and society, usually represented in the criminal justice system – the Courts, police or probation. This can raise uncomfortable tensions between parties and blurring of the respective roles of professionals involved, who may be unclear as to whether their function is about treating patients, controlling offenders, protecting the public or satisfying legal or political authorities. The final chapter examines some of the ethical dilemmas concerned, such as confidentiality and capacity to consent to treatment, and how the forensic psychotherapist can work constructively with external agencies such as the Courts or the police, without being unconsciously drawn into destructive collusions and pathological solutions, which may reflect the very behaviours the violent person presents for help in the first place.

Finally, I am not suggesting that a psychoanalytic approach provides an excuse for antisocial behaviour, or that it removes the need for appropriate punishment of the offender, but I propose that it offers a conceptual framework, in which his offending acts, which are always interpersonal, can begin to be thought about and understood in relation to unconscious processes. The violent person acts instead of thinking, and if we, not just as therapists and clinicians, but as members of the society we share with the offender whose actions we so fear, can offer compassionate inquiry and thoughtfulness instead of condemnation and rejection, our reflective stance may be internalized by both 'perpetrator' and 'victim', and help break the vicious cycle of violence and recrimination which is so characteristic of the world we live in.

1

VIOLENCE: PSYCHOANALYTIC PERSPECTIVES

Although psychoanalysis has been preoccupied with the nature of aggression and destructiveness since Freud, until recently very little has been written about the psychoanalytic understanding of actual violence. Similarly, although most psychoanalysts and psychotherapists are familiar with the murderousness and violent fantasies in the patients they see in their clinical practice, few will see patients who act on their fantasies to become violent. In the last two decades, however, there has been increased interest in the psychoanalytic understanding and treatment of violent and delinquent patients, patients with a history of criminality and those who enact sexual violence and other perversions in which violence is inherent. This parallels the increasing interest in psychoanalytically informed treatments for people with severe character pathology, such as those patients diagnosed with borderline or antisocial personality disorders who constitute an increasing proportion of the patient population referred to psychiatrists and therapists for help.

Examination of the recent psychoanalytic writings on violence reveals several related and overlapping themes. One is that there may be several different forms of violence, reflecting different forms of aggression, with different aetiologies and psychodynamic pathways. Another, paralleling the increasing importance of the object in the psychoanalytic understanding of aggression, is the understanding of violent behaviour through attachment theory. This reflects the increasing consideration in more recent psychoanalytic theory of disturbances, including trauma, in the very early development of the child, as being highly relevant to the development of mind and later character abnormalities or psychosis, that may be enacted in violent behaviours. Other psychoanalytic authors have focused more on understanding the unconscious phantasies underlying violent behaviour. Here, the psychodynamics of violence have been explored in relation to themes including the role of the father, thinking and the representation of self and object, violence as representing a core primal scene phantasy and violence as a defensive reaction to shame, humiliation and narcissistic injury.

Although the selective focus of a particular author may reflect the particular clinical field or theoretical framework in which they work, this has impeded the development of a more integrated and comprehensive theory or theories of violence, which respect the complexity of the issues involved. In this chapter I will give a very brief overview of how psychoanalysts have thought about aggression, and then focus on the ideas of the main contributors to the contemporary psychoanalytic discussion on violence, and, following authors such as Fonagy, and Cartwright, introduce a multi-dimensional framework through which the understanding of violence can be approached.

A psychoanalytic history of aggression

Few topics in psychoanalytic history have generated more heated debate and conflict and a vast and daunting literature than that of human aggression since Freud first postulated the death instinct. Historically this debate has been characterised by dichotomies. Is aggression an irreducible and innate drive or instinct, or is it a reaction to the environment? Can aggression be seen as constructive, an essential ingredient of normal development necessary for separation and individuation, or is it always destructive and pathological? Although such a polarisation of viewpoints can be understood as reflecting profound differences in psychoanalytic theory and technique, it may draw us into false dichotomies and the belief that there is only one type of aggression. These psychoanalytic disputes also obscure the essential contribution of Freud and psychoanalysis in locating aggression firmly within the human psyche: aggression is a fundamental aspect of our psychological make-up that orientates our relationships with others and ourselves and pervades our view of the world.

Freud's views on aggression were complex and developed throughout his lifetime. He initially saw aggression as being a component of the sexual instinct used in the service of mastery (Freud, 1905a), but later saw aggression as a response to both internal and external threats, such as loss, and used in the service of self-preservation (Freud, 1915, 1917). In 1920, he made aggression an instinct in its own right in the death instinct, a force that operates insidiously at all levels of the organism, in opposition to the life instinct (Freud, 1915). Freud proposed that the death instinct accounted for the repetition compulsion, and was incorporated into part of the superego as unconscious guilt.

Subsequent psychoanalysts can be divided into those, such as Klein and her followers, as well as the ego-psychologists in the United States, who understood aggression to be instinctual in origin, and those, such as Winnicott (1956, 1986) and Fairbairn (1952), who viewed it as reactive to environmental trauma and loss. Klein believed that innate envy and destructiveness were manifestations of the death instinct and predominated in early life, giving rise to persecutory anxieties of annihilation and primitive defences, unconscious phantasies and an archaic superego, which characterised the 'paranoid schizoid' position (Klein, 1946). At this early stage of development immature defence mechanisms such as splitting and projection predominate and the baby is unable to integrate conflicting experiences. This gradually develops into the more mature 'depressive position' with the tolerance of loss and ambivalence (Klein, 1935). By contrast, Winnicott (1971) saw aggression as a creative force necessary for healthy development by enabling individuation and separation. He posited a central role for the mother in his concepts of the 'facilitating maternal environment' and the maternal 'holding' functions. He believed that pathological aggression and antisocial behaviour arose as a reaction to early deprivation and trauma (Winnicott, 1956, 1986).

More recent psychoanalytic writers emphasise the role of the object and object relations in the genesis of aggression, but also accept that aggression may have an instinctual component, and that there may be different types of aggression which are exhibited in different forms of violence (Glasser, 1998). Many authors (e.g. Kernberg, 1992; Kohut, 1972) have focused on rage as a form of aggression that can emerge as explosive violence. Cartwright (2002) defines rage as the expression of a primitive explosive affective state, and identifies several psychodynamic factors such as shame, narcissistic injury, self-exposure, hate and reactive affective states that are consistently linked with the genesis of rage. These authors can be seen to have moved away from the polarisation of their predecessors towards a more coherent and flexible theoretical approach that embraces both biology and psychology, and specifically the role of the object. The research on attachment by Bowlby (1969) and his followers, and how the infant's relationship and proximity-seeking behaviour to his mother or primary object is both instinctual and also determined by the object's behaviour, has increasingly influenced thinking on the aetiology of aggressive behaviour. The conclusion is that the capacity for aggression is innate, but that aggressive behaviour or violence occurs in response to threats that the self perceives in relation to internal or external objects.

Definitions of violence

A significant area of confusion in the literature concerns the definition of violence. Many authors have not clearly distinguished aggression from violence, using the two terms interchangeably. Other related nouns such as anger, rage, destructiveness, sadism, cruelty and brutality are also often poorly differentiated and defined. Various psychoanalysts, including Mervyn Glasser, Adam Limentani and Donald Campbell, working at the Portman Clinic in London, a National Health Service out-patient clinic that provides psychoanalytically informed treatments for violent, delinquent and perverse patients, have been pioneers in the psychoanalytic investigation of violence. They distinguish violence from aggression by specifying violence as a behaviour that involves the body. Glasser (1985) defines violence as an actual assault on the body of one person by another, involving penetration of the body barrier, 'the intended infliction of bodily harm on another person'. Glasser's definition here clearly distinguishes violent behaviour from violent thoughts and fantasies, a distinction that is very important in clinical practice when considering issues of treatability and risk. However, the use of the word 'intended' implies that violence is always consciously motivated. Limentani (1991) qualifies this by pointing out that the motivation for such behaviour is not always conscious, but may be unconsciously driven. De Zulueta (2006) defines violence as giving meaning to a form of interpersonal human behaviour. She emphasises that it is a thinking 'subject' doing something destructive to an 'other' human, and that the study of human violence hinges on understanding how humans develop in terms of how they both think and feel about themselves and the 'other'.

In this book I will confine the definition of violence to the act of bodily harm involving a breach of the body boundary, whether consciously or unconsciously motivated, inflicted by one person onto another person. The focus of my exploration is the internal world and interpersonal world of the violent person and his objects, and

I am therefore not considering violence towards animals or property, although these may hold unconscious symbolic meaning for the offender. Restricting my definition to bodily action does not detract from consideration of the emotional and psychological aspects of violence, as some authors have suggested (e.g. Mizen and Morris, 2007). On the contrary, one of the essential messages of this book is that acts of violence have psychic meaning. Such meaning may not be consciously available but may reside in the unconscious, and it is one of the tasks of the psychoanalyst or forensic psychotherapist to discover and understand the unconscious psychological phantasies, symbolic meanings, affects and motivations that lie behind the external violent act.

Different forms of violence

Following on from the hypothesis that there are several types of aggression is the proposition that there are different forms of violence. Glasser (1998) makes an important distinction between two different modes of violence, which he called 'self-preservative violence' and 'sado-masochistic violence'. It is worth considering Glasser's classification of violence in some detail, as it is useful in clinical work with violent patients. The crucial distinction between his two different forms of violence involves the role of the object.

Self-preservative violence is a primitive response triggered by any threat to the physical or psychological self. Such threats might be external and include the danger of castration, attacks on a person's self-esteem, frustration, humiliation or an insult to an ideal to which the person is attached. The person can also feel threatened by internal sources such as feeling attacked by a sadistic superego or fear a loss of identity by feelings of disintegration and internal confusion. The violent response is fundamental, immediate and aimed at eliminating the source of danger, which may be an external object or an attack on the person's own body which is experienced as an external persecutor in self-harm or suicide.

Sado-masochistic violence is derived from self-preservative violence in that it is a result of the sexualisation (a bodily process) of self-preservative violence. Sado-masochistic violence is most commonly observed in the perversions, in people who exhibit a preferred and persistent deviant sexual behaviour that is pervasive and reflects a global structure involving the individual's whole personality (see Chapter 4). The difference between these two forms of violence is most readily understood by considering their relationship to the object (i.e. the person towards whom the violence is directed). In self-preservative violence, the object at the time of violence is perceived as being of immediate danger but holds no other personal significance and its responses are of no interest. In sado-masochistic violence, by contrast, the responses of the object are crucial – the object must be seen to suffer, but to do so it must be preserved, rather than eliminated as in the case of self-preservative violence. Sado-masochistic violence also involves pleasure, which is not a component of self-preservative violence, where anxiety is always present. A simple example of the difference between the two types of violence would be the soldier who kills the enemy in a battle, believing that such an action is necessary to prevent himself from being killed (self-preservative violence) in contrast to the soldier who captures the enemy and tortures him to make him suffer (sado-masochistic violence).

Although it appears that Glasser is describing two very different forms of violence, he saw these as the two poles on a continuum of violent behaviours.

> One can envisage a continuum starting at the one end with ordinary social teasing and moving via the cat and dog, sado-masochistic relationships which characterize some couples, to the perversion of frank sado-masochism; this in turn shades into sexual assault such as rape, moving through crimes of violence to homicide, which is the other extreme of the continuum.
>
> (Glasser, 1996a, p. 287)

Glasser emphasised that the appreciation of the object as a person decreased as one moved from the sexual to overtly violent.

Other recent authors have proposed typologies of violence similar to Glasser's. Perhaps the closest is Meloy (1992), who distinguishes between affective violence and predatory violence, roughly corresponding to Glasser's self-preservative and sado-masochistic violence respectively. Meloy writes from an attachment viewpoint and cites evidence from empirical research to argue that different neurophysiological pathways underpin these two different forms of violence, which are not linked as Glasser suggests with his continuum. Affective violence is a defensive response that occurs when the autonomic nervous system is activated following a perceived threat to the individual. Like Glasser, such a threat may be internal or external. Predatory violence lacks emotional involvement, is purposeful, calculating and involves what he calls a 'suspension of empathic regard' in the individual concerned. This type of violence occurs in psychopathic characters, and will be discussed further when we examine personality development and psychopathy in later chapters.

We can see here how both Glasser and Meloy propose two different forms of violence, based on two underlying types of aggression. Although these different forms of violence may not encompass all forms of violence, I think both Glasser's and Meloy's divisions of violence into self-preservative/affective versus sadistic/predatory are very helpful clinically. This will become clearer with the clinical examples and consideration of the treatment of violent patients later in this book.

Attachment, trauma and loss

Several authors, such as De Zulueta (2006), highlight the role of early trauma and loss, which are often evident in the histories of violent individuals. Rejecting the idea of innate destructiveness, De Zulueta integrates Bowlby's (1969) attachment theory, object relations theory and Kohut's (1985) self-psychology with primate and infant research as well as neurobiological research on trauma victims and violent offenders to propose a psychobiological theory of violence rooted in early loss, deprivation and trauma. She believes that violence can be understood as a failure in adequate caregiving or 'faulty attachments'.

Following Bowlby, researchers into the study of attachment have shown that the early relationship to the primary caregivers is critical to the development of personality, mental representations and affect control (Carlson and Sroufe, 1995). The development of the self occurs through the internalisation of different types of attachment relationships with significant early caregivers, usually the mother, to form internal working models or representations of object relationships. These attachment patterns have very important and long-term · effects on how the individual relates to others throughout life. In normal development, the infant is biologically programmed to ensure close proximity to his primary attachment figure via a range of attachment behaviours. If the attachment figure leaves, this provokes an angry protest in the infant with the aim of alerting the caregiver to the infant's distress and need for closeness. Prolonged absence or loss of attachment figures can cause this natural angry protest to develop into more pathological destructive aggression. Trauma such as child abuse or neglect, early parental loss or emotional deprivation can have serious adverse effects on the developing attachment relationship between the infant and his caregivers. Normal secure attachments are necessary for the development of affect regulation, impulse control, empathy and the capacity to reflect or mentalize (see below). If the child has internalised pathological attachment relationships, his reduced capacity to regulate his feelings means that he is more likely to express emotion in primitive ways such as violence towards self and others. De Zulueta (2006), Meloy (1992) and others propose that destructive reactions to perceived vulnerability and loss are an indication of loss and damaged attachments in early life.

Mentalization

Fonagy and his co-workers (Bateman and Fonagy, 2004; Fonagy and Target, 1995; Fonagy et al., 1991a, 1993) have further developed the model of how early trauma and disrupted attachments involving physical and emotional abuse may lead to aggression and violence, introducing the concept of 'mentalization'. This is the capacity to reflect and to think about one's mental states, including thoughts, beliefs, desires and affects, and to be able to distinguish one's own mental states from others. Relative failures of mentalization may result in such mental states being located and managed in the realm of the body, being experienced as psychosomatic bodily states and processes, including the use of violence. This lack of differentiation between mind and body means that the body is now experienced as a substitute for the mind and mental states.

Fonagy believes that aggression is biologically rooted, but arises in response to perceived threats to the psychological self. The normal development of a child's theory of mind, or appreciation of the mental basis of human behaviour, is dependent on the inter-subjective process of emerging psychological awareness between the child and his primary caregivers or attachment figures. The child becomes increasingly aware of his own mind through his growing awareness of the mind of his mother through her capacity to demonstrate to him that she thinks of him as a separate person with his own distinct intentions, beliefs and desires. If the mother's or primary caregiver's thoughts are frequently malevolent or fail to view him as a separate being, the child cannot develop a capacity to feel safe about what others think of him, which may lead to a more generalised failure to see others as thinking beings at all. In such abused or neglected infants, aggression arises as a defensive response to defend the fragile emerging self from the assumed hostility of the object. If the abuse or neglect is ongoing, a fusion will occur between aggression and self-expression of the child. The expression of aggression is further potentiated by the reduced capacity of the child to mentalize – if he is unable to see others as having mental states as different from himself, this will reduce the inhibition of his aggression and violence towards others as he is unable to empathise or appreciate another person's suffering.

Fonagy and colleagues (Fonagy and Target, 1995) emphasise that some people with a fragile capacity for mentalization that predisposes to violent action with minimal provocation may not have had a history of overt abuse. They argue that nevertheless, such individuals may have experienced more subtle damaging interpersonal experiences with their primary attachment figures, in which the mother is unable to have a place in her mind for her infant, or feeds back a distorted, damaged image to the child, who will then develop an identity around an alien persecutory internal object that is unable to think or feel and has to be defended against by violent means. Fonagy's work here draws on Bion (1970) and Winnicott (1971) in emphasising the essential role of the mother in her containment or mirroring in facilitating the infant to develop a healthy capacity to find his own mind in the mind of the object. If this does not occur, the child resorts to pathological solutions, including the use of aggression or even violence to protect the fragile self from perceived threats to undermine this. This includes a desperate struggle for separation from the object, but paradoxically, the more the child strives for separation, the more he experiences fusion with his object, as the latter is experienced as part of his self-structure. This can lead to developmental crises in adolescence or early adulthood when the need for separation and independence is at its height, and a failure to achieve this can precipitate violent or suicidal behaviour as a pathological attempt to free the individual from the internal persecutory object.

Gilligan (1996), in his work with high-security inmates, corroborates the devastating effects of such a poor development of self, sense of identity and agency that results from early trauma and parental abuse. These offenders' early experiences of being rejected, ostracised, abused or made to feel as if they did not exist predisposed them as adults to be sensitised to feeling ostracised, bullied or ignored, leading to unbearable feelings of shame and humiliation which need to be defended against by violent means. Following the many authors (Parens, 1993; Schafer, 1997; Shengold, 1991) who have highlighted the role of painful affects involved in narcissistic injury in precipitating rage-type aggression, Gilligan proposes that all forms of violence are precipitated by feelings of shame and humiliation. Gilligan reminds us that words alone can constitute trauma, that the violent person may not have been the victim of actual violence, but of verbal and emotional abuse that can equally damage the developing mind.

The internal object world, the role of the father and superego

The above writers on attachment locate the origins of violence in the pathological early relationship between mother and infant, which prevents the child developing a sense of separate identity, and violence is used as a desperate measure to create space between self and other. Many other psychoanalytic authors have also focused on the role of the maternal object in creating a pathological internal object world in which pre-oedipal object relations predominate and predispose to destructive aggression and violent enactment. Here the pathological effects of the overprotective mother, who over-gratifies the infant and confuses her narcissistic needs with his, may be as detrimental as the absent or abusive mother. This leads to fears of being overwhelmed or consumed by the object, which can only be averted by an aggressive response. Thus Shengold (1991) describes the narcissistic mother who over-stimulates her child and views him as an extension of herself rather than a separate being, replacing the child's own development of self by his mother's idealisations. The child's sense of emptiness and disillusion that occurs when he inevitably discovers that the world is not such an ideal place is referred to by Shengold as 'soul murder'. Such individuals are more vulnerable to reacting with rage-type aggression and violence to perceived self-damage, shame and narcissistic injury, like those described by Gilligan above.

Glasser (1996a) also considered the relationship to the maternal object as being fundamental in the genesis of aggression and violence. He described a particular constellation of interrelated feelings, ideas and attitudes that he called the 'core complex'. A major component of the core complex is a deep-seated and pervasive longing for an intense and intimate closeness to another person, a wish to merge with them, a 'state of oneness' or a 'blissful union'. Such longings occur in all of us, but where there has been an early pathologically narcissistic relationship to the mother they persist pervasively in a primitive form unmodified by later stages of development. Merging no longer has the quality of a temporary state but is feared as a permanent loss of self, a disappearance of the person's existence as a separate, independent individual into the object, a fear of total annihilation. To defend against this annihilatory anxiety, the person retreats from the object to a 'safe distance'. But this flight brings with it feelings of emotional isolation, abandonment and low self-esteem. These painful feelings prompt the desire for contact and union with the object once more, so that the core complex has the qualities of a vicious circle.

Aggression is a central component of the core complex. The annihilatory fear of a loss of separate existence provokes an intense aggressive reaction on the part of the ego. In order to preserve the self, the object – usually meaning the mother at this very early developmental stage – has to be destroyed. But this of course would mean the loss of all the goodness of the mother, the security, love and warmth that she offers. The infant has only two options – to retreat into a narcissistic state or to resort to self-preservative aggression against the obliterating mother. This, Glasser proposes, is the origin of self-preservative violence. We will see in later chapters how Glasser formulates that in the perversions there is an attempt to resolve the vicious circle of the core complex by the sexualisation of aggression, the conversion of aggression into sadism. The mother is now preserved and no longer threatened by total destruction, as the intention to destroy is converted into a wish to hurt and control. This can lead to sado-masochistic as opposed to self-preservative violence.

The role of the father in separating the child from the dyadic relationship with the mother has been considered of great importance by many authors in understanding the genesis of violence (e.g. Bateman, 1999; Campbell, 1999; Fonagy and Target, 1995; Limentani, 1991; Perelberg, 1999a; Stoller, 1979). In normal development the father provides an essential role of creating a space to facilitate the child as seeing himself as separate from mother. The 'good enough father' can be internalised by the child to form an intrapsychic paternal or 'third object' that acts as an intermediary object by breaking up potentially pathological symbiosis and fusion between self and primary object. The role of the third object in the creation of internal space is also essential to the development of thinking, the capacity for symbolisation and mentalization (Britton, 1992; Fonagy and Target, 1995; Segal, 1978). Many violent individuals have histories of absent or emotionally unavailable fathers, or abusive fathers who did not provide any source of love or containment that the child could turn to. In such individuals there is a lack of an adequate paternal introject and the person feels trapped intrapsychically in a dyadic relationship with the mother where there is no possibility of another/third perspective. In her clinical experience, Perelberg (1999b) notes the precariousness of male identifications in violent patients where the internal representations of father remain primitive.

Such poor internalisation of a paternal object has implications for the development of the superego in violent individuals, an area which has also been of interest to a multitude of psychoanalysts since Freud. Freud (1923) viewed the superego as a result of identification with the father in the boy to avert castration anxiety, and identification with the mother to avoid loss of her love. The concept has been developed in many different ways since Freud, but a broad generalisation would understand the superego to be the internalisation of parental values, goals and restrictions, to form an internal intrapsychic structure that represents the conscience of the individual, which can be experienced as supportive, punitive or absent.

Freud (1923) believed that the superego was absent in psychopaths; Fenichel (1931) believed there was some evidence of primitive, if ineffective superego functioning in such individuals; whereas Klein (1927), by contrast, saw the superego in cases of violence as being overly harsh and punitive. Klein understood violence as the external manifestations of an attempt to relieve an internal sense of persecution between superego and ego, creating an unconscious sense of intolerable guilt that leads to the eruption of violence. Klein's views here echo Freud's understanding of criminal behaviour as being the enactment of an unconscious sense of guilt.

The superego may be involved in different ways depending on the type of violence (Cartwright, 2002). Both Sandler (1960) and Glasser (1978) emphasise the superego as containing approving and permissive as well as prohibitive features. Glasser divides the superego into two sets of functions: the proscriptive superego (superego as conscience) which provides moral and ethical restrictions, prohibitions and boundaries, the transgression of which makes the person feel guilt; and the prescriptive superego (superego as ego-ideal) which sets ideals, standards and goals of behaviour, the failure of which to attain causing feelings of shame, low self-esteem and inadequacy. The proscriptive superego may be used to justify socially sanctioned violence such as war, whereas Shengold's (1989) victims of soul murder and Gilligan's (1996) violent offenders who are very sensitive to feelings of shame may have deficits in the prescriptive superego predisposing them to rage-type violence. In psychopathic violence, the ideals of the prescriptive superego may actually be perverted so that negative goals are seen as rewarding (see Chapter 4).

The role of phantasy

One of the fundamental propositions that psychoanalysis has to offer in thinking about violence is that the violent act has meaning, and this meaning is unconscious. In other words, the violent behaviour is motivated by unconscious phantasy. Throughout this book I use the term 'phantasy' to refer to unconscious fantasy, and 'fantasy' to refer to more conscious fantasising or day-dreaming. Drawing on her psychoanalytic experience with violent patients, Perelberg (1995, 1999a) proposes that violent acts have underlying specific phantasies or unconscious narratives that motivate them. She notes that in Freud's writings there are associations between his ideas on violence and the mythology of the origins of humankind, unconscious phantasies of the primal scene (i.e. the child's primal unconscious phantasy of sexual intercourse between the parents) or the Oedipus complex. Perelberg expands Freud's ideas by linking violence to a core phantasy of the primal scene, involving the pre-oedipal mother, in contrast to Freud's emphasis on oedipal phantasies. Perelberg proposes that in affective or self-preservative violence the person's unconscious phantasy of the primal scene is of violence and the relationship to the pre-oedipal mother is engulfing and also violent. These beliefs have developed in the context of a pathological intrusive early symbiotic relationship with the mother as described above. The violent act is therefore an attack on the mother's body, the mother being experienced in phantasy as not only being in possession of the child's body, but also the child's intellectual and affective experiences. Perelberg proposes that the function of violence is survival in the face of a maternal object that is experienced as obliterating, with no conception of a paternal object present. Glasser's (1996a) concept of the core complex here is of relevance.

Others have seen violence as a fantasised attack on the mother's body (Bateman, 1999; Campbell, 1999; Fonagy and Target, 1995). Fonagy argues that the underlying phantasy motivating violence in such individuals who have a reduced capacity for mentalization is aimed at destroying the contents of the mind of the other. In other words, thoughts, feelings and desires in others that are separate from themselves are perceived as so threatening that they must be destroyed. The phantasy of being overwhelmed or consumed by unmanageable experience appears to be a common denominator in motivating self-preservative or affective violence. Hyatt-Williams (1998), writing from a Kleinian perspective, emphasises the phantasies of annihilation and evacuation that underlie violent acts aimed at defending against deathly psychic indigestible experiences of trauma or obliteration.

However, the phantasies underlying sadistic or psychopathic violence may be different. Cartwright (2002) distinguishes between conscious fantasies and unconscious phantasies in different forms of violence. The phantasies that may underlie affective violence described above are unconscious and constitute deep structures of the mind, from where behaviour and thought emanate. Conscious fantasising, for example day-dreaming, describes surface mentation that has a sublimatory function. Cartwright argues that the perpetrators of socially sanctioned violence such as soldiers may have conscious fantasies about what they might do to the enemy, but these fantasies are not based on deeper unconscious phantasies. In affective or explosive rage-type violence, conscious fantasies about attacking the object may be lacking, but there may be pervasive unconscious murderous phantasy constellations. By contrast, in sadistic violence conscious violent fantasies are inevitably present which motivate their acts of violence. Here the normal censorship between conscious and unconscious has been partially breached, allowing what are normally unconscious phantasies to become permissible in the conscious mind. A similar process can occur in psychosis.

Defence mechanisms and defensive systems

The eruption of violence may be thought of as a failure of adequate defence mechanisms to inhibit aggressive impulses. Psychoanalysts have traditionally associated violent acts with deficits or collapse of the ego's defensive system (Hyatt-Williams, 1998; Menninger, 1963) so that the ego is overwhelmed with unmanageable affect. Violence in itself, however, may be considered a defence. Thus it can be thought of as a defensive way of maintaining attachments (Bowlby, 1969), as a defence against intolerable guilt (Symington, 1996) or as an identification with the aggressor (Anna Freud, 1936). Shengold (1991) believes that the rage that soul murder victims feel is a result of identification with the aggressor and the legacy of trauma. Both Gaddini (1992) and Glasser (1997) describe failures of identification in violent patients, with the use of more primitive defensive manoeuvres akin to imitation or what Glasser calls 'simulation', which can raise particular technical difficulties in treatment, as we will see.

What is commonly seen in violent patients is a deficiency of the more maturely developed defence mechanisms, such as repression, that would usually inhibit aggressive impulses, and an over-utilisation of more primitive defence mechanisms, such as projection, splitting and projective identification, that serve to perpetuate the violence by incorporating it into their means of defence. Projective identification, first described by Klein (1946), is a defence mechanism in which the person projects or externalises their internal feelings and object relationships, which they cannot bear to recognise as internal to themselves and therefore attribute them to others. The person who has been invested with these unwanted aspects may unconsciously identify with what has been projected into them and may feel unconsciously pressurised to act out in some way. From an interpersonal perspective, it can be seen how projective identification can escalate between two people into violence. Hyatt-Williams (1998), formulating his extensive work with violent prisoners from a Kleinian and Bionian perspective, describes how these individuals' minds are dominated by persecutory anxiety, which they are unable to tolerate, and they therefore use projective identification to a pathological degree in an attempt to expel such toxic states of mind from conscious experience. However, such a defensive manoeuvre may be ineffective, in that once projected, the intolerable mental state may then be experienced by the person it is projected into as unpleasant, and may act in an aggressive way towards the projecting person. This may then be experienced as an even more intolerable and indigestible emotional state that cannot be contained by either party, and continues to be projected between both perpetrator and victim, causing irreconcilable arguments and an escalating violent situation. Meloy (1992) also describes how the mechanism of projective identification can be used to cause violence, with a desperate need to control the object, which may only terminate in murder. These processes will be examined further when we consider domestic violence in Chapter 5.

Such primitive defences, which have been aptly termed 'action defences' (Lecours and Bouchard, 1997), are habitually used in people with borderline or antisocial personality disorders, to form defensive systems that work together with a constellation of object relations, phantasies and impulses, to form pathological defensive organisations (Hyatt-Williams, 1998; O'Shaughnessy, 1981; Steiner, 1982) that constitute part of the character of the individual, and function to ward off psychic pain and unbearable states of mind. Such splitting off and projection of unpleasant experience from consciousness is at the expense of psychic stasis and causes arrest of the normal development of the self and emotional growth, impeding any learning from experience. This can cause a psychotic splitting of the personality so that areas of the mind containing violent affects and primitive object constellations remain encapsulated and underdeveloped. This is similar to Winnicott's (1960) ideas in the development of a 'false self', which he believed was present in antisocial characters. For Winnicott, the false self develops through compliance with a narcissistic mother, who does not recognise the infants needs, but substitutes her own, which the infant complies with, but at the expense of development of the true self, which remains hidden.

Such paranoid defensive organisations, however, remain rigid and brittle, and prone to over-react to stimuli, which may lead to de-compensation of the personality and ensuing violence. Cartwright (2002), in his investigation of rage-type murder, proposes that vulnerable individuals have a defensive organisation that he calls the 'narcissistic exoskeleton'. This consists of a rigid split in the psyche between a constellation of idealised object relations and internalised bad objects, where the former assumes the position of the outer personality, forming a defensive field in which the phantasy of the external world as being an all-good reflection of the self is rigidly maintained. The internal world, consisting of bad-object relations which are associated with aggression, is disowned. This is similar to Winnicott's (1960) concept of the 'false self' defensively hiding the 'true self'. Cartwright describes people who appear from the outside to be successful, stable, perhaps sometimes rather controlling, but non-aggressive, individuals who, seemingly out of the blue, commit explosive violence or even murder. He explains this by a breakdown in their narcissistic idealised defensive system that functions to deny and control the existence of the hidden aggressive bad-object system, which then intrudes into and overwhelms the mind and personality, cannot be subject to thought given its poor representational capacity and therefore has to be evacuated physically in violent action. This collapse in defences is precipitated by conflict or threats experienced by the person in relation to separation or antagonism to the victim, which may have begun long before the murderous event.

The external setting and situational factors

The consideration of violence from a psychoanalytic viewpoint in no way diminishes the importance of external factors in the genesis of violence. Although this book is concerned with exploring the internal world of the violent person, an understanding of how external events and circumstances affect this internal world is of critical importance, particularly in the prediction of violence. Situational factors impact on the offender's internal world, but the offender in turn manipulates external objects to fulfil an internal purpose (Cartwright, 2002).

Trauma and severe provocation may be seen as weakening and overwhelming the person's defensive systems so that underlying aggressive impulses erupt into violence. How a person experiences provocation is of course highly variable, dependent on their individual make-up of internal objects, defences, phantasies and previous experiences. Verbal insults, which most of us would be able to ignore, may be experienced as deeply traumatic and threatening to someone with fragile self-esteem, causing feelings of shame which may precipitate a violent reaction. Where violence ensues following apparently little environmental provocation, more emphasis can be placed on internal pathological states in contributing to the violent act.

Drug abuse, which is often associated with violence, can alter defences in different ways, leading to different types of violent reaction. Acute ingestion of stimulant drugs such as cocaine can cause a collapse of ego defences and precipitate a paranoid rage reaction leading to violence, which would be classified as affective (Meloy, 1988). On the other hand, rather than weakening defences, chronic drug misuse may bolster a person's pathological defences to which violent actions are integral. Thus Meloy describes how the clinical properties of both methamphetamine and cocaine exaggerate the pathological defensive character of the psychopath, by heightening his sense of omniscience and omnipotence and justifying his inclination to engage in predatory violence by inducing paranoid delusions.

Analysis of the external crime scene or index offence, and in particular the characteristics of the victim, can shed light on the internal pathological world of the offender, who may be unconsciously re-enacting past conflicts in his violent acts. Here the victim and other situational factors may hold an unconscious representational role for the offender, mirroring an internal unconscious phantasy that is enacted in the external crime scene. Parallels may be seen between the constellation of the violent incident and significant traumatic events in the offender's past (Mizen and Morris, 2007), so that the index offence can be understood as a repetition compulsion of previous patterns of relating and traumatic experiences. For example, the critical and nagging wife may be experienced unconsciously by the offender as his critical and abusive mother, so that his resulting violence towards his partner has unconscious matricidal motivation. Cartwright (2002) suggests, however, that defensive

murder may not always constitute a re-enactment of previous conflicts, but may be a manifestation of a breach of usual patterns
and re-enactments and therefore represents the emergence of a new
immediate, albeit pathological and fatal, solution to what is felt to be
an impossible solution.

Towards a multi-dimensional framework

All of us have aggressive impulses but not all of us are violent.
The ideas summarised in this chapter show that the pathways that
lead from aggression to violence are not linear but are dependent
on several factors. Given the complexity of the aetiology of violence, any formulation is necessarily schematic, and can only form
an overall framework, which should be flexible and open to modification. Nevertheless, I find it helpful, following Cartwright (2002),
to consider violence from a multi-dimensional viewpoint, where
violence is mediated by a number of different intrapsychic factors. Moreover, different constellations of intrapsychic characteristics
interacting with specific situational factors may cause different types
of violence.

The different dimensions considered in this chapter include the
following: the role of loss and trauma, the internal object world
including the role of the father and construction of the superego, the
capacity for representation and mentalization, unconscious phantasy, the defensive system and the interaction with environmental
factors. What have not been considered in any depth as yet are
the influences of sexuality, gender, race and society, which will be
explored further in Chapters 4, 5 and 6 respectively. Clearly, each different dimension or intrapsychic factor does not act independently in
influencing the emergence of violence, but will interact and influence each other. For example, a history of early maternal abuse
may significantly traumatise the developing mind so that the adult's
capacity for mentalization is poor, and the development of mature
defence mechanisms impaired so that primitive defensive systems
predominate. This process may be compounded by an absent father
and the development of a harsh superego with low self-esteem and
increased sensitivity to feelings of shame, which may make the person interact with others in a predominantly paranoid way. This
in turn lowers the threshold for feeling provoked by interpersonal
interactions, and increases the risk of violent enactment. Recognition and analysis of these different dimensions is helpful not only
in understanding the offender who is known to be violent, but also

in the assessment and management of future risk of violence, as we will see in Chapter 7.

Summary

- Although there are many different definitions of violence, the working definition of violence in this book is an act of bodily harm involving a breach of the body boundary, inflicted by one person towards another. The motivation for violence may not be obvious, but violence can be seen as a communication with unconscious symbolic meaning.

- There are different types of violence based on different underlying types of aggression, and mediated by different intrapsychic factors. A useful distinction is between self-preservative violence, where the person acts in self-defence in response to a perceived threat, and sado-masochistic violence, which is used to torture, control, but ultimately preserve the object of the violence.

- The early relationship to the mother, or primary object, is critical to the genesis of violence. Early abuse, trauma and loss can cause pathological attachment relationships in the infant, leading to later difficulties in affect regulation and a deficient capacity for representation and mentalization, which predispose to poor modulation of aggression. Violence can be seen as a defensive response to feelings of shame and humiliation, which have their roots in disorders of attachment.

- The role of the father in separating the child from the dyadic relationship with the mother is also important in the normal development of aggression and superego functioning, deficits in which can predispose to violent behaviour.

- Violence can be seen as the result of a failure in the normal defensive mechanisms against aggression. Violent individuals tend to use primitive defence mechanisms such as projection, splitting and projective identification, forming defensive pathological organisations in the mind, which predispose to violent enactment.

- External events and situational factors interact with the internal world of the offender to precipitate violence, which may represent the re-enactment of previous conflicts.

2

VIOLENCE, MENTAL ILLNESS AND PERSONALITY DISORDER

Mr B, a white British mini-cab driver, had a highly disrupted childhood during which he was physically abused by his mother, and in and out of foster care. Father was a distant figure, an alcoholic and promiscuous 'businessman' known as 'Jack the lad'. Mr B was disruptive at school, and as a teenager became involved in delinquent activities such as stealing cars, and misusing illicit drugs. In his 20s Mr B became closer to his mother, but had a series of relationships in which he was domestically violent to his partners. After being arrested following a drink driving offence, he was held in custody, where he accused the prison guards of poisoning his tea. On his release, he committed a robbery with a knife, and then approached a woman and killed her with multiple stab wounds.

In prison he was found to be expressing odd ideas and appeared thought disordered, was thought to be psychotic and transferred for an assessment to a secure hospital. Following treatment with anti-psychotic medication his psychotic symptoms disappeared rapidly over the next few weeks, and over the next 10 years in hospital he showed no further evidence of psychosis, even during a prolonged period when his anti-psychotic medication was stopped. Personality assessment showed he had narcissistic and antisocial personality traits and he scored highly on the Hare Psychopathy Checklist (see below). Despite having received psychodynamic therapy for 5 years in hospital, female nursing staff described him as glib, superficial and dismissive. He was diagnosed with a personality disorder, but although there had been no evidence of psychotic illness since his admission, he continued to remain detained under the Mental Health Act under the category of 'Mental illness' rather than 'Psychopathic Disorder' because his (male) psychiatrist felt well-disposed towards him and was reluctant for him to be 'labelled a psychopath'. This doctor also decided to treat him prophylacti-cally with anti-psychotic medication, in preparation for his release into the community in case of future 'breakdown'.

Diagnostic classifications

Violence is often linked with madness in the public imagination, fuelled by depictions of psychotic violence in film and literature, or by the media highlighting failures of psychiatric care in which acts of violence are committed by mentally disordered patients. This asso-ciation may be exaggerated in the mind of the public by members of the legal and psychiatric professions who seek to use a mental disor-der as a medico-legal defence for the violent offender in the criminal courts. This perpetuates the belief that severe acts of violence such as homicide are so heinous that they could only be carried out by someone who is sick. However, most mentally ill people are not vio-lent, and repeated studies have shown that there is only a small, albeit significant, association with mental illness. Studies measuring the rates of psychiatric disorders in prisoners show that this is much higher than in the general population (Hollin, 1989) with a majority of prisoners diagnosed with either antisocial personality disorder or substance abuse (Blackburn, 1993). Although it is generally accepted that people diagnosed with certain types of personality disorder have a higher risk of violence, the evidence is flawed by inconsis-tencies in how personality disorder is defined. This confusion was amplified by the existence of a legal category of 'psychopathic disor-der' in the Mental Health Act (1983) to describe a 'persistent disorder or disability of mind resulting in abnormally aggressive behaviour or seriously irresponsible conduct', which, although psychopathic dis-order was not recognised as a medical entity, cemented the equation of personality disorder with socially deviant behaviour in the public mind. Although the revision of the Mental Health Act (2007) removes the reference to the specific category of psychopathic disorder, the definition of mental disorder has been broadened so that someone with personality disorder can now be detained even if they are not displaying abnormally aggressive or seriously irresponsible conduct.

So what do we mean by mental illness or disorder, and how does this account for the violent behaviour of an individual? Psy-chiatrists have tended to be more interested in the risk of violence in people with a clear-cut mental illness, particularly psychosis, and less interested in those who are diagnosed with a personal-ity disorder, perhaps because of an erroneous perception that the latter were less likely to be treatable. Although both depressed and manic patients have an increased risk of violent behaviour, the medical diagnosis consistently associated with the highest risk of violence is schizophrenia. In such psychotic patients, it is argued that violent behaviour is motivated by that person's psychotic symptoms (Link and Stueve, 1994; Taylor et al., 1994). Specific psychotic symptoms, known as 'threat/control-override' symptoms, for example command hallucinations, delusions of thought insertion or that one's mind is controlled by external forces, have been linked to an increased risk of aggression (Swanson et al., 1996). Here, the violence is explained solely by the existence of an underlying psychotic, usually schizophrenic, mental illness. Such a hypothesis raises important moral, ethical and legal questions, as this would imply that a person who commits an act of violence while mentally ill may not be responsible for their actions at all.

However, an association between particular psychotic symptoms and violence may be explained in other ways, such as pre-existing personality traits and underlying attitudes such as suspiciousness (Monahan et al., 2001). Furthermore, concurrent substance misuse greatly increases the probability of violence in people with schizophrenia, but is also a risk factor in non-mentally ill people. With an increasing body of evidence to show that cannabis is an aetiological factor in schizophrenia, it is therefore not clear whether to attribute violence in a psychotic person addicted to cannabis to the drug itself, the psychotic illness, the pharmacological effects of cannabis on the mental processes producing the psychotic illness, or the effects of cannabis on pre-existing personality traits and behavioural tendencies. Here, psychodynamic explanations may be more useful in understanding the underlying mechanisms, in that psychotropic drugs, whether illicit, or prescribed for the psychotic illness, may act on the ego defence mechanisms which regulate impulse control.

The discourse and debate generated by such differences of opinion within the psychiatric world, particularly in Britain, are constrained by a historical collective mentality that has tended to focus on epidemiological research and empirical observation rather than constructing psychological theories of mind linking personality with mental illness. This is reflected in contemporary psychiatric diagnostic classification systems based on descriptive phenomenology, which use a categorical approach to classify disorders on the basis of observable behaviour and symptoms, rather than theories of causation. The World Health Organisation's *International Classification of Mental and Behavioural Disorders, Tenth Edition (ICD-10)* (World Health Organisation, 1992), the diagnostic system used by most British psychiatrists, is 'atheoretical' with the deliberate omission of aetiological explanations of its mental disorders. In the other main diagnostic system, the American Psychiatric Association's *Diagnostic and Statistical Manual of Mental Disorders (DSM-IV)* (American Psychiatric Association, 1994), every diagnostic category is given an operational definition, as well as being a 'multi-axial' classification with separate axes allowing the systematic recording of five different information sets (clinical syndrome, personality and developmental disorders, physical conditions, psychosocial stressors and level of social and occupational functioning in the last year). While these manuals may appear to be impressive tomes and are useful in aiding communication and ensuring diagnostic consistency, they are limited by being lists of syndromes and symptoms potentially devoid of meaning and explanation.

Personality disorder

The limitations of a diagnostic system which categorises syndromes according to behavioural symptomatology become even more evident when we consider personality disorders. Personality disorders are variations or exaggerations of normal personality attributes and traits. The DSM-IV defines personality disorder as enduring patterns of cognition, affectivity, interpersonal behaviour and impulse control that are culturally deviant, pervasive and inflexible, leading to distress and social impairment, and in some cases antisocial behaviour. In both the DSM-IV and the ICD-10, several categories of disorder are identified and operationally defined according to specific criteria. This medical model of categorical classification of personality disorder implies qualitative distinctions between normality and abnormality and clear boundaries between categories. However, individuals, whether violent or not, do not neatly fit into this all-or-none system, and people with personality difficulties often fulfil criteria for more than one personality disorder. Moreover, the ICD and DSM classifications differ in their categorisation, and have evolved over the years with the introduction of new disorders and the removal of others, so that a person with violent behaviour may variously fulfil criteria for antisocial, dissocial, emotionally unstable, borderline, narcissistic or sadistic personality disorder according to which side of the Atlantic they reside and in which era they lived. Indeed, it could be argued that the clinician's adherence to a diagnostic system that isolates syndromes of character abnormality as opposed to the 'normal personality' is a defence against acknowledging the possibility that psychic disturbance, including aggression, may be present in us all.

The alternative to a categorical system is a dimensional approach that assumes quantitative differences, or varying degrees of dysfunction. The dimensional approach shifts the focus of personality disorder from surface psychopathology to a consideration of underlying structural abnormalities and deficits in the character. Such an approach is more compatible with psychoanalytic conceptualisations, and may more accurately represent the organisational structure of personality dysfunction. It is likely that a dimensional approach will feature more prominently in the next version of the American diagnostic manual, DSM-V. Dimensional measures of personality traits such as the Millon Clinical Multi-axial Inventory (Millon et al., 1994), developed in the United States, are increasingly being used in forensic settings in the UK.

Borderline and antisocial personality disorders are those most often associated with violent behaviour, and indeed violent behaviour is one of the defining features of these personality types. Violent behaviour is also associated with the paranoid and schizoid disorders defined by DSM-IV. However, instead of considering isolated symptoms in these disorders of character, it is more instructive to look at the underlying structural dynamics and developmental deficits they may share. Kernberg's (1984) concept of the personality organisation provides a helpful explanatory construct in understanding the development of personality traits that predispose an individual to impulsive and violent behaviour. Kernberg has proposed a two-dimensional approach to the systematic understanding of character organisation. On one dimension are the various personality traits such as narcissism, obsessionality, hysteria and dependency; and on the second dimension there are three levels of personality organisation, which are discriminated on the basis of identity integration, defensive organisation and reality testing. Meloy (1988) believes that most homicidal acts are committed by people with borderline and psychotic personality organisations.

Observation of Mr B's (above) relationships in hospital showed that he would form rapid friendships with new patients or members of staff who would be flattered by his attentions and impressed by his wit and charm. However, Mr B would inevitably become hostile and contemptuous of others as soon as his own wishes and demands, for example increasing his ground leave, were frustrated or denied. In group therapy he would tend to impress and dominate the group with grandiose accounts of his exciting car-jacking exploits as a teenager, but would appear disinterested and lacking in empathy for the other patients' problems. The clinical team treating him was split into those (mostly male staff) who experienced him as a 'loveable rogue' and others (predominantly female) who considered him to be a seductive but deceitful psychopath who was fundamentally untreatable.

The borderline personality organisation describes a character structure made up of poorly differentiated and un-integrated self- and object-representations, resulting in a diffuse and incoherent identity, and the use of predominantly primitive defence mechanisms such as splitting, projective identification, idealisation, denigration and omnipotent control. Relationships tend to be superficial, narcissistically driven and are characterised by lack of empathy and awareness of the other person as a separate individual with differing needs and opinions. Using the dimensional approach to violence advocated in the previous chapter, we could describe these individuals as having a poor capacity for representation and mentalization, and a defensive system that is over-reliant on more primitive modes of functioning, both risk factors for poor impulse control and violent behaviour.

Despite Mr B's long treatments with individual and group psychotherapy, he remained volatile, and quick to take offence to perceived slights and insults by other patients, resulting in him frequently provoking arguments with patients and staff. Whilst these were now always verbal and not physically violent, as he had been during the early years of his admission, it was clear that Mr B found it difficult to tolerate a different point of view from his own. This can be seen as a reflection of a persistently reduced capacity in Mr B for representing and differentiating his own thoughts and affects in his mind from the thoughts and feelings of others. Instead of being able to tolerate ambiguities and differences, which could be used to modify and elaborate his own thoughts, other people's attitudes were experienced by Mr B as a concrete intrusion into his mind that was unacceptable and must be expelled in violent action – currently as verbal outbursts, but previously as bodily violence with fatal consequences. This failure in mentalization and poor impulse control may be the result of Mr B's early childhood history of trauma, neglect and multiple disruptions, in which his mother was unable to provide a background of safety from which Mr B could develop a secure attachment, but instead violently intruded upon Mr B's body and mind. Mr B's alcoholic father's emotional unavailability and physical absence prevented Mr B from being offered any source of alternative identification or respite from the abusive relationship with his mother. As a young adult, Mr B was not consciously aware of his rage at his mother, but enacted this in the violence towards his girlfriends, culminating in his psychotic homicidal attack on a female stranger.

The research on the causes of personality disorder suggests that there is no single known cause, but that a complex interplay between biological, social and psychological factors interferes with normal development of the personality (Alwin et al., 2006; Rutter, 1987; Stone, 1980; Zanarini and Frankenberg, 1997). Although studies showing genetic, temperamental, neuroanatomical and biochemical factors are implicated in personality disorder, repeated studies have also shown that the incidence of childhood neglect, abuse, trauma and loss is much higher in people with diagnosable personality disorders than in the normal population. Psychological and social dysfunction within the families of people with personality disorder is also evident to a high degree, with higher instances of parental depression and alcoholism, poverty, unemployment, domestic violence and family breakdown. It appears that multiple adverse life experiences combined with biological vulnerability are necessary to produce a significant level of personality disorder. For example, the recent body of research on so-called callous-unemotional disorder of childhood, which is thought to represent an innately disturbed group of children who develop into antisocial and psychopathic adults (Barry et al., 2000; Lynam and Gudonis, 2005), shows that their developmental trajectory can nevertheless be influenced by the environment, as the genes involved in antisocial and aggressive behaviour interact with specific environmental factors, such as physical abuse, to determine outcome (Hodgins, 2007). This viewpoint is consistent with the psychobiological attachment model outlined in the previous chapter in which it is proposed that violent behaviour originates in experiences of trauma, abuse and loss that interfere with normal attachment and the development of mind, with subsequent adverse experiences compounding the earlier traumas and faulty attachments. This is not to say that all people who are violent have a diagnosable personality disorder, but that certain developmental deficits and abnormalities in character that are seen in personality disorder may also predispose to violent behaviour.

The medical team looking after Mr B spent much time debating his psychiatric diagnosis. Although the medical records from his short time in prison after his index offence recorded that he was expressing persecutory ideas, appeared suspicious of the prison officers, and that his speech sounded odd, suggesting thought disorder, none of the clinical staff had observed any such behaviour since his transfer to the high secure hospital 10 years previously. This transfer had been accepted on the basis that Mr B had a diagnosable psychotic illness, having been made subject to a hospital order with restrictions on the grounds of mental illness. Mr B's emotional instability, his aggressive outbursts, superficial short-lasting relationships and lack of concern for others all pointed towards a diagnosis of a borderline or antisocial personality disorder. Some staff even suspected that he had feigned a psychotic illness in order to escape a custodial sentence, whilst others, such as his psychiatrist, were reluctant to officially call him personality disordered out of concern that this could confuse his diagnosis should he become psychotic again. He was eventually referred to as having a 'dual diagnosis', with no further thought that his previous psychotic illness and current personality disorder could be linked by the same underlying psychic processes.

Psychosis

Psychiatrists have tended to think about mental illnesses and particularly psychotic disorders as disease entities that are quite separate in both their presentation and their aetiology from character pathology. Again, this is reflected in the prevailing medical diagnostic model based on distinct categories of disorder, rather than viewing psychological disorders on a dimensional continuum. If a person fulfils diagnostic criteria for both a mental illness and a personality disorder, they are known as having a 'dual diagnosis' in which separate pathological processes are attributed to both mental illness and character abnormality, instead of considering that they might share underlying pathological mechanisms, whether psychological or organic. If a patient with a dual diagnosis is also violent, whether the violence is attributed to the mental illness or to the personality disorder can have serious implications for that patient's possibilities of treatment as many psychiatrists until recently have resisted providing therapy for people with personality disorder, preferring to think of them as untreatable.

Moreover, the tradition of descriptive psychopathology in clinical psychiatry prioritises an interest in the form of a patient's symptoms and signs rather than exploring their content, which is often deemed irrelevant or incidental. This is enshrined in Jaspers's (1959) concept of the 'un-understandable' primary delusion of schizophrenia, where the content of the delusion is deemed ultimately meaningless, and the 'normal' person, in this case the assessing psychiatrist, is not able to understand where the psychotic person's abnormal beliefs originated and decides that further exploration would be unnecessary. This, of course, ignores the possibility that such a delusion may be replete with unconscious meaning, and that exploration of the psychotic person's inner world, their unconscious desires and conflicts may yield very meaningful connections with that person's history. For example, the primary delusion of a schizophrenic spinster, who believes that men are entering her flat in the middle of the night to anaesthetise and rape her, may appear at first sight to have no connection with her uneventful middle-class upbringing, but on further inquiry may be a reflection of her doubts about her femininity, the unconscious conflicts about her sexual desires related to oedipal wishes and fears about her own aggression towards men. Here we can see parallels between the psychotic symptom and violent behaviour, both of which may on surface examination appear to be unreasonable, but when viewed through a psychoanalytic lens the logic of unconscious meaning is exposed. Both delusions and violence can therefore be thought of as symptomatic pathological solutions to underlying unconscious conflicts, which may need to be addressed as part of the treatment of the disturbed person.

Psychoanalysts have historically understood psychosis as being the result of structural deficits in the ego and a regression to more primitive modes of functioning and use of primitive defence mechanisms. Freud (1911a, 1924) saw psychosis as an extreme form of regression to infantile modes of thinking, a condition where primary process thinking, such as occurs in normal dreaming, supervenes. The ego is too fragile to handle instinctual desires which overwhelm it, and there is a generalised loss of normal ego functions, for example, the loss of the ability to differentiate self from other, inner reality from outer reality, thought from perception, perception from memory and past from present. There is also a loss of conceptual thinking or failure to symbolise, so that the psychotic person can only think in concrete terms. Freud saw psychosis as a withdrawal of the person from the external world into a narcissistic state, and because of this he believed the psychotic was unable to form a relationship with or transference to the analyst and was therefore untreatable. He believed that the delusions and hallucinations experienced in psychosis were an attempt by the psychotic person to repair a fragmentary inner world. 'In regard to the genesis of delusions, a fair number of analyses have taught us that the delusion is found applied like a patch over the place where originally a rent had appeared in the ego's relation to the external world' (Freud, 1924, p. 151).

Melanie Klein and later psychoanalysts went on to develop and challenge Freud's ideas, in particular that psychotic patients were not treatable with psychoanalysis. Klein believed that rather than having no transference to the analyst, the psychotic patient had an intense transference, but one that was characterised by pathological projection and projective identification, so that the apparent absence of transference was actually the transference (Klein, 1952). She believed that psychotic illnesses represented the revival of severe infantile anxieties and primitive defence mechanisms, such as splitting, idealisation and projective identification, so that the patient lacked a secure identity as he had projected parts of himself into others (Klein, 1946).

Winnicott (1959–1964) focused attention on early environmental deficits and traumas, which he thought predisposed to psychosis, in particular the very early relationship between the mother and infant. This contributed to the notion that faulty mothering caused schizophrenia by the 'schizophrenogenic' mother, and while this is a simplification of the ideas at the time, mothers felt unduly blamed and this added to a growing disillusion with psychoanalysis so that these ideas became discredited. As with personality disorder, however, there is now a revival of a more sophisticated model that proposes that both organic factors (e.g. genetic, brain damage at birth) and experiences of trauma, loss and attachment disturbances interfere with the normal development of mind and make it more vulnerable to later psychotic breakdown. The symptoms of psychosis can be seen as the ego's attempts to repair an underlying breakdown of the personality or disintegration of the ego. Such an ego is characterised by confusion of self and object, loss of reality testing, use of very primitive defence mechanisms and the failure of repression which allows previously unacceptable unconscious thoughts and affects to enter and overwhelm the ego.

Mr S was a 22-year-old physics university student, somewhat socially isolated but doing well academically. He was an only child, describing himself as shy and introvert with few friends at school. His parents had divorced when he was 3, after which he had rarely seen his father. He described a very close relationship with his mother whilst growing up, sleeping in the same bed with her until puberty. Medical records of his mother revealed that she had suffered from depression when Mr S was a child. Following graduation, he returned to live with his mother to apply for graduate jobs. During this time he had his first sexual experience with a female student, who broke up the relationship after only a few weeks.

During that summer he was interviewed for a Masters course, and the interviewers reported that he appeared suspicious and told them that he had been implanted with a radio chip at his dentist. Over some weeks he became convinced that his house was under surveillance and that his life was in danger. He began sleeping on his mother's floor for safety, but then started believing that his mother was controlling his mind and that she was setting him up. One evening, after his mother urged him to see the doctor, he took a kitchen knife and killed her with multiple stab wounds. He then turned the knife on himself, inflicting serious injuries in an attempt to disembowel himself. In prison he was found to be 'grossly psychotic', was diagnosed with paranoid schizophrenia and transferred to a medium secure psychiatric hospital, where he responded to anti-psychotic medication.

We can speculate that Mr S's mother may have been both emotionally withdrawn from him whilst depressed during his childhood, as well as using him for her own narcissistic needs as a substitute for her absent husband. Mr S had no father figure with whom to identify, and this absence of third object meant that Mr S could never truly achieve the psychic separation and individuation necessary for healthy development. This may have left him with deficits in his capacity for mentalization or symbolisation, and a more fragile mind that was susceptible to psychotic breakdown.

Bion (1957) saw the psychotic person's mind as not being totally psychotic, in that the primitive level of functioning of the psychotic part does not totally overwhelm the whole ego or personality as in, for example, delirium, but that the psychotic patient has non-psychotic parts of the personality, which the analyst or therapist can work with. However, Bion (1959) thought that psychotic patients were so terrified of their own thoughts that they mount destructive attacks on their thoughts and any meaning, coining the phrase 'attacks on linking'. The psychotic part of the mind makes use of primitive projective defence mechanisms to relieve itself of emotional pain, loss or depressive experience. These unbearable thoughts and feelings are evacuated to produce the psychotic symptoms. Thus hallucinations and delusions can be thought of as projected unbearable feelings and thoughts that are then experienced by the psychotic person as originating in the external world.

One can speculate that Mr S's experience of a depressed and narcissistic mother and absent father interfered with his pre-oedipal and oedipal development and led to the formation of an overly harsh superego. His psychotic breakdown occurred shortly after he was rejected by his girlfriend. It appears that this first sexual experience and subsequent rejection awoke previously repressed unresolved oedipal aggressive and sexual feelings towards his mother and feelings of loss and abandonment by his father, which were intolerable to Mr S's conscious mind and had to be projected into the external world. The projected aggressive feelings were then experienced as coming back at him in his beliefs that he was being poisoned. His delusion of surveillance can be understood as the projection of Mr S's harsh superego, which severely judged him for his forbidden sexual impulses.

The psychotic mind's poor representational capacities and inability to symbolise (concrete thinking) render the psychotic person reliant on the excessive use of primitive defence mechanisms such as projection and projective identification to rid themselves of intolerable psychic pain. But most psychotic patients are not violent, so why does a psychotic person become violent? Recent psychoanalytic writers working with psychotic and violent patients propose that the psychosis itself holds a defensive function, in defending against underlying aggressive impulses. When this defensive shield is breached, such aggression can emerge as violence.

Projection and projective identification are powerful defence mechanisms but may only be partially successful. The projection of unacceptable thoughts and feelings perceived as 'bad' into another person may then make that person appear frightening to the psychotic person who believes that the only way to get rid of their 'badness' altogether is to annihilate the person invested with his projections. Lucas (2003) describes the process of psychotic homicides as the psychotic person projecting their unbearable persecutory and depressive feelings concretely into a stranger, and then seeking relief through attacking and murdering him. In projective identification, the person who is the object of the psychotic projections may himself experience these as unpleasant and unwanted, unconsciously identify with these projected states of mind and act aggressively towards the psychotic person. The latter may then react violently in the belief that he is defending himself.

Sohn (1995) describes working with patients diagnosed with a psychotic illness who have carried out apparently unprovoked violent attacks on strangers, in which projection and projective identification processes fail altogether. He proposes that in these psychotic patients, projective identification cannot be used to rid the self of frightening states of mind because these states of mind are experienced as concrete mental objects that have to be kept in the mind to avoid the worse dread of a completely empty mind. Sohn suggests that these patients' aggressive instincts have interfered with their capacity to symbolise, which includes the symbolisation of 'loss', in other words that they are left with the terror of a mind devoid of content. Sohn speculates that these patients did not experience an original maternal object into which they could project their feelings. This lack of symbol formation or mentalization, and inability to project means that the only way of ridding the mind of these intolerable feelings is by violent physical action. Hyatt-Williams (1998) proposes that an essential feature of murderous acts is the collapse of symbolic thinking, releasing previously encapsulated unmetabolised death experiences, that he calls 'the death constellation', which overwhelm the mind and have to be massively projected in homicide, or introjected resulting in suicide.

As Mr S descends into the terrifying world of psychosis, boundaries between self and other, internal and external, ego and id, become confused and eventually collapse. Previously repressed aggressive and sexual feelings enter his mind, are experienced as intolerable and have to be projected into others. He turns to his mother for support, but in his mind, her role as protector breaks down as she is increasingly invested with his projected badness. She is no longer perceived as a separate human being but now becomes the terrifying object that has to be destroyed. Her murder, however, brings no relief, as she can no longer function as a receptacle for Mr S's projections. Mr S's subsequent disembowelment can be seen as a regression to a state of mind in which self and object merge, where Mr S now desperately attempts to rid himself of a terrifying maternal object viscerally experienced as located in his abdomen, so that he is literally pregnant with his mother who has to be aborted. These massive projections, which he enacts in homicide and attempted suicide, however, remain unsuccessful as he is left with the dread of an empty mind, which is then defensively filled again with psychotic symptoms.

Hyatt-Williams (1998) believes that murder only occurs concretely after it has been committed many times in phantasy, often unconscious phantasy that has never entered the person's conscious awareness. The potential murderer employs many efforts, both conscious and unconscious, to keep these murderous impulses encapsulated in the mind to avert action. Such defensive efforts include the person seeking refuge in what Doctor (2008) calls a 'psychotic retreat', which not only keeps the aggressive feelings in check, but also makes them unable to mourn and process their history of loss. Doctor proposes that the early abuses and traumas experienced by such patients are experienced as threatening to life itself, creating an emptiness or void · at the centre of their very being that is filled with 'psychotic debris' in order to encapsulate their murderous rage. Here the psychosis is used as a defence, the psychotic experience vividly replacing the real individual history of trauma and impoverishment. Only when this psychotic defensive arrangement is threatened by the fear of death, it breaks down and releases the rage which is enacted in extreme violence.

It may be tempting to attribute all acts of extreme violence or murder to psychotic processes operating in the mind. However, it is important to distinguish violence committed in the context of a psychotic illness, where the psychotic violence is motivated primarily by a matrix of long-standing delusional beliefs as in the case of Mr S, and explosive or rage-type violence, in which the person may appear to be transiently psychotic but has no previous history of psychosis. In such rage-type violence or murder, the psychotic-like symptoms are better understood as dissociative experiences linked to trauma in the context of a borderline-type personality (Cartwright, 2002). In many cases of violence, the person may fulfil criteria for a diagnosis of personality disorder and although there is no evidence of a pre-existing clear-cut psychotic illness, a psychotic-like mental state at the time of the offence may result in the person receiving an additional diagnosis of schizophrenia, as in the case of Mr B. An alternative explanation, however, to this double pathology or 'dual diagnosis' is that the psychotic symptoms are the result of a breakdown in the 'psychopathic' defences of the individual concerned (Hale and Dhar, 2008). This will be explored further in the next chapter when we examine the notion of psychopathy, as both a severe variant of personality disorder and a defensive structure, in more detail.

Summary

- Although the majority of mentally ill people are not violent, violent behaviour has a small but significant association with schizophrenia, the reasons for which are unclear.
- Current psychiatric diagnostic classifications are based on a categorical rather than dimensional model, which limits their usefulness in understanding common underlying causes and mechanisms in personality disorder and mental illness. A dimensional approach is more compatible with psychoanalytic conceptualisations of underlying pathological personality

structures, the more primitive of which predispose to violent behaviour.

- The aetiology of personality disorder and mental illness is complex, but both involve genetic predispositions interacting with early adverse environmental experiences to produce pathology in adolescence or adulthood.
- Like violence, psychotic symptoms can be seen as communications with unconscious meaning, pathological solutions to underlying unconscious conflicts.
- Violent behaviour in both individuals with personality disorder and those with mental illness may be explained by the use of primitive defence mechanisms such as projection and projective identification and their failure to contain aggressive impulses.

PSYCHOPATHY

The psychopathic criminal is a familiar and enduring figure used by authors, filmmakers and journalists to frighten and seduce their audiences – the cold, calculating serial killer, the mafia gangster, the ruthless business magnate or the Nazi SS officer. The psychopath's superficial charm, ruthlessness, pathological lying, disregard of emotional attachments, lack of remorse and shame and capacity for extreme and sadistic violence have intrigued both lay people and professionals in the world of mental health for the past two centuries. This has culminated in a new risk-obsessed millennium in which the detection of psychopathic traits in convicted prisoners and psychiatric patients has been refined and enshrined in risk assessment tools that are marketed to predict which individuals are most likely to be violent.

Historical conceptions of psychopathy

Since the French psychiatrist Pinel first documented in 1801 a group of patients who behaved in impulsive and destructive ways with no apparent defect in reasoning, a disorder he called 'manie sans delire', the historical vicissitudes of the psychopathic concept within psychiatry trace a path that alternated between clinical understanding and moral condemnation. The latter is reflected in a trend of pejorative diagnostic terminology in psychiatry, with Koch's (1891) concept of 'psychopathic inferiority', Meyer's (1904) 'constitutional inferiority', Kraepelin's (1887, 1889, 1896, 1903–1904, 1915) notions of 'degeneration' and Prichard's (1835) 'moral insanity'. Psychopathy here was thought of as a biologically rooted entity that was degenerative in moral stature. The beginning of the twentieth century, however, heralded a psychogenic interest in the disorder. Psychoanalysts now became interested and tried to maintain an objective scientific attitude divorced from moral judgement. In Freud's (1916) paper 'Some character-types met with in psycho-analytic work' he described a subgroup of people whom he referred to as 'criminals from a sense of guilt'. These were individuals who were drawn to committing forbidden antisocial deeds to relieve an unconscious sense of guilt. This stimulated a series of clinical reports by psychoanalysts including Aichorn (1925), Alexander (1923, 1930, 1935), Fenichel (1945), Friedlander (1945), Greenacre (1945), Horney (1945) and Reich (1945), about people who displayed antisocial and delinquent behaviour, which highlighted the failures of the superego, deficits in early identifications and early disturbed parent–child relations.

Others emphasised the developmental deficits evident in the mind of the psychopath, but also considered psychopathy as a defensive structure. Winnicott's (1956, 1986) distinction between experiences of privation and deprivation is of relevance here. In privation, there have never been any good objects or experience, which can only lead to hopelessness, whereas in deprivation there have been some early good experiences, which are subsequently lost, producing 'antisocial tendencies' of anger, resentment and violence, which can be seen as a more hopeful attempt to regain the lost object. Similarly, Bowlby (1944) coined the term 'affectionless psychopaths' for children whose apparent indifference to others concealed their terror of 'the risk of their hearts being broken again'.

Cleckley's (1941) book *The Mask of Sanity* remains one of the most renowned and respected classic works on the psychopath. He attributed psychopathy to a concealed psychosis, an idea that he evolved in subsequent editions and can be linked to Kernberg's (1984) later conceptualisations of personality organisations. Within psychiatry, Cleckley's influence has been felt most in the clarity of his clinical description of the psychopath. He described 16 behavioural criteria for psychopathy, including guiltlessness, lack of remorse and shame, incapacity for object love, emotional shallowness, impulsivity, egocentricity, inability to learn from experience and lack of insight. These primary traits of the psychopath have been more recently empirically defined and measured by Hare (1991) in the development of his widely used risk assessment tool, the Psychopathy Checklist (see below). Cleckley was also influential in his assertion that the psychopathic personality was not only found in the criminal population, but was also prevalent in successful and respected professionals including businessmen, scientists and doctors.

In the latter half of the last century, two divergent paths emerged in the scientific investigation of the psychopath. Psychoanalytic theorists continued to examine the psychogenic and intrapsychic origins of psychopathy with an increasing emphasis on the importance of narcissistic psychopathology and disturbances in early object relations or pre-oedipal pathology, while psychiatrists became more interested in genetic and neurobiological empirical research that validated organic theories of psychopathic character development. In this chapter I will focus on contemporary psychoanalytic contributions to the concept of psychopathy and its relation to violence, in particular the work of Meloy who is prominent in those working in the field of psychopathy in formulating a coherent integration of ideas related to physiological and cognitive deficits in psychopathy with related psychoanalytic concepts. Meloy's biopsychogenic model proposes that although neuroanatomical, neurophysiological and twin and adoption studies suggest a genetic basis, early disturbed object relations and other environmental influences are also necessary to produce psychopathy.

Definitions of psychopathy and the Hare Psychopathy Checklist

The term psychopathy continues to be loosely applied within mental health. Perhaps because of its pejorative connotations, current diagnostic classifications exclude the term, with the ICD-10 using Dissocial Personality Disorder (World Health Organisation, 1992), and DSM-IV using Antisocial Personality Disorder (American Psychiatric Association, 1994). In the UK until recently a person could be detained in hospital against his will under the category of 'psychopathic disorder'. This was a legal category within the Mental Health Act for '... a persistent disorder or disability of mind (whether or not including significant impairment of intelligence) which results in abnormally aggressive or seriously irresponsible conduct ...' (Mental Health Act, 1983). It was generally accepted that the term 'psychopathic disorder' did not represent a single clinical disorder, but was a legal category describing a number of severe personality disorders, which contributed to the person committing antisocial acts. The recent reform of the Mental Health Act (2007) has replaced all previous separate definitions of disorder, including the term 'psychopathic disorder', with a single category of 'mental disorder' applied throughout the act.

But it is with the invention of the Hare Psychopathy Checklist (PCL) that the concept of psychopathy has achieved most influence in the assessment and management of violent patients in forensic psychiatric services, and to a lesser extent in the management of violent offenders within the criminal justice system. Hare empirically validated Cleckley's original clinical description of a 'psychopath', to produce a reliable operationalised risk assessment instrument consisting of a 20-item questionnaire. High scores are empirically associated with a considerable increase in the likelihood of violent recidivism (Hare, 1991). While the PCL and its later versions have proved to be useful and immensely popular risk assessment tools, some argue (e.g. Mizen and Morris, 2007) that this has turned into a 'psychopathy industry', and that the emphasis on descriptive characteristics detracts from further exploration of underlying dynamic factors that may contribute to the psychopathic construct. The danger is that once a person is labelled a 'psychopath' he will be seen as dangerous and untreatable, categorically different from others, rather than a human being with particular personality traits that have developed for specific defensive reasons, and who may not be resistant to therapeutic change.

Developmental origins and the internal world of the psychopath

Mr J, a good-looking man in his 30s, was a serial fraudster who preferred his victims to be vulnerable young single females. Over several months he would gain their confidence and affections with lavish gifts and fine dining, entertaining them with false tales of success in a glittering career in the city. Once he had seduced them into a sexual relationship, he would begin to steal money by fraudulent misuse of bank accounts and credit cards, and if they attempted to leave him he would become physically abusive and harass them. Using a variety of aliases, he conned car show room managers into lending him expensive vehicles 'for advertising shoots'. When he was finally arrested on a string of assault, harassment and fraud charges, he claimed that he was the victim of the women he had conned, advocating that they had harassed and seduced him.

Any account of development of the psychopathic personality needs to explain behaviours and attitudes that may appear to be antithetical to basic human nature – the lack of empathy and emotional attachment, the reversal of moral values, the addiction to violence and extreme states of excitement, the triumphant manipulation and deception of others – psychopathic characteristics that are too easily dismissed as being based on evil intent, rather than consideration of very complex underlying psychopathology leading to 'violence and disorders of the will' (Richards, 1998).

Personality organisation

Meloy (1988) defines psychopathy as an intrapsychic process in which aggression has a central organising principle in both its structure and its function. He emphasises that psychopathy represents a category to be used for diagnostic purposes, but is also a continuum, a psychological disturbance that varies in type, severity and treatability from one person to the next. This continuum is located within the spectrum of narcissistic personality disorders, psychopathy being an aggressive subcategory (Kernberg, 1975). Following Kernberg's (1984) levels of personality organisation, narcissistic personality disorders, including psychopathy, represent personality function and structure at a relatively high level of borderline personality organisation. Nevertheless, although in borderline personality organisation, unlike psychotic personality organisation, reality testing is maintained, there is a lack of integration of identity of self, and a predominance in the use of primitive defence mechanisms. The psychopath may appear to function at a sophisticated level – the mask of sanity – but this conceals serious and pervasive deficits in ego structure and functioning.

Meloy proposes that the developmental origins of psychopathy begin in disordered attachment. This originates within the infant who is biologically endowed with excessive aggression or has other neurologically determined deficits in the capacity to attach, as well as an autonomic hyporeactivity or under-arousal. Early experiences of parental abuse, lack of maternal attunement and containment, and neglect interact with these biological abnormalities to set the scene for the development of psychopathy. In other words, although psychopathy is biologically predisposed, early deficits and conflicts in primary object attachment experiences are also necessary to determine this character disorder.

Failures of internalisation

Meloy postulates very early disturbances in separation and identification processes in the development of the psychopath. For the normal infant, differentiation between internal and external, and the sense of a separate self gradually emerge in the context of a mother who provides a background object of primary identification

(Grotstein, 1980) and containment without unnecessary impinge-ment. For the infant psychopath, however, early physical and emo-tional abuse introduces him prematurely to adverse experiences leading to precocious separation in which he experiences a domi-nance of uncomfortable sensations. Meloy suggests that this overly harsh sensory-perceptual experience with the mother may combine with what he calls an 'atavistic fear of predation', which predisposes to the formation of a narcissistic outer shell that conceals an inner vulnerable self. This is similar to Winnicott's (1960) notion of a 'false self' that develops prematurely at the expense of the hidden 'true self', as well as Cleckley's (1941) understanding of the psychopath as showing a mask of sanity to the world which conceals a hidden core of psychosis.

The infant therefore develops an early basic distrust in the environ-ment in the absence of consistent and reliable nurturing experience. This lack of containment adversely affects the processes of internal-isation. The predominance of painful and malevolent experiences for the infant means that he develops an unconscious disavowal for the need for soothing internalisations. What occurs instead is that the infant identifies with the 'stranger selfobject' (Grotstein, 1982), a preconceived unconscious phantasy that anticipates the presence of the predator in the external world. This primary archetypal iden-tification is reinforced by the actual experience of the parent as an aggressive 'stranger', and becomes the core narcissistic identification of the grandiose self-structure of the psychopath.

Internal object relations and the grandiose self

These abnormal internalisations of the psychopath coalesce to form a pathological defensive structure of the self, the 'grandiose self-structure' (Kernberg, 1976). The grandiose self exists in all narcissistic personality disorders, but in the psychopath constitutes the very core of the self, and determines all interpersonal and affective function-ing. It is the primary identification for the psychopath, and must be maintained at all cost to ensure the psychopath's narcissistic equilib-rium. This is achieved by continual idealisations of himself as 'preda-tor' and denigration of others as 'prey'. Because the psychopath's personality organisation remains organised at a pre-oedipal or bor-derline level, internal object representations are not integrated and are experienced in extremes, as good or bad, positive or negative. The psychopath experiences his own self-representations as positive, and attributes negative qualities to others. In this way unpleasant affects and phantasies associated with bad objects are disavowed and projected into those around him.

However, this omnipotence of self and denigration of others in phantasy alone are not sufficient to maintain the grandiose self as a primary identification in the psychopath, unlike the more benign narcissistic personality disorder. The grandiose self can only be maintained by actual behavioural denigration of others, including violence. Meloy speculates that this failure of omnipotent phantasy is because the psychopath becomes immune to his own phantasies, exacerbated by chronic autonomic low arousal, so that unbearable affects of emptiness and envy start to reach consciousness and can only be evacuated by denigration and dismissiveness of others, and in some cases violent destruction of the object.

Mr L was a 25-year-old builder who invented grandiose stories about himself to improve his self-esteem. He claimed that he owned a Porsche and bragged about how this enabled him to pick up girls with whom he had sexual intercourse and then rejected. He started a relationship with a young woman who eventually realised that he was telling lies, and she ended the relationship. Mr L became depressed and was referred to the GP counsellor, but did not come back after an initial consultation in which he related his early history of sexual abuse by his father. Shortly after this, whilst walking through the park he saw an attractive young woman, whom he approached to ask out. When she rejected his advances, he bludgeoned her to death with a rock. In prison he maintained that his actions were justified as he had to 'shut her up', as she was mocking him.

The internal world of the psychopath is populated by primitive internal objects, or 'part-objects', in which good and bad are not integrated. The grandiose self is tenuously maintained by the psychopath attributing only the positive object representations to himself. Bad objects and negative or unpleasant affects and representations are projected into others. The psychopath's relationships with others remain narcissistically driven, external objects experienced as existing only for gratification. The self is idealised, others are denigrated. This creates a primitive, pre-oedipal internal world in which object relations have a dyadic structure, and are governed by primitive defence mechanisms such as splitting, denial, omnipotence and projection, with a lack of more mature defence mechanisms such as repression and sublimation. Thus the psychopath lives in a two-dimensional world, in which self and object are not fully differentiated into whole and separate entities. Affect regulation is inadequate, with emotions that are felt intensely, but can rapidly dissipate and change. The emotions felt by the psychopath are those familiar to the pre-oedipal toddler – envy, shame, boredom, rage and excitement. More mature affects, such as guilt, fear, depression, remorse and sympathy, which involve an appreciation of whole objects and a capacity for attachment, are missing.

Mr D had been referred for psychotherapy to explore his aggressive behaviour and previous violence. He had been convicted when younger for shaking his new-born baby, which had caused irreversible brain damage. Following his release from prison it was felt that he lacked remorse and minimised his offence, as he maintained that he had not intended to hurt the child. During his first consultation he expressed his fury and contempt towards a female cousin who had previously been experienced by Mr D as very supportive, but he had now cut off all contact with her as she had recently formed a relationship with a man whom he described as a paedophile and according to Mr D would be a risk to her teenage daughter. Here we can see how Mr D's own aggression and violence towards his child are not owned, but projected into his cousin's partner, who, with the cousin, become the receptacles for Mr D's unacceptable impulses. Mr D is unable to integrate conflicting representations of himself or others, but resorts to splitting and projection, locating all negative affects and aggressive impulses in the cousin and her partner, who have to be 'cut off completely' to maintain his own sense of grandiosity and righteousness. This maintains a simple dyadic state of mind in which people are either good or bad, preventing any deeper exploration of his own feelings of ambivalence and loss.

The psychopathic superego

The psychopath's paucity of deep and significant identifications with others means that he makes widespread use of pseudoidentificatory processes involving conscious and unconscious 'simulation' (Glasser, 1986) and 'imitation' (Gaddini, 1969) of other people's attitudes and actions. Simulation is the unconscious modelling of the attitudes and behaviours of the object with no corresponding change in the structure of the self. Imitation is a primitive unconscious defensive process that develops in the absence of the object with the aim of establishing a phantasy of magical and omnipotent fusion between self and object representations to ward off painful sensory experiences. Greenacre (1958) referred to the psychopath as an imposter, the 'as-if' quality that he possesses. However, he is often not aware of this lack of authenticity or 'false self' (Winnicott, 1960), unlike the less disturbed narcissistic personality disorder who is aware that at times he feels like a fake.

These pathological identifications and failures of internalisation, including the failure to internalise values, also affect the development of the superego. Psychoanalysts have been intrigued by the reversal of values in the psychopath, an apparent inversion of normal conscience, in which good intentions are punished and evil actions and intentions are rewarded. This has been called the inverse or mirror conscience (Richards, 1998; Svrakic et al., 1991). This identification with badness or evil means that psychopaths do not have the internal constraints that normally inhibit gratification of impulses. In severe narcissistic pathology, the superego is not fully developed, but consists of sadistic superego precursors or fragments that are the projected aspects of early persecutory objects (Kernberg, 1984). Svrakic et al. (1991) suggest that in the more antisocial or psychopathic person these pathological superego precursors have been more fully developed into an organiser that gratifies destructive behaviours and punishes positive behaviours, which explains why the identity of a 'negative hero' or 'anti-hero' supports the self-esteem or grandiose self of the psychopath. This identification with sadistic persecutory objects also explains the psychopath's use of sadism to achieve pleasure.

Thus, aggressive introjects and identifications have replaced those based on parental ideals, resulting in the psychopath attributing negative value to notions such as attachment, morality, love and empathy. As the pre-psychopathic child grows older, he increasingly identifies with role models based outside of the family circle, selecting older peers and mentors who are aggressive and destructive, such identifications consolidating the sadistic superego. Pre-oedipal simulatory and imitative processes develop in later childhood and adolescence into more conscious simulation of higher social affects and learnt manipulative deception to gain social advantage. The empathic failure of identification with others means that the psychopathic person is not inhibited in his behaviour by the normal social taboos against violence, in that the psychopath is not aware of the emotions and suffering of others, or becomes excited at making the other suffer. The psychopath attempts to maintain omnipotent control of his objects by both conscious deception and unconscious mechanisms such as denial and projective identification. Meloy (1988) reminds us, however, that psychopathic patients who appear to be malingering or intentionally lying reflect a complex interplay of conscious choice and unconscious defence in the psychopathic mind.

Mr Y was a homosexual man in his 20s who had been serially sexually abused as a child, both within and outside of his family, whilst he was in care homes. He eventually ran away from care to work as child prostitute in the nearby city. As a teenager and young adult he engaged in a range of offending behaviours, including theft, burglary, fraud and violent assaults. In his 30s he developed more sophisticated conning where he picked up well-heeled men in gay bars. After having sex with them he would steal their wallets and cars, and using this money and the expensive stolen vehicles he seduced rent boys. Eventually arrested and charged with abduction, false imprisonment and sexual assault, he presented in prison as virtually mute and claiming total amnesia following a head injury as a result of an assault by one of the rich gay men who had given evidence against him. He convinced the inexperienced prison doctor that he was suffering from brain damage and unable to testify. Shortly afterwards he was observed giving detailed instructions to his own lawyer regarding his defence.

Meloy (1988) has coined the term 'malignant pseudoidentification' for the process whereby the psychopath consciously imitates or unconsciously simulates certain behaviours of the victim to foster the victim's identification with the psychopath, thus increasing the victim's vulnerability to exploitation. This is often achieved by successful fraudsters or conmen, who may carefully select their victims by recognising subtle narcissistic vulnerabilities of the victim via transference and countertransference phenomena. As in the example above, mental health and legal professionals are not immune to the psychopath's covert seduction. The psychopath attempts to increase the professional's empathy with the psychopath by simulating or mirroring the affects and mannerisms of the professional, flattering the victim's narcissism via pseudoidentification. The professional is attracted by the apparent helpfulness of the psychopathic individual and can become almost deluded into believing that a special bond has been established between herself and the psychopath. Newly qualified professionals and those who see themselves as altruistic, denying their own narcissistic investments, may be particularly prone to harbouring legal or therapeutic 'rescue phantasies', which renders them vulnerable to a malignant pseudoidentification with the psychopath.

Countertransference reactions

The extreme behaviours and attitudes exhibited by the psychopath evoke strong reactions or countertransference feelings in others.

Hale and Dhar (2008) believe that the defining characteristic of psychopathy is the capacity to bring out the worst in the clinician or institution in contact with the psychopath. They view psychopathy as a defence mechanism in which bad feelings are projected into others, who must suffer in order to maintain the psychopath's precarious psychic equilibrium. The psychopath distorts reality and the feelings of those around them to protect his sense of sanity. The projected confusion of reality and phantasy can lead to the feeling that the psychopath is playing or interfering with one's mind. Meloy (1988) highlights the countertransference reactions that commonly arise in clinicians who are faced with a psychopathically disturbed person. These include feelings of moral outrage and therapeutic nihilism; feelings of hopelessness and guilt when change does not occur; excessive fear, and its counterpart, the denial of real dangerousness; devaluation and loss of professional identity; and excessively punitive and sadistic responses when the therapist unconsciously identifies with the patient's hatred and aggression. The role of countertransference in the assessment and treatment of psychopathic and other violent individuals will be discussed further in later chapters.

Psychopathic violence

Mr F, a 45-year-old man, had been a schoolteacher and 15 years previously had used this position of authority to intimidate and sexually abuse a 15-year-old girl, Ms P. Always attracted to extreme violence and now working as a security guard, Mr F had become obsessed with asphyxia, specifically becoming sexually excited at the idea of strangling a woman and watching her die. Mr F started watching short films that he found on the Internet where actors appear to have intercourse and then strangle their partners. After rehearsing this in his mind, Mr F persuaded Ms P, now 30, and who continued to have a sporadic dependent relationship with Mr F, to allow him to partially strangle her with a piece of wire during intercourse. After some time he then persuaded her to place an advertisement in the local paper seeking a female flat mate. After a young woman had replied and moved in with Ms P, with Ms P's co-operation, Mr F posed as an electrician, entered the flat and proceeded to attempt to rape and strangle the woman. The woman managed to escape. Mr F was arrested and charged with rape and attempted homicide. Mr F expressed no remorse for his offence but admitted that he had taken cocaine to 'enhance the sensation'.

The psychopath's attraction and addiction to violence is facilitated by several intrapsychic factors. First, his lack of attachment and

and alcohol addiction. Eventually rescued by a supportive girlfriend, he was persuaded to give up his life of crime and drugs, managed to stop his violent activities but became increasingly depressed and tormented over several years by intrusive thoughts of self-recriminations and 'guilt' about what he had done to his victims. Feeling suicidal he presented to his doctor who referred him to a psychiatrist. During the first consultation he presented as very depressed and worried the clinician with his suicidal ideation. During this interview he revealed details of past violent exploits for which he had never been caught, making the psychiatrist feel somehow special and excited to be seeing such an interesting patient and offered him therapy rather than reporting him to the police. At the following appointment a fortnight later, the psychiatrist was astonished when Mr P announced that he had cured him. His depression of the past 2 years had apparently vanished. Mr P declared that he no longer felt any guilt, he had a 'free conscience' and was very grateful to the doctor for 'curing him'.

Here we can see how Mr P's grandiose self-structure was dependent on his circle of powerful criminal friends who created a world of omnipotence and excitement that bolstered Mr P's psychopathic ego. When this world collapsed after the incarceration of the members of the gang, Mr P's own psychopathic defence mechanisms began to collapse, and he entered into a downward spiral of drug abuse until he was offered salvation by his girlfriend. However, Mr P was unable to sustain work in the real world, working as a waiter where he felt humiliated and had no recourse to the violent retribution that would be justified according to the rules of the criminal world in which he had grown up. Although he appeared to present with depressive symptomatology, on closer examination it can be seen that he was not experiencing genuine feelings of guilt, loss and concern for his victims, but had replicated the sado-masochistic criminal world in his mind, masochistically torturing himself by a sadistic superego with his intrusive thoughts of self-recriminations. Contact with the psychiatrist appeared to have fulfilled the function of the confessional: Mr P had 'off-loaded' his sins onto the doctor resulting in the rapid resurrection of his psychopathic defences and previous functioning. This represents a manic solution, rather than any real acknowledgement of painful feelings of guilt, loss and rejection.

Summary

- Historically there has been a dichotomy between those who saw psychopathy as being due to constitutional deficit, and those who viewed it as a defence against early trauma. More recent research indicates that while there is a genetic and biological basis to the disorder, early adverse environmental influences are also needed to form disordered attachments, the basis of psychopathy in adult life.

- The personality of the psychopath is organised at a borderline level, with the use of predominantly primitive defence mechanisms such as projection and splitting, failures of internalisation and identificatory processes to produce superego abnormalities and the defensive construction of a grandiose self that is maintained by continual idealisation of self and behavioural denigration and manipulation of others, including violence.

- The psychopath evokes extreme feelings or countertransference reactions in others, which may unconsciously influence how professionals treat him. Such reactions include feelings of moral outrage, therapeutic nihilism, fear, anger and sadistic responses and a sense of specialness.

- The psychopath's attraction to sadistic or predatory violence is facilitated by his lack of empathy, his low level of emotional arousal, his identification with sadistic objects and the use of stimulant drugs that bolster his psychopathic ego.

- The psychopathic grandiose self is a fragile structure that may break down so that the person is overwhelmed by underlying persecutory anxieties and presents with a transient psychotic state, which can be mistakenly diagnosed as schizophrenia. This breakdown in psychopathic defences can also cause a shift from sado-masochistic to self-preservative violence.

4

VIOLENCE, SEXUALITY AND PERVERSION

Aggression plays an integral part in all sexual activity. Although one might think of sexual intimacy as being the expression of loving feelings and the wish to be truly close to the other, aggressive impulses are necessarily involved to facilitate separation and to manage anxieties about being both overwhelmed by and losing the other person. Adult sexual relations and sexuality involve a complex interplay of conflicting feelings of love and hate, wishes to merge with the other versus wishes for independence and creative versus destructive impulses, all of which represent the culmination of a complex developmental trajectory from unconscious infantile and oedipal wishes, phantasies and conflicts, through adolescent revivals and crises, to adult modes of relating.

An unconscious fear of aggression and violence can be the basis to psychosexual disorders. For example, erectile failure in men, or vaginismus in women, may be based on unconscious anxieties about sexual intercourse as a violent act, and failure to perform during sexual intercourse may be due to unconscious fears of damaging or of being damaged by their partner. These unconscious fears may be derived from primitive unconscious phantasies of the primal scene as a violent act and the pre-oedipal mother as engulfing and violent. As mentioned in Chapter 1, Perelberg (1995, 1999a) proposes that this represents a core phantasy in violent individuals, but this phantasy may also be present in people who are not overtly aggressive or violent, or even consciously unaware of their aggressive feelings. However, when aggressive impulses become more prominent in sexual relations, with conscious or unconscious wishes to hurt, control or dominate the object, the person is not suffering from a psychosexual disorder but a sexual perversion. In this chapter we will explore the idea of perversion as a defence against aggression and unbearable anxiety.

Definitions of perversion

Perversion has become a pejorative term that accounts for its removal from current medical diagnostic classifications to be replaced with the term 'paraphilia' in DSM-IV (American Psychiatric Association, 1994), and the phrase 'disorder of sexual preference' in ICD-10 (World Health Organisation, 1992). This reflects the changing attitudes towards unusual sexuality and sexual practices over time. What may be acceptable behaviour in one era becomes unacceptable in the next, and vice versa. In recent years one could argue that there has been an increased sexualisation of society with sexual matters being more overtly portrayed in art, fashion and literature, discussed in the media, made a compulsory part of children's education and changing legislation and social policy to a degree that would have been thought quite shocking only a few decades earlier. On the one hand, there has been a normalisation of sexual orientation and behaviours previously thought of as perverse, such as homosexuality, transsexualism and transvestitism, leading to the legalisation of same-sex marriage and rights for transsexuals. Adult pornography has become mainstream, and sexual clubs catering for certain fetishistic or sado-masochistic preferences are thought of by many to be harmless and enjoyable variations of the myriad of human sexual desires. On the other hand, there has been a global epidemic of panic and moral condemnation of sexual crimes towards children such as incest, child abuse and paedophilia, the most recent anxiety and confusion being generated by the rapid proliferation of Internet child pornography. The public outrage and horror at the atrocities that can secretly occur next door in suburbia, such as the highly publicised cases of the West family in this country, the Dutroux case in Belgium and the Fritzl case in Austria, create an atmosphere of terror and excitement which stifles considered debate and therapeutic understanding of not just these rare extreme cases, but of other sexual practices which have become more culturally acceptable. Sexual offences such as paedophilia or rape would be seen by most people as violent coercive acts; however, the aggression that lies behind other sexual activities such as fetishism, exhibitionism or voyeurism may not be so obvious. What may appear to be primarily sexually motivated may actually conceal hidden destructiveness and violence.

In the 'Three essays on the theory of sexuality', Freud (1905a) defined perversion as 'sexual activities which either (a) extend, in an anatomical sense, beyond the regions of the body that are designed for sexual union, or (b) linger over the immediate relations to the sexual object which should normally be traversed rapidly on the path towards the final sexual aim' (p. 150). Here we can see that Freud considered perversions as abnormal sexual behaviours, some of which, such as masturbation or fellatio, which Freud considered perverse and symptoms of pathology, would now be considered normal by most people in our society. It is when the behaviour becomes more important than the sexual partner that it may be considered perverse. For example, a man may become excited when his wife puts on lacy underwear as part of their foreplay during love making. When the underwear becomes more important than his partner, and engaging in sexual intercourse with his wife is merely to sustain the fantasy about the underwear and enact the fetish, rather than engaging in an intimate relationship with another person in her own right, the man's behaviour can be called a perversion. The person with a perversion feels taken over by their compulsive, sometimes bizarre, sexualised behaviour, which only provides temporary relief from underlying anxieties, and therefore is endlessly repeated. The perversion may dominate a person's life, or remain split off and hidden in a person who appears to be functioning normally in his work and relationships, such as the well-respected married vicar, who is discovered to be sexually abusing altar boys.

An important distinction that psychoanalysts have made is between perversion as an aberrant behaviour and perverse psychic mechanisms. A person may show no overt perverse pathological symptoms, but uses habitual modes of relating and defence mechanisms that constitute perverse character traits. Stoller (1975) emphasised that everyone was more or less perverse and may use perverse mechanisms to defend against trauma by sexualisation. In his paper 'Character perversion' Arlow (1971) described patients who have replaced an original symptomatic perversion with personality traits that defend against voyeurism and fetishism to the extent that reality testing is damaged, but they no longer show any overt perverse behaviours. Ruszczynski (2006) asks us to think not only of perverse behaviour but also of a perverse organisation of mind, in which a particular constellation of anxieties, defences and internal object relations become projected into the external world in the perverse behaviour. He reminds us that the perverse act, like the violent act, may violate another person's body, but also violates and corrupts the other's mind, by sexual and aggressive means.

The definition of 'perverse' becomes more complicated when its use is extended beyond the sexual realm. Freud used the word perversion exclusively in relation to sexuality, and he did not associate perversion with the non-sexual instincts. Before Freud's time, however, the term perversion was used to in relation to other instincts. As Laplanche and Pontalis (1973) note, there is a multitude of forms perversion can take: perversions of the 'moral sense' (delinquency), of the 'social instinct' (prostitution) and of the 'instinct of nutrition' (bulimia or dypsomania). As we shall see in Chapter 5, Welldon (1988) posits a perversion of the maternal instinct. Contemporary psychoanalysts have understood perversion to be due to abnormal aggressive and narcissistic development, rather than primary sexual or libidinal deviation. A global definition of perverse might include any destructive attack on the truth, reality or creativity that is being presented as the opposite. For example, the mother who insists that her child must eat only organic vegan food for his health and to prevent cruelty to animals, although this restricts the child's diet so much that he becomes malnourished, or the man who convinces his wife that he needs to spend long hours working to provide financially for the family, but is actually avoiding intimacy with his wife and children, may both be considered to be acting perversely. Some non-sexual criminal behaviours such as shop-lifting and fraud may also be thought of as perverse. It is important to highlight the hostility, secrecy, collusion and self-deception that are integral to any perverse activity.

Polymorphous perversion

Freud (1905a) believed that all of us start out in life perverse and that a person's character is built up from defences or reaction-formations (where an unacceptable impulse is transformed into the opposite) against perverse infantile sexual impulses and dispositions. Contrary to the prevailing view that sexuality began at puberty, Freud believed several component or 'partial' sexual drives operated in the first few years of life, and worked unconsciously in pairs of opposites, such as looking and exhibiting, masochism and sadism, activity and passivity. The drives underwent a series of developments though oral, anal, phallic and genital stages, at each stage specific drives and erotogenic zones (the areas of the body that received most pleasure at each stage of development) being prominent. He described the normal child as polymorphously perverse, and it is not until the oedipal period at around ages 4 or 5, according to Freud, that the sexual drives abated because of the influence of several unconscious factors such as shame and disgust, leading to reaction formations, the development of a sense of guilt and more mature ego defences such as sublimation and repression. The partial infantile sexual instincts become more integrated because of the innate force of genitality in the phallic phase, and become permanently organised because of the biological influences of puberty. Freud at this stage believed that adult perversity was the result of component infantile sexual impulses that had escaped integration, repression and sublimation, because of a combination of biological and developmental factors including child sexual trauma. Freud linked certain specific adult perversions with specific infantile partial sexual drives: for example the child's urge to look turned into voyeurism, the urge to show into exhibitionism and the urge to touch into frotteurism. Freud's understanding of neurosis was that it was the result of repressed infantile sexual wishes – neurosis was therefore the opposite or 'negative' of perversion.

Mr L was convicted and received a probation order for an offence of voyeurism in which he had hidden in women's changing rooms and masturbated to the sight of naked women. He was referred for treatment and offered a place in a psychotherapeutic group for men and women convicted of sexual offences. In the group he appeared reticent and passive, revealing very little about himself, and although when he did speak he was considerate and polite, he was experienced by the female members of the group as secretive and rather sinister. This could be understood as a re-enactment of his offending behaviour in the group setting, in which he is experienced as spying on the female members of the group and violating their privacy, by hearing their personal stories but not revealing his own. Later, when this dynamic had been understood by the group and pointed out to him, Mr L revealed that as a child of a single mother, with three sisters but no brothers, he remembered being both terrified and fascinated by the atmosphere of repressed femininity and female sexuality that surrounded him, but from which he felt completely excluded.

Perversion as a defence against castration anxiety

Freud (1927) moved closer to the idea of perversion as a defence with his paper 'Fetishism'. Here he proposes that an adult's perverse sexual obsession with an article of female clothing such as a high-heeled shoe was a defence against the anxiety of castration. The young boy does not want to believe that his mother does not have a penis, as this means he might lose his too. The child who becomes an adult pervert correctly observes that she has no penis, yet retains a contradictory belief that she must still have one. This is disavowal, a defence against external reality, the contradiction of simultaneously knowing and not knowing allowed by the primary process of the unconscious. Freud proposed that the fetish item, such as the shoe, was a symbolic substitute for the woman's missing penis, and that the adult man's fetishistic activity was both a token of triumph over the threat of castration and a protection against it.

Mr H was referred for psychotherapy for a long-standing foot fetish. He demanded that his girlfriends did not wash their stockings and socks so that their feet would be dirty and smelly, which Mr H found immensely exciting. Sexual intercourse itself was unsatisfactory and secondary in importance in Mr H's mind to the sexual gratification he obtained from smelling and touching the foot. Mr H was from a large family, having eight siblings, those closest to him being sisters. Mother was described as strict and 'wearing the trousers', whilst father was mostly absent, away at work, and when at home, was denigrated by mother. We might speculate that Mr H's foot fetish is evidence of his confusion about sex and gender, his difficulties in establishing a secure male identification growing up surrounded by the female sex and his attempt to defend himself from castration anxieties induced by his mother by maintaining control over the woman's foot as a symbol of the penis that he convinces himself the woman must have, and therefore so must he.

The idea of disavowal as a defence mechanism used in perversion led to the understanding, by various theorists such as Lacan (1966), as perversion being located between neurosis and psychosis. In neurosis, the primary defence mechanism is repression, the pushing out of consciousness of thoughts and wishes that do not fit in with one's view of one's self. In psychosis, repression fails completely and the person is overwhelmed by the unconscious and creates a delusional world to make sense of chaos. In perversion, disavowal allows contradictory beliefs to be held simultaneously – the perverse person may hold a circumscribed delusional belief misrepresenting reality, such as the paedophile's conviction that children enjoy adult sexual attention, but the rest of the personality appears intact and functioning normally, unlike the psychotic person whose ego has completely collapsed. This leads us to the idea of perversion as a defence against psychosis and aggression.

The erotic form of hatred

As well as highlighting oedipal conflict and castration anxieties in his conceptualisation of perversion, Freud, in 'A child is being beaten' (1919), emphasised the role of aggression in the defensive regression to earlier developmental stages in perversion, particularly the anal stage with its component instincts of sadism and masochism. Glover (1933) proposed that perversions were the culmination of a pathological development of a reality sense. He suggested that the development of the infant's sense of reality could be distorted by primitive anxieties, including those arising from the infant's innate sadism, which made him misinterpret reality in a paranoid way. One solution to combating this fear is to neutralise sadism by investing it with libido (libidinization). Glover proposed that perverse symptoms in an adult represented a regression to excessive localised areas of libidinization in the mind, which, although this may sacrifice some relations to reality and adult genital function, preserved reality over a wider area. Perversions therefore 'help to patch over flaws in the development of reality sense' (Glover, 1933, p. 499). Glover's ideas here are relevant to later theories that perversion defends not only against aggression, but also against psychosis. In other words, a perversion represents a split-off localised area of the mind that is delusional, but this prevents the whole mind becoming grossly psychotic. It is not uncommon for patients who present with perverse behaviour to have a history of psychotic illness, where the perverse symptoms surfaced as the person was recovering from the psychosis and can be seen as necessary defences against future psychotic breakdown.

Stoller (1975) defined perversion as 'the erotic form of hatred'. He believed that hostility was the primary motivation in perversions. This hostility was hidden behind the overt sexualisation and represented a phantasy of revengeful triumph over childhood trauma. Perversion is therefore the pursuit of gratification through hostility to defend against infantile anxieties and trauma. Such trauma may not be overt abuse, but represent the dangerousness of the early attachment to the mother. Much of Stoller's work is based on his study of transsexual patients and their mothers, which led him to emphasise the difficulty men have in separating from their primary identification with their mothers to establish a normal masculine identity, and he suggested that 'in men, perversion may at bottom be a gender disorder' (Stoller, 1974, p. 429). Stoller's work is important in that it acknowledges Freud's ideas about fetishism and castration anxiety, but locates the origins of perversion earlier, in the pre-oedipal attachment to the mother.

Glasser (1996a) expanded these ideas that perversion is a defence against pre-oedipal anxieties and aggression towards the maternal object, and an inability to negotiate the normal developmental stages of separation and individuation. As described in Chapter 1, Glasser's concept of the 'core complex' is critical to understanding how perversions arise. The core complex is to some degree present in all of us, representing a very early core conflict between the wish to be close to the mother and the fear of being overwhelmed by her. However, where there has been an early pathologically narcissistic relationship to the mother, these conflicts become much more intense and persist in an unmodified form despite later stages of development. The wish to merge with the mother/other becomes very dangerous as it now represents a total loss of self, a permanent annihilation of the person as a separate independent being. This annihilatory anxiety provokes an aggressive reaction on the part of the ego. This aggression, however, cannot be directed at the mother as this would destroy her, so instead propels the person to withdraw into a narcissistic state which initially feels safe but soon becomes contaminated with feelings of total isolation and abandonment, giving rise to longings to be close to the maternal object once more.

Glasser proposes that the pervert resorts to a particular solution in an attempt to escape from the terrifying vicious circle of the core complex. This is the sexualisation of the aggression and hostility towards the needed maternal object, that is, the conversion of aggression into sadism. Although the object is now made to suffer and its suffering becomes a source of pleasure for the pervert, the relationship with the object is preserved. The object – originally the mother – no longer needs to be destroyed completely, but can be dominated and controlled.

Mr P was a middle-aged lonely homosexual man referred for individual psychotherapy due to his failure to establish long-term relationships, and his 'addiction' to sado-masochistic sexual practices such as bondage, which left him feeling increasingly isolated and depressed. During a session following the therapist's break, he described with relish the bizarre and exciting world of the sado-masochistic club he had attended the night before, and how excited he had become at being tied up and whipped. During this detailed and lurid account Mr P appeared to become more and more animated and was difficult to interrupt, leaving the therapist feeling dominated and controlled by him. The therapist eventually commented that Mr P's manifest sexual excitement about the previous night's activities appeared to obscure his recognition of the violence inherent in such acts. She suggested that Mr P may have experienced violent feelings himself in connection with feeling abandoned by her during the break, and he had to negate such unpleasant feelings by seeking out sexual contact in which he is whipped, but under his control. She pointed out that something similar was happening in the session with Mr P whipping and keeping her at a distance with his uninter-ruptable account of the night before. Mr P was able to acknowledge and link this to his feelings of rage towards his alcoholic mother who repeatedly aban-doned him by placing him in children's homes, only to 'rescue' him again each time she found a new partner with the illusion of creating a happy family.

The above clinical example illustrates how in the perversions the person manages their aggression towards the maternal object by con-verting such aggression into sadism via sexualisation. This sadism can manifest itself in sado-masochistic violence, such as with Mr P's sado-masochistic sexual practices. Although he assumes the position of the masochist in being whipped, he remains tightly in control by being able to tell the person whipping him to stop at any moment. He therefore remains in control of the object, unlike his experience with his original maternal object, and at the same time inviting violence to be inflicted upon himself fulfils the role of punishment to alleviate his unconscious guilt over wanting the maternal object to himself. In his relationships, he manages his core complex anxieties by keep-ing all his relationships at a distance thus avoiding his fears of being overwhelmed and controlled by intimate contact, and by refusing to commit to them in the long term he pre-empts being rejected by his partners. Any anxieties and aggression that are provoked by fears of separation are quickly defended against by his widespread use of sexualisation, evident not just in his external relationships but also in his relationship with the therapist. Individuals often seek treatment when their defence mechanisms, including such sexualisation, start to become less robust, as in the case of Mr P, who was increasingly left feeling unsatisfied, disgusted with himself and despondent fol-lowing his sexual practices. In more extreme cases, such a weakening of a person's habitual defensive structure can cause sado-masochistic violence to break down into self-preservative violence, as in the following clinical example.

Mr H, the foot fetishist introduced above, sought therapeutic help because of his difficulty in maintaining relationships. If his girlfriend did not comply with Mr H's demands for her not to wash her feet, as well as the very prolonged foreplay involving Mr H stroking her feet prior to sexual inter-course, Mr H would become angry, leading to arguments and the girlfriend inevitably leaving. The last girlfriend had left following an argument in which Mr H, according to him, 'lost control and I found myself attempting to kill her with a knife'. Mr H started therapy, but could not tolerate the therapist challenging his view of himself as a calm non-violent person, and left after only a few sessions. Here we can speculate that Mr H's foot fetish is an attempt to neutralise Mr H's anger towards his mother, not only for her castrating powers, but also because she neglected Mr H by having inter-course with his father to produce more children. Mr H's infantile fears of separation and rejection emerge in his adult relationships but are kept in check as long as he can control his partners in his sado-masochistic fetishis-tic foreplay. When the girlfriend resists and threatens to leave him, Mr H's fears of separation are realised, as he fears he cannot survive without the (maternal) object. This is experienced as a fatal attack on Mr H's psychic equilibrium, and his sado-masochistic means of control of the object via the fetish breaks down into self-preservative violence. At the moment of attack-ing his girlfriend, Mr H's aggression is in response to a fear of annihilation, even if the aggressive act is aimed at destroying the very object on which he so depends.

The work of Glover, Stoller and Glasser has important implications for the understanding of the perversions. The perverse person's sex-ual phantasies and behaviours do not indicate adult sexuality but reflect the use of sexualisation to defend against very primitive ter-rors in relationships. Whereas Freud identified castration anxiety as being the motivating force behind perverse behaviour, here we can see that much earlier anxieties about separation, abandonment and helplessness are paramount.

A defence against generational and sexual difference – the facts of life

The perverse person's failure to negotiate these primitive anxieties as part of normal development causes his internal world to be arrested at a pre-oedipal stage of omnipotent and narcissistic relating and fusion with the maternal object. Healthy growth and development, which imply separation from the object and becoming an indepen-dent individual, are feared and attacked by the pervert's use of denial and disavowal. This amounts to a perverse attack on reality or the facts of life, the disavowal of separation and difference. Money-Kyrle reminds us of three fundamental facts of life: 'the recognition of the breast as a supremely good object, the recognition of the parent's intercourse as a supremely creative act, and the recognition of the inevitability of time and ultimately death' (Money-Kyrle, 1971, p. 443). The first fact of life is the recognition that the infant is dependent on external sustenance for survival – it challenges the belief that the person is self-sufficient, and requires the toleration of both dependence and separation. The second fact is the recognition of generational and sexual difference, that the mother is not only a separate individual but can also unite with another person of the opposite sex, the father, to create babies, a relationship which excludes the child. The third is the recognition that we all grow old, we cannot arrest the passing of time, we are not omnipotent, but must face loss and be able to mourn.

We can how in the perversions, reality is attacked and pathological solutions are sought which attempt to deny such fundamental facts of life. Thus the paedophile negates generational differences by taking a child as his sexual partner, the transsexual denies the reality of biological gender difference by his belief that he can become a person of the opposite sex and the person who engages in sado-masochistic sexual intercourse in which pain is sought for sexual gratification denies the fact that sexual intercourse can be creative and produce new life. Chasseguet-Smirgel (1984) describes the world of the pervert as an 'anal-sadistic universe' in which such generational and sexual differences are disavowed. She sees perversions as a magical omnipotent attempt to deny the inevitable trauma of discovering the difference between the sexes and generations, in creating a world in which such distinctions are erased. In such a world, penis, faeces and child are all equal and interchangeable, a world of perverse 'pseudocreativity' rather than real creativity. The Internet provides an ideal medium in which such perverse phantasies can be elaborated and perpetuated in the two-dimensional world of Internet pornography, which includes child pornography, where the viewer has complete control over the objects of his phantasies. Intimacy with a real person, who might have their own wishes and demands, is bypassed. McDougall (1985) calls these pseudocreative inventions of the pervert the 'neo-sexualities' – the seemingly endless permutations of perverse behaviour, the most bizarre and unimaginable scenarios that are used for sexual gratification. However, McDougall reminds us that the underlying themes in these plots remain the same – not only the failure to master castration anxiety, but an unending attack on the breast-mother while attempting to idealise a maternal image that negates any difference between the sexes.

In summary, the understanding of perversion has shifted from Freud's original theory of component instincts of infantile sexuality that had escaped repression to a realisation that perverse behaviours and phantasies have a defensive function against not only castration anxieties, but much more primitive pre-oedipal anxieties and aggression towards the maternal object. Perversion can be seen as a disorder of narcissistic development in which true separation from the maternal object has not been achieved. Cooper (1991) believes that most, if not all perversions, defend against a core trauma of the experience of terrifying passivity in relation to the pre-oedipal mother who is perceived as malignant and omnipotent. It should be emphasised that many of the patients who seek treatment for their perverse behaviours or functioning have experienced real traumas, abuse or rejection, with parents who showed excessive aggression or neglect, and the sexualised behaviour with which they present is a symptom of their impossible struggle with their own destructiveness and cruelty that they in turn suffered from their original objects.

Summary

- The term perversion refers not only to aberrant sexual behaviour, but also to perverse character traits. All perverse activities contain aspects of hostility, secrecy, collusion and self-deception that may not be conscious.
- Freud's early theories of perversion as infantile sexual instincts that had escaped repression, and as a defence against castration anxiety, have been replaced by understanding perversion as having a defensive function against underlying aggression and psychotic anxieties. Difficulties in the very early relationship with the mother are thought to be important in the aetiology of perversions, which can be thought of as narcissistic disorders.
- Glasser proposed that the pervert resorts to a particular solution in an attempt to escape from the terrifying anxieties of abandonment and engulfment of the core complex, by the sexualisation of the aggression towards the needed maternal object. By converting aggression into sadism the object is not destroyed, but controlled and dominated.
- Perversions can also be thought of as an attack on reality and denial of generational and sexual differences.

VIOLENT WOMEN

The vast majority of violent crimes are committed by men. This statistic has been robust over time and in different populations. Around four-fifths of all violent incidents in the UK are committed by males (Home Office, 2004), and this pattern is very similar in France and Germany (Heidensohn, 1991), as well as in the United States, where recent statistics showed that 81.8 per cent of persons arrested for violent crime were male (US Department of Justice, 2007). The ratio of male to female homicide in England and Wales has remained stable at about 10:1 in recent years (Home Office, 2006). However, recent statistics suggest that overall numbers of male and female perpetrators of violent crimes against another person are increasing compared to other offences (Ministry of Justice, 2008), and more specifically, the proportion of recorded domestic violence incidents in which the offender is female has increased significantly in recent years (Home Office, 2004). As will be discussed in this chapter, the relationships between offender and victim show marked differences according to the gender of the offender – most victims of male violent perpetrators are not known to the offender, whereas the victims of violent women are most often close family members – their partners or children.

Historically, there has been little interest from criminologists in female violence and offending until recently, with early writers in the nineteenth and twentieth centuries emphasising biological factors that caused certain women to turn to theft and prostitution. It was not until the feminist movement of the 1970s and 1980s that there has been any serious and sustained interest in female criminology. Feminist criminologists focused their attention on the violence that occurs within the home, rather than on the street, which had been the domain of traditional criminologists. Such domestic violence is more hidden, shameful and involves women. These feminists have largely been responsible for drawing society's attention to women as the victims of violence, both physical and sexual, and usually committed against them by their partners. Here the understanding of violence and gender has shifted from seeing women as criminals, to seeing them as the victims of violence within a patriarchal society.

Violence against the body

Clinicians working with women have long recognised that women, as opposed to men, are more likely to direct their aggression towards themselves and their own bodies, rather than towards the bodies of others. Self-harm in the form of cutting is an obvious example of violence to the self. However, other psychopathologies that are more common in women, such as anorexia nervosa and bulimia, can also be viewed as aggression that has been internalised to attack the female body. In her seminal book *Mother, Madonna, Whore: The Idealization and Denigration of Motherhood* (1988), Welldon not only challenged the narrow feminist view that women were solely the victims of violence rather than perpetrators, but also challenged the traditional psychoanalytic cannon of knowledge on perversion and female sexuality. Not only did she suggest that women have aggressive impulses and can be violent, often in subtle or perverse ways, but she also suggested that the object of female violence could be their offspring. Here Welldon was challenging an unspoken but sacred and prevailing belief in society that mothers could not and would not deliberately harm their children. As she points out: 'Again, in the 1960s, we neglected to acknowledge what really happened with "battered babies"; nobody, even experienced physicians, could believe that those babies' injuries had been caused by their mothers. No-one seemed to understand these women as mothers: "women" were seen as capable of such actions, but not "mothers" ' (Welldon, 1988, p. 10). Even today, when there is indisputable proof that women can kill, women such as Myra Hindley, or Rosemary West, are demonized and not considered worthy of any psychological exploration or help.

Welldon's work draws on that of the psychoanalyst Pines, who described how women use their bodies, and in particular their reproductive systems, as vehicles for the expression of unconscious phantasies, wishes and conflicts. Pines (1972, 1993) explored how the specifically female activities of pregnancy, childbirth and miscarriage could be motivated by underlying conflicts related to a woman's difficulties with her own mother. Although some of the female patients whom Pines worked with came from deprived back-grounds, she was not specifically working with criminal or perverse women. Welldon, learning from her direct clinical experience of over 30 years of working with violent and perverse women at the Portman Clinic, proposed that certain mothers view their babies as narcissis-tic extensions of themselves, and use them for their own unconscious needs and expressions of unresolved conflict.

Welldon challenged the traditional psychoanalytic view of perver-sion as being based on castration anxiety and the belief that because women do not possess a penis, they cannot suffer from a perversion. Welldon emphasises the difficulties in separating from a terrify-ing and overwhelming maternal object in the genesis of both male and female perversions, and how the perverse behaviour embod-ies the aggression and revenge aimed at the maternal object in the guise of genital sexuality, when in fact the underlying phantasies are dominated by earlier, pre-genital factors. However, while in male perversions, the perverse act is aimed at an outside object, or per-son, Welldon discovered that in perverse women, the perverse act comprises an aggressive attack against themselves, either against their bodies, or against objects that are the products of their bodies: their babies. While both male and female perversions can be seen as revenge on a terrifying maternal object, in men this is located within the genitals, whereas for women it is the whole body. Motz (2008), in her book *The Psychology of Female Violence: Crimes Against the Body*, extends Welldon's work on female perversions to consider-ing the psychology of female violence in general, where the woman's body or creations of her body are unconsciously used for violent and perverse purposes.

All children face a complex developmental task in separating from their primary maternal object and becoming an independent person. In normal development, such a process is facilitated by the child's healthy aggressive impulses that are tolerated by the good-enough mother. When the mother cannot tolerate her child's self-assertive aggression, and retaliates, rejects the child or withdraws into depres-sion or psychosis, the child's immature mind is overwhelmed with its own and the object's aggressive impulses that the child cannot adequately process and can only deal with by pathological means, either by evacuation into others via projective mechanisms, or by turning the aggression inwards against the self. Little girls face an added difficulty in separation in that the body they are separating from is similar to their own. Following Grunberger (1985), Welldon believes that because the girl is born to someone who is not her 'true sexual object', she does not receive the same attention or investment from her mother that she would were she a boy, and is therefore more dependent on her. Perelberg (1997) also describes the little girl's struggles with separation from the mother and establishing a separate existence. When this process is incomplete, impeded by a mother who does not allow her daughter to be an independent being, the girl's identifications and internal objects remain confused and undifferentiated from the internal maternal object, and make the girl more prone to the internalisation of aggression in an attempt to achieve separation. Self-harm can therefore be seen as a symbolic attack on the internalised mother's body (Campbell and Hale, 1991).

The violent or perverse woman is likely to have experienced early difficulties in her history, often in the first 2 years of life, in the pre-oedipal relationship to her primary objects. She may have experienced neglect, rejection, separations, mentally ill or alcoholic parents and physical or sexual abuse. Her early relationship with her parents, particularly the mother, is critical in determining her capacity to be a parent or mother when she herself has children. As Welldon (1988) points out, we all struggle with our determination not to repeat the mistakes of our parents with our own children, and are repeatedly surprised at the power of our unconscious undermining our conscious efforts, the compulsion to repeat in our relationships the patterns of relationships that we were subject to. For the woman who has experienced actual abuse or neglect, the task becomes much harder. Many may not even be aware of the ambivalent relationship they have with their narcissistic, abusive or neglectful mothers, who are often described in idealised terms. In order to keep her relationship to her mother and hence ensure her own survival, the maltreated baby must resort to splitting. The punitive, humiliating and bad image of the parent has to be split off and repressed, and a defensively idealised parental image is retained in consciousness. The child, however, identifies internally with the repressed denigrated parental self, leading to feelings of shame, guilt and self-loathing. The girl's failed separation from her mother results in her internal objects being fused with a destructive maternal imago, which may remain successfully repressed until adolescence when, triggered by biological sexual changes, the girl's emerging feminine sexuality cannot be experienced as untainted by this internal malignant maternal object, and has to be attacked by self-harm, starvation or neglect.

Welldon suggests that sometimes women choose motherhood for unconsciously perverse purposes. While consciously the woman

wishes to reverse her own abusive maternal experience by having her own child, unconsciously the child represents triumphant
revenge on her own mother. By achieving motherhood, the woman
automatically becomes the master of her child, whom she can control
and dominate, as she was herself by her own mother. Many of these
women, in the absence of any internalised good objects, feel empty
and unconsciously use pregnancy as a way of feeling filled with good
objects.

When these women have their own children, they are not able to
treat them as separate individuals, but experience them as narcissistic extensions of themselves. Her baby becomes the unwitting object
of the woman's own infantile needs for emotional nourishment and
physical affection, as well as the container of her unresolved fear
and aggression directed at her own mother. Such aggression tends
to become manifest when her child's activities challenge her experience of being one undifferentiated being, blissfully fused with her
child. This commonly occurs at key developmental stages of separation – birth, weaning, learning to walk and going to school. In less
pathological cases, the mother becomes fearful of separation which
manifests in her anxieties about the child's safety and well-being
without her, which can be seen as a projection of her own anxiety
and aggressive impulses. An example might be the mother who is
reluctant to send her child to nursery, as she believes he is too anxious to cope without her. However, in more disturbed and damaged
women, such threats of separation reactivate their own unresolved
separation anxieties from their internalised maternal objects, provoking aggression that cannot be contained and becomes enacted
in actual violence towards the child. Motz (2008) describes how the
baby can become the receptacle for the mother's unconscious violent
impulses and unwanted toxic feelings, using their children as poison
containers (DeMause, 1990).

Both Welldon (1988) and Motz (2008) draw attention to transgenerational patterns of perverse mothering – how women who
were themselves neglected and abused by their mothers re-enact
this destructive behaviour with their own children. This intergenerational transmission of abuse can be partially explained by a social
learning model in which children learn from the behaviour modelled
by their parents. Attachment theory provides a richer understanding
of how such intergenerational transmission of parenting styles can
occur. The attachment pattern that develops between mother and
child is internalised by the infant to form an internal working model
that influences the child's developing sense of self, affect control

and relationships with others. Parental abuse and neglect can interfere with normal attachment so that disturbed attachment patterns
are internalised by the child, which will inhibit the child's capacity
to mentalize and interfere with her ability to control emotions and
relate to others as an adult, including her own children. Empirical
research with instruments such as the Adult Attachment Interview
has shown how adults with evidence of disturbed attachment to
their own parents are more likely to have children who are poorly
attached to themselves (Fonagy et al., 1991b, 1995).

*Ms W's mother was an 'invalid' for most of Ms W's childhood, being
morbidly obese and barely able to leave the household, and demanding that
Ms W and her younger siblings carried out all the housework, cooking and
looking after her. Ms W's father was mostly away at work or with his friends
in the pub, and did not interfere with his wife's control of the family. As a
child, Ms W was constantly anxious that her mother was going to die, and
tried her hardest to look after her and be a good girl. However, as she grew
older, she became more resentful, and left home at the earliest opportunity
after she became pregnant at 15. She moved in with her boyfriend and baby
son, and within 2 years gave birth to another baby, a girl. When her daughter was 3-months old, Ms W brought the baby to hospital as she was not
feeding properly. Medical examination revealed the child to be very underweight, and it was discovered that she had several old fractures to her leg,
which were thought to be non-accidental injuries. When social workers visited Ms W's house, they found it to be in a state of chaos and neglect, and
her older child also appeared underweight and dirty. Ms W initially accused
her partner and father of her children of violence towards both her and her
children, but he denied this and it transpired that the couple had separated
after the girl was born and had left the family home. Ms W then admitted
that she may have 'been a bit too rough' with her daughter when she was
crying, although she had 'not meant to hurt her'.*

*Here we can see how the poor parenting and neglect that Ms W expe-
rienced from her own mother was internalised and repeated with her
children. At an early age Ms W exhibited a pseudo-maturity in looking
after her mother and the household, at the expense of being nurtured herself
and developing sufficient internal structures for mentalization, separation-
individuation and affect control. The baby's inconsolable crying threatened
her view of herself as merged with her baby, and unconsciously reactivated
her own intolerable experiences in childhood. Lacking the ability to recognise this consciously, she instead resorted to violent action to annihilate the
pain. The aggression towards her infant can therefore be seen as an attack
on a hated internalised maternal object.*

In the last 25 years doctors, social workers and the legal profession have become much more aware of the extent of child abuse that occurs within families. The Children Act (1989) defines the criteria as to whether a child reaches the threshold of significant suffering or harm from the parents or caregivers, so that the local authority can institute care proceedings. This Act was revised in 2004 (Department of Health, 2004) to highlight the need for inter-agency communication and co-ordination, following the inquiry into the death of Victoria Climbie in 2000 (Laming, 2003), a little girl who was tortured and killed by her great aunt and aunt's partner. More recently such recommendations have been revisited in the highly publicised case of 'Baby P', a child who was abused and killed by his mother and stepfather, leading to public outcry and blame directed more at social services' failure to protect, than at the perpetrators themselves.

In cases of physical abuse towards children, paediatricians have developed expertise in deciding whether or not a child's injuries are 'non-accidental'. However, in such cases, many professionals implicitly assume that such injuries are the result of male violence (usually father or mother's partner) with the mother cast in the role of either not knowing, or being the passive victim of her partner's violence, rather than the active perpetrator of violence towards her own children. This is even more evident in cases where the child is killed. As Motz (2008) highlights, infanticide and maternal filicide bring together the twin taboos of child murder and female violence. However, the statistics are clear that while female violence in general is rare, when women kill, their victims are much more likely to be their partner or child. Studies of female homicide show that 80 per cent of victims are close family members – 40–45 per cent of female homicide offenders kill their children, and roughly one-third kill their partner (Wykes, 1995).

Infanticide

The reluctance to believe that women are capable of being murderous to their offspring often leads clinicians to prioritise biological explanations for female violence, and to attribute their actions to mental illness. The offence of infanticide illustrates this very well. The Infanticide Act was initially introduced in the UK in 1922, and reduced the offence of child murder to manslaughter in cases where it was believed that the mother had killed her child because she had not fully recovered from the effect of giving birth, which had caused a disturbance in the balance of her mind. The reduction in offence to manslaughter was due to an increasing reluctance to convict mothers of murder as this would automatically lead to the death sentence. The Act was revised in 1938 to include not having recovered from the effects of lactation (breast-feeding) as a further cause of a disturbance in the imbalance of mind at the time of the killing that could reduce the charge of murder to manslaughter. This means that in the UK the law has developed to have special provisions for the crime of infanticide, which, like that of manslaughter, gives judges complete discretion over sentencing. In practice, judges tend to be sympathetic and have been criticised for giving lenient sentences, often probation orders, with or without conditions of treatment, rather than custodial sentences.

Both medical and legal professions alike have been complicit in perpetuating the belief that infanticide, as well as other forms of female violence, must be due to hormonal imbalance to cause such a disturbance of the woman's mind that she would lose control and kill her child. The crime of infanticide is restricted to females, as it is assumed that men would not kill their children because of hormonal disturbance. Furthermore, it is often assumed that the woman must be severely mentally ill, often with a psychotic disorder, to be able to kill her new-born child, whereas in fact, many women convicted of infanticide have no psychiatric diagnosis. These biological explanations for female madness and violence are based on the implicit assumption that a woman would not take a rational decision in clear consciousness to kill her child, but must be acting under mental instability. Motz (2008) critically reviews the Infanticide Act, and suggests that the notion of female hysteria is implicitly woven into its structure. She suggests that the Act is unconsciously based on deep-seated fears of women's procreativity, the fear of menstrual women and mystique of childbirth being taboos that have held great influence in many different cultures and led to the belief that women are ruled by biological forces. Such a reductive biological argument rules out the possibility of female agency – that whether or not hormonal changes influence her behaviour, the woman may still be able to exercise choice in her actions. Motz reminds us that infanticide is a tragic act of violence, but one that may have seemed the only solution, however misguided, to the woman at the time.

Various researchers (d'Orban, 1979; Resnick, 1969; Scott, 1973) have attempted to classify infanticide based on the motivations of the mother into categories such as an unwanted child, mercy killing, psychosis, battering parent or Medea syndrome (where the woman kills her child as revenge or retaliation against her partner).

However, such classificatory systems do not take into account unconscious motivations and aggression. For example, where the mother is grossly psychotic and has delusional beliefs that her child will suffer immense harm and therefore must be killed to spare him, the infanticide is often described as being 'altruistic'. The term 'altruistic killing' may also be used when the baby is seriously brain damaged or deformed and the (non-psychotic) mother kills him to spare him suffering. As Motz (2008) points out, such a term denies the aggressive and narcissistic components to such 'altruistic' actions, where the mother unconsciously cannot accept that she has produced a disabled baby, which represents a damaged aspect of herself. The mother is narcissistically identified with her damaged baby and killing it may be the enactment of a suicidal phantasy. Motz argues that homicidal and suicidal urges are strongly linked in the unconscious, and that the early detection and treatment of maternal depressive illness as well as psychosis may reduce the incidence of infanticide. Even where the woman is clearly suffering from a psychotic illness in a case of infanticide or filicide, a psychoanalytic formulation may be helpful in understanding some of the predisposing factors contributing to a murderous act that may appear horrific and senseless.

Ms E was convicted of the manslaughter of her 6-month-old baby. Ms E herself was the child of a mixed-race couple. Her Nigerian father left her white British mother when she was a baby, and Ms E was brought up by her mother who regularly beat her and accused her of being 'bad' like her father. Ms E married in her early 20s, but her husband left her shortly after their baby was born. Ms E's explanation for killing her daughter was that she believed she was possessed by demons, and heard a voice telling her that she had to beat the child to get the demons out of her body. If the child's eyes changed colour she would know this had been successful. The child's eyes indeed did turn red prior to her death due to haemorrhage, and Ms E took this as confirmation that the demons were being exorcised. Ms E also exhibited delusions that her male neighbour was in love with her and she felt persecuted by another woman, who in Ms E's mind was her rival for the neighbour who loved her.

Although Ms E clearly fulfilled criteria for a diagnosis of schizophrenia, a psychoanalytic viewpoint might suggest again that Ms E was narcissistically identified with her baby, the unwanted daughter of the wrong colour rejected by her mother. As in the previous clinical example, Ms E's violence towards her daughter was an enactment of her aggression towards a part of herself that she experienced as bad, made concrete in the colour of her

and her baby's body. Furthermore, we can understand her delusional beliefs
as based on unconscious oedipal wishes – her longing for an absent man
(father), whilst being persecuted by a female rival (mother).

Munchausen's Syndrome by Proxy

Ms D was a 23-year-old woman charged with unlawful wounding with
intent of her 6-month-old baby son. Ms D described a childhood of emo-
tional neglect, in which her parents were experienced as cold and distant.
Between the ages of 9 and 13 she was sexually abused by an uncle but had
never told anyone about this prior to her trial. Ms D had formed a rela-
tionship with a man who was 20 years her senior, whom she described as
unsupportive and away a lot due to his work commitments. Her pregnancy
was unplanned and following the birth of the baby she found it difficult
to cope and frequently presented to her GP and health visitor for advice.
When the baby was 3-months old, Ms D injured her leg in a fall, and was
prescribed strong opioid painkillers by her GP. Following this she took her
baby to the doctor saying that the baby was overly sleepy and not breath-
ing properly, and he was admitted to hospital in a very ill state. Medical
staff were initially perplexed as to the cause of the baby's illness, but blood
tests eventually revealed significant quantities of opiates in the baby's blood.
When confronted, Ms D admitted that she had been putting her painkillers
in the baby's milk, and had been continuing to do so secretly even after the
baby's admission to hospital, to 'calm him when he was crying'. The baby
was removed from her care, Ms D was charged and remanded to prison,
where she took an overdose of painkillers. She was assessed by the prison
psychiatrist who recorded that she presented in an inappropriate manner,
like a 'giggly immature teenager', appearing unconcerned as to what had
happened to her baby. The psychiatrist found no evidence of a psychotic or
depressive illness.

One could argue that the nosological history of Munchausen's Syndrome by Proxy (MSBP) parallels the symptomatic presentation of
the disorder itself. First described by a British paediatrician, Meadow
(1977), MSBP is a disorder in which adults, almost always women in
the roles of mother, nurse or nanny, bring children in their care to the
attention of the medical profession with worrying physical symptoms and signs that are later suspected or discovered to be either
fabricated or because of injuries perpetrated by the woman herself
on the child. Although the syndrome was increasingly recognised
over the next 25 years, with the case of Beverley Allitt, a 24-year-old
nurse who was found guilty of killing four children and attacking

nine others in her care on the ward, being the most highly publicised, there nevertheless remained a reluctance by both the medical
and legal professions, as well as the general public, to believe that
women, especially mothers, were capable of causing such covert
harm to their children. Many of such doubters might argue that
the story of Munchausen's Syndrome by Proxy was itself fictitious,
that it does not really exist but was an invention of Meadow, who
was recently discredited and punished by his own medical regulatory body, the General Medical Council, for exaggerating the risk
of two cot deaths in the same family, in the trial of Sally Clarke, a
solicitor who was convicted in 1999 of murdering her two babies
on the basis of Meadow's evidence. After Meadow's evidence had
been discredited her conviction was eventually quashed in 2003 and
another mother, Angela Cannings, who had been convicted for murdering two of her three babies on Meadow's evidence that she was
suffering from MSBP, was also released on appeal. Despite a considerable accumulated body of respectable inter-disciplinary academic
research and knowledge of MSBP, including covert video recordings
of mothers harming their babies in hospital (Southall et al., 1997), the
opposition spokesman for health Lord Howe, speaking in the House
of Lords, asserted that MSBP was 'one of the most pernicious and
ill-founded theories to have gained currency in childcare and social
services in the past 10 to 15 years. It is a theory without science.
There is no body of peer-reviewed research to underpin MSBP. It
rests instead on the assertions of its inventor' (Lord's Hansard, 2003).
Since this controversy over the diagnosis, the term Munchausen's
Syndrome by Proxy has been recently largely replaced with the term
Fabricated or Induced Illness (FII).

Although many paediatricians, psychiatrists and social workers
continue to see such mothers whom they suspect of harming their
children, these professionals are often afraid to testify in court as
expert witnesses because of the risk that they too will be publicly
vilified and disgraced like Meadow. This creates a doubly tragic and
dangerous situation – one in which not only the children who are
being harmed are being overlooked and neglected, but also their
mothers, who at an unconscious level are also asking to be noticed
and cared for, using their children as substitutes for their distress.

Motz (2008) proposes that MSBP is one of the most disturbing
examples of a female perversion. In such women there is a profound
confusion of boundaries and identifications with her child, whom the
woman views as part of herself. Women with MSBP often have complex histories of childhood abuse or neglect, including sexual abuse,

self-harm, eating disorders and other somatic disorders. A significant proportion of women with MSBP have also been diagnosed with Munchausen's syndrome proper (Adshead, 1997; Rosenberg, 1987) with histories of multiple presentations of unexplained symptoms, hospital admissions and surgical procedures. Although these women may be viewed by professionals as deliberately fabricating their symptoms, there is most likely a spectrum between conscious fabrication and unconscious somatisation.

Motz (2008) draws parallels between women who self-harm and those with MSBP, in that in both their sense of identity is located within their body (and the body of their child) which is experienced as damaged and distorted because of their own early abusive experiences and difficult relationships with their own mothers. The violence that these women perpetrate on themselves and their children is in part an enactment of the aggression towards their parents who have betrayed them. However, in women with MSBP, presenting their children for medical attention, albeit for injuries inflicted upon the child by themselves, can also be seen as an attempt to protect and save the child from their unconscious murderous phantasies. Such women are unable to verbally articulate their anger, pain and distress, but may unconsciously seek understanding and containment from the medical professionals, who may represent the wished for third party or father who can intervene and rescue the child from the mother's murderous grip. Thus MSBP can be seen as a perverse solution to the mother's unconscious aggressive impulses, in which the child is harmed but he is also saved. Women with MSBP, such as Ms D above, consciously see themselves as concerned and caring parents and their violent impulses are split off and unavailable to their conscious mind. Thus in Ms D's case administrating opiates to her baby can be seen as her attempt to treat the baby's distress, which was experienced as indistinguishable from her own, while denying any aggressive intent. This reflects Ms D's identification with her baby as a distressed child in need of comfort, as well as representing a damaged part of herself that needed to be attacked. Her use of primitive defence mechanisms such as splitting and dissociation are exemplified by Ms D when she presented in a dissociated state in prison. Women with MSBP deceive others with their child's illnesses or injuries that they are secretly responsible for, but also deceive themselves by denying their own aggressive phantasies and impulses. Such profound deception therefore serves a dual purpose of making the woman feel omnipotent and triumphant over others, a defence against her experiences of feeling helpless and abused, but at the same time her self-deception protects her from acknowledging her propensity for violence. Professionals may unconsciously collude with this deception in their failure to acknowledge that a woman could harm her own child or refusal to believe that such a syndrome as MSBP can exist at all.

Domestic violence

Why do women stay in abusive relationships and become trapped in a cycle of violence? This has been the subject of much research and debate since the extent of domestic violence was highlighted by feminist criminologists 30 years ago. The plight of women abused by their partners is usually understood within a socio-economic framework. Thus, these women are seen as the victims of men who control and dominate their wives within the home via coercive and violent means, behaviour that is somehow tolerated or implicitly sanctioned by a patriarchal society. Such a society has made it very difficult for these women to leave abusive relationships, not only because of their financial dependence upon their husband or partner, but also because of the lack of support from the social and legal systems. The woman may be fearful of facing a custody battle in which she is charged with desertion, or face the possibility that social services will become involved, consider her an unfit parent and remove her children. She may be frightened of living in a refuge or temporary accommodation, with a partner who threatens to find her and retaliate.

Although such socio-economic explanations may be valid in accounting for some of the difficulties women may have in being able to separate from an abusive partner, psychologists have tried to explore the effects of prolonged or severe abuse on the victim and whether this contributes to her inability to leave her partner. The model of learned helplessness is often used to explain the abused woman's state of mind and her continued dependence upon her partner. Learned helplessness was first described in laboratory rats, who showed symptoms of apathy, passivity and loss of motivation to respond when they were repeatedly exposed to painful stimuli with no means of escape (Seligman, 1975). It is proposed that the battered woman who sees no means of escape from the abusive relationship responds in the same way, developing feelings of helplessness and hopelessness, lowered self-esteem, passivity and social isolation (Walker, 1984). This depressive state of mind and resulting cognitive distortions negatively interfere with her appraisal of situations in which she might be able to exert some influence, believing instead that she is powerless to alter her situation. This constellation of behavioural and cognitive patterns seen in women who were exposed to violence in intimate relationships has been called 'battered woman syndrome' (Walker, 1984). Battered woman syndrome has been utilised in a variety of professional and institutional contexts such as clinical intervention programs, but its most controversial use has been in the legal arena in the context of criminal defences.

The model of learned helplessness, however, does not take into account unconscious dynamic factors between victim and perpetrator that may also contribute to the process of victimisation. The victim–victimiser dyad may be understood as a unit held together by strong unconscious forces in which both partners participate, each gratifying their unconscious needs. To talk about the battered woman as needing to stay in a relationship in which her partner mistreats her can be easily misunderstood as saying that she consciously chooses to or deserves to be abused. Motz (2008) points out, however, that ignoring the female victim's role in the relationship would be to denigrate her and accept her passivity. Exploring the roots of her active participation, albeit unconscious, in the violent relationship is not to blame her, but can provide deeper understanding of her inability to leave, despite repeated experiences of abuse.

The defence mechanisms of projection and projective identification are helpful in understanding the unconscious interpersonal dynamics that can occur in the abusive couple. It is perhaps easier to see that the man rids himself of his own feelings of inadequacy and impotence by projecting them onto his female partner, so that in his violence towards her he is attacking a hated and denigrated version of himself. It may be more difficult to consider the abused woman's part in unconsciously allowing herself to be the receptacle of her partner's violent impulses. However, many of these women, because of their own early histories of abuse, neglect and attachment difficulties, may already have an image of themselves as damaged. Many will also have witnessed parental violence and seen their own mothers as victims. Feelings of anger and aggression towards the abusive parents are associated with intense guilt, and so are split off and directed against themselves, so that the parent is preserved as a good object. Becoming the recipient of abuse in relationships as an adult both appeases the battered woman's sense of guilt for her aggression towards her own caregivers and also recreates the abusive relationship of her parents. Both man and woman in the abusive couple may play an unconscious role for each other, based on their own early object relationships. Thus the violent man may experience his female partner as a controlling and overwhelming maternal object from whom he can only feel separate through violence. The abused woman may unconsciously participate in this role through secret feelings of triumph and power in the knowledge that her partner is dependent on her.

Such relationships can be viewed as containing sado-masochistic elements, with both partners dependent on the other, and both assuming unconscious sadistic and masochistic positions. As discussed in previous chapters, one of the hallmarks of sado-masochistic violence is that the object is preserved and not destroyed – within these couples, both partners unconsciously ensure that neither is destroyed nor abandoned. These relationships are often characterised by cycles in which the man is violent and the woman threatens to leave, followed by the man begging for her forgiveness and the woman deciding to give him another chance. In her threats to leave, the woman may unconsciously identify with both an abandoning object and an abandoned child, represented in the present in her partner, but based on her own experiences of being abandoned as a child, the pain of which she unconsciously wishes to protect her partner from. Her internal oscillation between these two positions constitutes a central unconscious conflict that impedes her ability to separate from her partner. The relationship between battered wife and battering husband is one in which all the violence is overtly located in the man. However, this conceals unconscious dynamics in which both partners are locked in a sado-masochistic prison from which neither can escape. The woman's aggression may only become evident when she becomes violent herself, and in rare cases, kills her partner.

Summary

- Violence towards others is much more common in men than women. Women tend to direct their aggression towards their own bodies, including their reproductive systems, which are used as vehicles for the expression of unconscious conflict, often stemming from a neglectful or abusive relationship with their mothers and leading to transgenerational patterns of abuse.
- Welldon challenged the notion that perversions did not exist in women. While both male and female perversions can be seen as an attack on a terrifying internalised maternal object, in men this

is located within the genitals, whereas for women it is the whole body, and the products of their body, that is, their children.

- Some cases of infanticide and maternal child abuse occur when the mother views their baby or child as a narcissistic extension of themselves, and uses them for the expression of their own unconscious needs and unresolved conflict, which may result in violence towards the child. MSBP can be thought of as an extreme example of a female perversion. In such cases, the woman's murderous fantasies are split off and not available to her conscious mind.
- Some women involved in violent relationships may be unconsciously enacting underlying dynamics in the couple that contain dependent, aggressive and sado-masochistic elements in both partners. Casting the woman solely as the victim, rather than acknowledging her own, albeit unconscious, aggressive participation in such relationships, denies women a sense of agency for their actions.

6

VIOLENCE AND SOCIETY, RACE AND CULTURE

So far, we have considered violence from the perspective of the individual person, and the influences that lead to his or her aggression becoming manifest. However, history shows us that the most frightening and uncontained violence is perpetuated by groups of people, and we are currently witnessing how the unprecedented social violence of the twentieth century's wars and genocides continues to evolve into new forms of terrorist and urban violence in the twenty-first century. This chapter will give a brief overview of group and social violence, and from a psychoanalytic perspective examine some of the underlying processes that contribute to human beings becoming more violent when they come together – from the small group violence of playground bullies, juvenile gangs and the football crowd, to violence of a much larger scale in military actions and warfare, and how socially sanctioned mass violence can be perverted to become sadistic violence intentionally aimed at non-combatant civilians in acts of genocide and terrorism. There is of course a multitude of important political, socio-economic and ideological influences that combine to produce socially violent events to which I cannot do justice, but I will touch upon issues of race and ethnicity which underscore many acts of violence, again looking at this from a psychoanalytic viewpoint.

Group violence

A Frenchman, Le Bon, provided one of the first major explanations of group behaviour in his book *The Crowd* (1895). He suggested that in a large group, the personal characteristics of individual members were subsumed into a common feeling or collective spirit, masking individual differences in class, education and attitudes. He proposed that this occurred via a process of mass hypnosis of the group by a charismatic leader, so that although individual members act consciously, the group as a whole acts unconsciously, not responding to reason and argument, but reacting to suggestion, imagery and allegory.

In 'Group psychology and the analysis of the ego' (1921), Freud explained this mass psychology of the group by proposing that all the group members mutually identify with each other and collectively project their superegos onto the group leader, whom they then obey, whatever he commands them to do. Freud suggested that the delegation of each individual member's ego-ideal to the group leader removed their normal superego constraints, liberating them to express aggressive instinctual urges, so that the group as a whole would willingly carry out acts of violence which the individual would be normally morally inhibited from doing. Freud thought that such group violence was facilitated by the libidinal links between members of the group, which provided them with a sense of companionship and purpose, as well as their idealisation of the group leader, which made them feel exhilarated and special.

Bion (1961) expanded Freud's ideas in his studies of the dynamics of small and large groups (see Chapter 10). He proposed that when a small group of people come together for a purpose, task-oriented leadership and functional organisation sustain the group's adherence to reality and they are able to operate in a rational mode. Bion called this type of effective, reality-based group a 'work group'. However, when unrealistic demands are made on the group, or overwhelming threats to its security emerge, three types of primitive reactions occur in the group, which he respectively called the 'dependent basic assumption group', the 'fight-flight basic assumption group' and the 'pairing basic assumption group'. The first two basic assumption groups are due to respective unconscious narcissistic and paranoid regressions of the group in the face of threat (Kernberg, 2003a). In the dependent basic assumption group, the members become dependent on a self-assured and narcissistic leader, who thrives on admiration and the position of authority. The group members feel entitled to be looked after by such a parent-figure and regress to behaving like greedy rivalrous siblings. In the fight-flight basic assumption group, the group members respond to danger by becoming more paranoid, and select a leader who is suspicious, aggressive and dominant. The group members divide into those who support the leader, and those who fight him – an 'in-group' and an 'out-group' – so that the group itself is splintered into rival factions, and the entire group has a hostile and paranoid atmosphere. An external threat can re-unite the group to act against a common enemy in an aggressive way. Kernberg (2003a) suggests that both groups are characterised by the predominance of primitive defence mechanisms – the dependent narcissistic group by primitive idealisation, projected omnipotence and parasitic dependency, and the paranoid fight-flight group by projective identification, splitting and acting out of aggression. Here we can see how collectively the group regresses to function in a similar way to the personality disordered individual, via primitive defensive operations, as described in the previous chapters. In Bion's third group, the 'pairing basic assumption group', two members of the group form a special relationship which becomes the focus of the group's fantasies of an ideal couple who will save the group from despair, over-dependency on the leader or potential destruction from the paranoid group. Kernberg likens this to a flight into a primitive oedipal structure.

Subsequent observations (Turquet, 1975; Rice, 1965, 1969) of large groups replicate Bion's findings. Large groups can work well if there are clearly defined task-orientated structures and goals, such as learning, constructing something or policy-making; but when these fail, or the group was never structured, it can disintegrate into an anxiety-ridden, chaotic mass, where the outbreak of individualised violence exacerbates the sense of danger, disorder and confusion. In such groups, primitive defence mechanisms are again prevalent, and the more mature rational efforts of individuals to quell the panic are not only ineffectual, but actively resented. The group recovers from this regression by selecting either a narcissistic or a paranoid leader, corresponding respectively to the dynamics of the narcissistic and paranoid regressive small groups described above (Kernberg, 1998, 2003a). If the group chooses a leader with narcissistic features, it will tend to become a 'feast crowd' (Canetti, 1960), enjoying being dependent on a 'wise' leader, who quells any sense of rivalry or resentment. This group becomes conventional in temperament, but at the cost of individual autonomy and depth of feeling and opinion. If, however, the group promotes a paranoid leader, the aggression of the individual members is mobilised by the leader against an external threat or enemy, and the group is transformed into a mob. Such an unstructured paranoid group is prone to outbreaks of actual violence, as, for example, in the football crowd, and, if restructured on more permanent ideological paranoid lines, can be transformed on a small scale into an organised gang, or on a much larger scale into a political mass movement. Kernberg (2003a) highlights how intensely aggression is activated in groups of any size, and how the normal processes of socialisation and role-relationships within the family and the more mature defensive ways of dealing with primitive impulses such as sublimation, reaction formation and repression and a tolerance of ambivalent feelings all become lost in the dynamics of the group, which regresses to functioning at the paranoid schizoid level described by Klein (1946).

Mr R was a 25-year-old man from a conventional middle-class home. He described himself as having been a rather shy and inhibited child, frightened of the scuffles in the playground and careful not to get into fights with other boys. He did well at school academically and was known as somewhat of a 'swot'. Although he was disinterested in football, a university friend persuaded him to go to a football match with him. They sat in a very crowded stadium amongst the fans of the home team that his friend supported. The other side was winning and the people around Mr R started becoming agitated and verbally abusive. Mr R initially felt frightened but then started feeling mesmerized by the fans' chants and became exhilarated when one of the fans sitting near him appeared louder and more dominant than the rest and leading the fans' protest against the other side. The fans started throwing objects, including cans of beer, and Mr R joined in. Following the match in which the home team lost, a fight broke out in the crowd leaving the stadium and Mr R suddenly found himself being arrested by the police, having assaulted another person near him. Afterwards, Mr R was astonished at his outbreak of violence, having always considered himself to be an anxious and passive person.

Racism and violence

Whether or not a group starts functioning in pathological ways obviously depends on a number of influences, not only the composition of the group and characteristics of the leader, but also external socio-economic, cultural and historical factors. Sociological writers have emphasised how groups can resort to violence because of genuine grievances and discontent about unfair conditions such as relative deprivation (Gurr, 1970), oppression of a minority or racial tensions (Baldassare, 1994). Racial violence merits particular examination, not only because of its long and tragic repetition through different eras of human history, but also because the underlying motivations of racial violence, which are based on fear and hatred of difference, can be generalised to other forms of violence perpetrated by one group against another.

Definitions of race vary according to the context, and the language in which issues of race, culture and ethnicity are described is often imprecise and confusing (Bhui and Morgan, 2007). In its legal usage, a racial group is a group of people defined by their race, colour, nationality or ethnic or national origins (Race Relations (Amendment) Act, 2000). In biology the word race is used to distinguish distinct populations of a species; however, many regard race as a social construct, with no basis in nature. An ethnic group is a group of human beings whose members identify with each other, on the basis of common cultural, linguistic, religious, behavioural or biological traits, real or presumed, as indicators of contrast to other groups. Concepts of race vary by culture and over time. Dalal (2002) suggests that attempts to conceptualise racism – whether from biological, religious or psychological standpoints – are inherently biased by the phenomena of racism itself, processes of racialisation originating in the external world of power structures and instituted and perpetuated in racialised thinking in the mind. He defines race as 'a form of hatred of one group for another'.

Psychoanalysis has itself been criticised for being ethnocentric in its theories emerging in a Judeo-Christian culture and therefore implicitly racist in its assumptions. Freud's ego-psychological goals of psychoanalysis of replacing id with ego can be seen to echo the Enlightenment's idealisation of scientific rationality associated with Europe and North America, over the irrational and underdeveloped Third World, which was the basis for colonial mentality (Altman, 2000). Kovel (1988) proposes that racism not only antecedes the notion of race, but actually generates the races and creates psychology for its own purposes. Dalal (2002) criticises both Freud and Klein for their emphasis on primary instincts in their accounts of human mental life, which he believes is reductionist and ignores the influences of society and culture, which are so important in constructing racism.

More recent psychoanalysts, however, have written explicitly about racism, describing 'racist states of mind' and proposing that racism is present in all of us. What is common to the above definitions of race and ethnicity is the construction of a group of people defined by their 'sameness' as compared to other groups of people who are different. It could be said that such struggles with similarity and difference are a universal feature of human mentality. This can be understood psychoanalytically as stemming from early infantile conflicts regarding separation from a maternal object with concomitant fears of dependency and change. Keval (2005) describes the

racist state of mind from a Kleinian perspective, as a type of pathological defensive organisation of the personality (O'Shaughnessy,
1981) or 'psychic retreat' (Steiner, 1993), as described in Chapter 1,
constructed to provide shelter from unbearable anxieties that are
provoked by the experience of separateness. All sorts of differences
within and outside of the self can be the targets of such anxiety,
because these signal the possibility of psychic growth, development and change, with accompanying feelings of loss and mourning,
which must be defended against. Keval describes how such differences can include the colour of someone else's skin, which must then
be attacked. The awareness of such a difference triggers unconscious
anxieties about being separate – at the most primitive level, being
separate from the maternal object, and later, separate from a third
object in the oedipal situation. Various authors (Davids, 1992; Fanon,
1986; Kovel, 1988; Tan, 1993) point to a specific phantasy underlying
racist thinking and feeling of fusion with an object, and how the racist
state of mind is a hostile attempt to control the object and prevent
any separation from it. Awareness that the person is different causes
unbearable feelings of shame and humiliation, leading to a form
of narcissistic rage that can erupt in brutal violence. These analytic
authors' explorations of the dynamics of racist thinking link with
some of the ideas we have already considered regarding aggression
and violence, namely Glasser's (1996a) concept of the core complex,
where the conflicts regarding separation from and engulfment by a
maternal object cause an aggressive response that must be defended
against, and Gilligan's (1996) thesis that violence is triggered by
emotions of shame and humiliation.

Keval proposes that the minor differences that are attacked in
racism are part of a defence against the recognition of major differences, such as the sexual differences and the differences of generations, and ultimately a defence against thinking and curiosity. He
refers here to the work of Money-Kyrle (1971), who described the
three fundamental facts of life as discussed in Chapter 4: the dependence of the small infant; generational and sexual difference; and
the passing of time, getting old and dying. Just as perversion can be
thought of as an attack on reality and the recognition of these facts
of life, separation and difference, racism can also be seen as a pathological solution which defends against acknowledging dependence,
separation, growth and death.

Although Keval is describing overt racist attitudes stemming from
pathological states of minds, several analytic writers stress the existence of such racist thinking in the unconscious of us all. Dalal

(2006) proposes that the liberal world view's strivings for equality end up stripping people of their particularities, whether of gender, status or ethnicity, and become blind to difference in an unhelpful way. He described his difficulties as a black therapist, and his experience of racism as one dimension of his personal and social experience being ignored by white colleagues, who had convinced themselves that they did not discriminate against colour. This has prompted white analysts and therapists (e.g. Altman, 2000; Morgan, 2007) to look at their work with patients from different ethnicities and to closely monitor their own countertransferences for evidence of implicit racist attitudes, for example that black men may be more threatening to work with. Bhui and Morgan (2007) advise that an important component of working therapeutically with multi-racial and multi-ethnic populations is to recognise the racial transference, which may be an expression of underlying conflict, as well as representing the patient's experience of racism. Davids (1998), a black British psychoanalyst, stresses, however, that the problem of ignoring the patient's cultural background is not so much due to defective psychoanalytic theory, but due to a reluctance on the part of the analyst to acknowledge the patient's difference, which reflects a fear of entering the domain of internal racism – both the patient's and the analyst's. If one is prepared to go into this charged area, there is no reason to give up existing psychoanalytic theories.

Dr G, a female forensic psychologist, was the therapist for a psychoanalytically informed treatment group for violent men in a prison run on therapeutic lines. Of eight group members, two were black – Joe, a second-generation Afro-Caribbean man, and Al, who was from Nigeria. The other group members and Dr G were white. Joe was coming to the end of his sentence for assault on his girlfriend and was due to be released into the community in a few weeks time. By contrast, George, a man who was serving a long sentence for armed robbery, was not expecting to be considered for release for at least another 2 years. George had always appeared in awe of Joe and admired him for his sporting achievements prior to being in prison (Joe played rugby semi-professionally).

The group had been discussing the triggers to their violent actions. Joe spoke poignantly of feeling humiliated by his girlfriend's taunts that she did not find him attractive and was reminded of feeling as a child that his mother was perpetually disappointed in him in some way. For the first time, he became tearful in the group. There was a silence, in which Dr G felt moved and thought that the other members felt similarly. To her surprise George suddenly accused Joe of faking his tears, that he was trying to disguise the fact that he was a 'typical black man who enjoyed beating his wife'. Joe became incensed, and turning to Dr G, asked her to intervene and insist that George be asked to leave the group for making racist remarks that were unacceptable and also illegal. Al, the other black person in the room, tried to mediate by saying that George had recently made other offensive remarks, such as saying to Dr G that he didn't think female therapists were up to working with violent men, and accusing another (white) group member of being intellectually arrogant. Al advised Joe not to take George's remarks seriously.

Dr G felt confused and said that she could not expel someone from the group for an illegal action when everyone in the group was there because they had done illegal things. She said it was important for the group to try to understand why George had felt like attacking Joe and suggested that it was difficult for group members who did not know when they would be released to see others, like Joe, moving on and leaving prison. John nodded to this remark, but Joe remained very angry and said that if George did not leave the group, then he would leave the group, even though his actual release date was a few weeks hence.

Following this session, Dr G reflected on what had happened, and wondered whether, due to her own unconscious racist assumptions, she had minimised the impact of George's racist remark on Joe, by implicitly agreeing with Al that George's insults should not be taken too seriously. Dr G suspected that Al was protecting himself from feeling racially attacked. In the next group meeting Joe again raised the issue of racism. This time, Dr G more explicitly suggested that George's remarks had been motivated by envy of change as well as not wanting to face the loss of a friend, and that he had chosen his words knowing that they would hurt Joe the most. Dr G went on to say how perhaps Joe, and even Al, felt that others did not understand what it felt like to be so visibly different and therefore open to attack, but perhaps they all could empathise with experiences of feeling different and ostracised, and this seemed to define the mood of the group at the moment, which was threatened by change with one of its members leaving. George then apologized for what he had said to Joe the previous week, and admitted that he was feeling very despondent, ostracised and alone in prison, having just received a letter from his girlfriend saying she had met someone else.

Much of the recent psychoanalytic literature on racism is based on observations from the consulting room in work with therapist–patient dyads of different ethnic backgrounds. We can extend their insights to the phenomena of racial group violence by observing how the same racist defences that operate in the individual become intensified by the regressive pull of the group. People construct groups to deal with difference and similarity. In Bion's fight-flight basic assumption group, the group becomes divided into in-groups and out-groups, where undesirable aspects and parts of the self are collectively projected from one group to the other, and must be attacked and destroyed. One of the most striking and devastating examples of this was in Hitler's attempt to create a 'pure-blooded' nation: 'This systematic concentration of pure blood, together with the expulsion of all that is foreign or undesirable, is the only way to succeed in eliminating impurities in the body of the nation' (Darre, 1930, p. 216, quoted by Chasseguet-Smirgel, 1990). The holocaust and other genocides are extreme examples of how individuals can collectively commit acts of horrific and mass violence, which can be seen to defend against very primitive anxieties of difference and otherness, but many acts of socialised violence on a smaller scale are also motivated by the fear of difference – be it racial violence, violence against a different gender or violence against people with a different sexuality.

Kernberg (2003a) identifies several important factors that contribute to the large-scale organised violence of war, genocide and terrorism, including the regressive pull of ideologies, the personality features of social and political leadership and the effects of historical trauma and social crises. An ideology reflects the value system of a social group, including national, political and religious belief systems, which gives the group a sense of purpose. Kernberg proposes that all ideological systems are located on a continuum between two respective poles of narcissistic and paranoid dimensions, and that 'normal' civilization is continually at threat from both. In a narcissistic ideology, such as in the Soviet Union during the Brezhnev years, the dominant Marxist ideology was like a state-imposed religion that, if formally and obediently adhered to, would provide economic and political security for its citizens, but at the cost of providing any meaning or freedom. A paranoid ideology, exemplified by the Cultural Revolution in China, or the National Socialist ideology of Hitler's Germany, is more overtly aggressive and dangerous, and predisposed to violence. Here, primitive defence mechanisms predominate in the group such as splitting, projection and projective identification: the world is neatly divided into good and bad, and the bad must be destroyed. Arendt (1951) warned that totalitarianism destroyed not only the public space, but the individual space as well, in the capacity to think and symbolise. Paranoid ideologies also restrict the autonomy not only of the individual but also of the sexual couple, severely discouraging intimate relations between individuals in the service of the community. The power of such paranoid ideologies to consolidate a group is facilitated by a leader who, at an individual level, has a pathological paranoid character, or, at worst, combines paranoid and narcissistic personality traits in the syndrome of what Kernberg terms malignant narcissism.

However, a group may also be profoundly affected by historical trauma, which becomes integrated into the individual egos of the population and shapes the behaviour of the group. Long-standing rivalries with neighbouring populations, lost wars and major political upheavals can coalesce in the formation of shared myths, rituals and language in a society. Volkan (1988) has written about how historical trauma interrelates with individual and group identity and conflict and how such group representations can be perpetuated from generation to generation in the collective psyche by influencing the early ego identifications of the small child. The child's early self-representations become integrated with social and cultural characteristics to form individual ego identity, and similarly the child's superego structures are formed not only by the internalisation of parental values, but also those of the group. In groups consolidated by historical trauma, further social trauma becomes indistinguishable from individual personal trauma with an unconscious identification between traumatised individual and traumatised group, so that attacks on the group are experienced by each individual personally, as a narcissistic wound that needs to be defended against. This can lead to a vicious circle of inter-group violence where violent conflicts are perpetuated over many years, sometimes centuries, leading to further re-traumatisation of the group and the wish for revenge, seen very clearly, for example, in the conflict in the Middle East. The pain of the group is evacuated in further violence, and the possibility for there to be a process of mourning is averted (Segal, 1997). Such cycles can only be halted with the recognition that within each group and individual reside both victim and perpetrator, which is of course a central tenet of the psychoanalytic understanding of violence and perversion put forward in this book.

Dehumanisation, genocide and terrorism

As in wars and other large-scale outbreaks of violence, the phenomena of genocide and the smaller groups involved in terrorism involve the centrality of a leader or individuals with pathological personality characteristics around whom the wider group gathers and is influenced by group mechanisms to carry out violent acts on another group. But when such violence becomes extreme and indiscriminate, involving the wished for or actual elimination of whole populations of people including civilians and children, something more is happening than the regressive group processes that can cause ordinary individuals to commit acts of mass murder under the influence of state ideologies, paranoid leadership and the effects of historical trauma as described above. In both genocidal and terrorist acts, as well as torture, a process of dehumanisation is assumed to occur in the minds of the perpetrators to explain violence that can seem so heinous and extreme that it defies explanation. Here human victims are treated as inanimate objects to be disposed of indiscriminately and at the capricious will of the torturer. Such violence appears no longer to be defensive or reactive to circumstances but has become sadistic to the point that all meaning is lost. Kernberg (2003b) describes how even the hatred expressed in the murderous actions towards a defeated enemy, the wishes to humiliate and make him suffer, contains some understandable human characteristic, but the chronic, mindless and unpredictable cruelty as occurred in the Nazi concentration and extermination camps takes violence into another realm. This is a world of 'absolute social power' (Sofsky, 1997), of total 'deobjectalization' (Green, 1993) and Chasseguet-Smirguel's (1984) 'anal universe' where all generational and gender boundaries are dissolved, incest and murder are condoned and moral and superego restrictions do not exist. Kernberg suggests that certain highly disturbed narcissistic individuals, freed from normal social restraint, readily participate in the world of extermination camps by gaining sadistic erotic pleasure from the murderous and incestuous invasion of other peoples' bodies. However, he points out that even in these cases, some remnants of humanity could be said to exist in the erotisation of sadism. In the most extreme cases of psychopathic malignant narcissism, this is lost, the person loses any erotic or libidinal interest in the victim, aggression and violence become completely mechanised and civilization and humanity are obliterated by the total immense meaninglessness of death. It is difficult to explain the existence of such extreme aggression and violence without reference to Freud's original concept of the death instinct.

In the wake of 9/11 and the rise of suicide bombers in the Middle Eastern conflict, more psychoanalysts have shown interest in contributing to the understanding of terrorism. Like other types of socialised violence, acts of terrorism are multi-determined by different factors such as the effects of extreme ideologies, religious fundamentalism and historical trauma, and so cannot be analysed without reference to the particular historical, political and cultural contexts in which the terrorist attacks are perpetrated. Akhtar (quoted by Hough, 2004) suggests that in terrorist groups, as in street gangs and cults, there is idealisation of the in-group, denigration of others and intolerance of difference. In cults, aggression can be directed inwards resulting in mass suicides, whereas both terrorist and gang groups direct their aggression externally, the former to fulfil political and ideological aims, the latter for social dominance and gain. In times of social turmoil, all three types of group can coalesce and become indistinguishable from each other. Terrorism also specialises in psychological warfare, creating anxiety and panic in societies.

Psychoanalysts have attempted to categorise the psychopathology of terrorists but even at this individual level, considerations of cultural and political context cannot be dismissed. Terrorist acts may be considered to involve dehumanisation as described above, involving a lack of empathy or concern for the other, but a terrorist who is viewed as an inhuman brute by one society is hailed as a hero by another. The few psychoanalysts and psychiatrists (e.g. Post, quoted by Hough, 2004; Taylor, 2008) who have interviewed remanded and convicted terrorists report that not all show emotional disturbance or evidence of personality disorder or mental illness, although the latter may be induced by the effects of prolonged incarceration without trial, such as in Guantanamo Bay. Some terrorists do have a history of severe individual trauma and have compensated for a sense of rejection and abandonment by transforming their victimhood into a sadistic and vengeful grievance, which is rationalised and reinforced by a fundamentalist ideology giving them an external focus for their aggression (Post, 2001). However, again such individual psychopathology is insufficient to explain the increase in new forms of terrorist activities such as suicide bombers, where the effects on the group of fundamentalist ideology and the trauma and humiliation of entire communities combine with individual pathology to form what Varvin (quoted by Elmendorf and Ruskin, 2004) calls the 'terrorist mindset'. This can be seen as an extreme form of the 'racist mindset' described above, where fear and hatred of the 'other' leads to the creation of mass panic and random atrocities against civilians. It can be difficult for psychoanalysts and therapists working in war-torn countries or communities where acts of violence or terrorism are being perpetrated by one group against another not to become partisan and identify with what might appear to be the obvious victims of such violence. However horrific and devastating these acts of violence are, terrorist violence, like all other forms of violence, can be seen as a communication, which is more than the conscious message that the terrorist wishes to convey to the world, containing within it a myriad of individual and collective unconscious fantasies, traumatic memories, defences and wishes, which must be understood before any lasting resolution of such conflicts can occur.

Summary

- Both large and small groups can function effectively on a task but when threatened tend to regress to primitive modes of collective narcissistic and paranoid defensive functioning which subsume individual efforts. Mass chaos and panic is averted if rescued by a leader, but if the latter has paranoid features, the aggression of the group can be mobilised against an external threat, real or imagined, which may culminate in group violence.
- Racism can be seen as an attack on and denial of separateness and difference. Anxieties about otherness, exemplified by skin colour, may lead to racist states of mind, which are defensive pathological psychic organisations that defend against acknowledgement of separation, growth and maturity. Such unconscious anxieties are present in all of us, but may be amplified in groups to produce mass hatred of one ethnic group against another, leading to military or genocidal violence.
- Organised mass violence such as war, genocide and terrorism arises from the effects of several factors, which include the regressive pull of ideologies, the personality features of social and political leadership and the effects of historical trauma and social crises.
- Extreme acts of genocide, terrorism and torture may involve a process of dehumanisation in which the victims of violence are viewed as inhuman objects to be sadistically disposed of at the perpetrators' will. However, terrorist violence always reflects a complex interplay of historical, socio-political and religious factors, in which victims and perpetrators may not always be distinguishable.

7

A PSYCHOANALYTIC APPROACH TO RISK ASSESSMENT

We live in a risk-obsessed culture. Children are no longer allowed to play freely because of the risk of being run over or being abducted by paedophiles, teenagers in our inner cities are afraid of being stabbed by each other and we are all at risk of being killed by the insane, or so the media would have us believe. Society's increasing aversion to any form of risk, and the resultant 'blame culture', has had a disproportionately powerful impact on the field of mental health. Mental illness is often negatively portrayed in the media, and its association with violent behaviour exaggerated. Many view people with psychosis as dangerous, despite the fact that rates of homicide by the mentally ill have remained stable for years and constitute only a small proportion of the total numbers of homicide.

But the media is not solely to blame for focusing public fear on the mentally ill. Since the first high-profile homicides in the UK in the early 1990s, politicians have successfully campaigned for risk assessment and management to become a central focus for mental health policy and practice. In 1994, the government demanded that public inquiries should be held for all homicides that had been committed by people who had recently had contact with mental health services. Although these exposed some failures of communication and care among professionals concerned, psychiatrists and other mental health workers felt unfairly blamed. Focusing attention on apparent failures in the professional network looking after individual patients concealed the shortcomings of earlier politically driven changes in the care of the mentally ill, such as the rapid closure of the old asylums and release of the mentally ill into a community ill-equipped to contain them. However, the increasing prioritisation of public protection over the individual rights of the mentally ill by successive government agendas continues, leading to new legislation, working practices and use of specialised instruments to assess risk. Sceptics might argue that risk predication has become an industry marketing a burgeoning array of risk assessment tools that create confusion for the clinician. Nevertheless, government policy stipulates that specialist mental health services should routinely assess each patient's risk of violence and harm, which was incorporated into the Care Programme Approach (CPA) introduced in 2000. Mental Health Trusts were encouraged to develop their own 'local' risk assessment tools, which many view as a futile, 'tick-box' exercise, encouraging defensive practice rather than thoughtful evaluation of individual patients.

Public expectations that risk should be eliminated altogether, an impossible task, has demoralised psychiatrists and other clinicians working with the mentally ill. The pressure to function as 'agents of social control' has a detrimental impact on clinical practice, engaging with patients and stifling innovation and creativity (Royal College of Psychiatrists, 2008). Such a blame culture appears to be particularly embedded in England, compared to other countries such as Scotland, the United States, Australia and New Zealand, although countries such as Holland and Sweden, where high-profile politicians were recently victims of homicide by the mentally disordered, appear to be undergoing similar shifts in public opinion. While the majority of those who work in mental health would now accept that risk management has to be an integral part of clinical practice, it is recognised that accurate risk prediction is impossible at an individual level. Approaches to risk have become more sophisticated and influenced by research in other fields. Although psychoanalysis is not a discipline traditionally associated with issues of dangerousness, this chapter will consider how psychoanalytic thinking can contribute to the debate on the assessment and management of risk.

Models of risk

There are two main models of risk assessment – the mathematical or actuarial, and the clinical (Buchanan, 1999). Clinicians have traditionally assessed risk on the basis of individual clinical judgement measuring dynamic aspects of the patient, but this unstructured approach has been criticised for its low validity, low inter-rater reliability and poor predictive value. Some dynamic variables such as long-standing intimacy problems and chaotic lifestyle are correlated with risk, but other dynamic variables which are regularly used in assessing risk have been clearly shown not to be linked with risk and are therefore misleading. These include victim empathy and remorse for the offence, which, despite the lack of empirical evidence in reducing offending, are incorporated into many treatment programmes as a goal in treating offenders, promoting moral over scientific treatment.

The unreliability of the predication of dangerousness by clinical judgement has led to the prioritisation of the actuarial model of risk assessment. This is an epidemiologically based approach that originated in the insurance industry and studies relevant populations to develop structured risk assessment schedules standardised to particular populations, for example, prison inmates, or patients in a medium secure unit. The actuarial tool collects static data about the patient known to predict future violence, such as a history of violent behaviour, being male, being of lower intelligence, low socio-economic status and drug or alcohol abuse.

The actuarial approach, however, also has its limitations. Actuarial factors are often ignored and seem to have little appeal to clinicians, perhaps because they appear irrelevant to clinical work as they are based on historical or demographic factors that cannot be changed. This means that no patient's risk rating could ever be improved with a risk assessment solely based on actuarial factors, making the idea of treatment redundant. Moreover, the actuarial approach is founded upon the behaviour of a group rather than an individual (Hart et al., 2007). The actuarial method is rendered virtually meaningless when trying to predict individual behaviour extrapolated from risk predictions based on a group, because it tends to ignore individual variations in risk by failing to prioritise clinically relevant variables and minimising the role of clinical judgement.

An unhelpful polarisation has developed between those who think the actuarial approach should be rejected altogether, arguing that it is used as a defence against the anxiety of clinical contact with disturbed patients, and those who idealise the scientific or empirical actuarial approach, rejecting what they may see as irrational or subjective processes in clinical methods. The actuarial approach cannot identify the triggers to the violent act in any particular individual, nor can it examine how the complex interplay of a violent person's history, environment and current relationships, including professional care, interacts to influence his behaviour. However, the actuarial approach is very important and surprisingly compatible with psychoanalytic thinking, in that it prioritises the importance of history. History is the best predictor of how someone will behave in the future, rather than the person's clinical presentation which may be very misleading. The importance of the past and notion that history repeats itself are of course central to classical psychoanalytic thinking. Focusing on the 'here and now' in risk assessment, which, interestingly, parallels a more recent trend in psychoanalytic technique, may be at the expense of gaining crucial information from reconstructing significant historical events.

Subjectivity

Both clinical and actuarial methods are affected by subjective judgement. Much of what goes on in the name of risk assessment is very subjective, based on individual ideas and emotive factors rather than established scientific findings. Most errors are made in the overestimation of risk, which can have as serious consequences to the freedom of the individual as mistakes made in underestimating risk, which are more publicised and can lead to defensive practices.

Recent research shows that even clinicians who are well-trained in using structured and actuarial tools tend to make a subjective response even if they are well-trained in structured and actuarial risk assessment. Blumenthal et al. (2009) have investigated the relative contribution of actuarial and emotive information in determining how experienced forensic mental health professionals rate the risk of violence. They showed that these professionals were unaware how they often minimised the importance of well-known actuarial factors, and that their judgement was disproportionately influenced by emotive factors, for example 'liking' or feeling frightened of the patient.

Psychoanalysis can help us understand these subjective responses to the patient by consideration of the unconscious communications that occur between clinician and patient. The limitations of both clinical and actuarial risk tools have led to the development of more sophisticated 'third generation' instruments that combine standardised and clinical methods to assess risk. This combined methodology is known as the structured clinical assessment of violence risk (SCAVR), and perhaps the most widely used SCAVR instrument is the Historical Clinical Risk-20 (HCR-20) (Webster et al., 1997). The HCR-20 measures a number of actuarial or historical items, and more current clinically rated dynamic aspects of the patient, including his plans, current social circumstances and external stressors.

However, like other risk assessment tools, the HCR-20 does not measure factors related to the patient's inner world – his unconscious motivations, wishes and phantasies, object relations or defence mechanisms. Consideration of the patient's internal world and unconscious dynamics have until recently been neglected in the risk assessment debate (Glasser, 1996b), but nevertheless have a significant influence on the offender's future risk of violence, as well as the judgement of the clinician who assesses that risk. The emotive responses evoked in the clinician by the patient may be understood in more detail by considering psychoanalytic ideas such as countertransference, the dynamic relationship including the unconscious communications between the offender and others, especially those involved in his care, and the defence mechanisms utilised in these communications. All of these concepts can help to explain how experienced professionals may at times be unknowingly seduced into making erroneous risk assessments.

Violence as communication

One of the most important messages of this book is that violence is not a senseless act, but on the contrary, one that is redolent with unconscious meaning. Violence can be understood as a form of 'acting out'. In his paper 'Remembering, repeating and working through' (1914), Freud says,

> ... the patient does not remember anything of what he has forgotten and repressed, but acts it out. He reproduces it as not as a memory, but as an action: he repeats it, without, of course, knowing that he is repeating it. For instance, the patient does not say that he remembers that he used to be defiant and critical towards his parents' authority; instead, he behaves that way to the doctor.
> (Freud, 1914, p. 150)

Freud went on to show how acting out was related both to the transference and to the resistance. The transference could be regarded as a repetition of the patient's past and could result in acting out involving the person of the analyst. 'The greater the resistance, the more extensively will acting out (repetition) replace remembering ... if, as the analysis proceeds, the transference becomes hostile or unduly intense and therefore in need of repression, remembering at once gives way to acting out' (Freud, 1914, p. 151).

Although Freud regarded acting out as a clinical psychoanalytic concept specific to psychoanalytic treatment, the concept has since been widened to include a whole range of impulsive, antisocial and dangerous actions of patients, not solely related to the clinical context, but describing habitual modes of action and behaviour resulting from the personality and pathology of the individual. The violent act can therefore be viewed as a behaviour that has replaced thinking, a communication, the meaning of which may be inaccessible to the conscious mind of the offender and those with whom he has contact. But the latter, including the professionals caring for the patient thought to be dangerous, nevertheless may be aware that they are affected by him, and may experience thoughts and feelings about him that are unexpected. Examination of the clinician's countertransference can be very useful in ascertaining information about the patient's internal world, state of mind and interpersonal relationships which may have direct bearing on his propensity to act out.

Countertransference

Countertransference refers to the emotional response that the therapist or clinician has towards the patient. This reflects the individual therapist's own conflicts and personal history, but is also a reflection of what the patient feels, or is doing to, the therapist, consciously or unconsciously. Countertransference is by definition unconscious and therefore conscious feelings about a patient may be misleading and disguise more unconscious unacceptable feelings. For example, excessive tiredness occurring in the therapist may be a defence against more unconscious hostile feelings that the therapist has towards the patient. Freud (1910, 1912) originally saw countertransference as a manifestation of unresolved conflicts in the analyst, which acted as an impediment to the work of analysing the patient. However since the 1950s, with the work of Heimann (1950) and others, there has been a shift in psychoanalytical theorising towards an appreciation of the patient's contribution to shaping the analyst's countertransference, and how the countertransference can be a valuable tool in providing clues to the patient's unconscious and internal world. Awareness of the therapist's countertransference has now become an essential part of the process and technique of modern psychoanalytic therapy and can be used to inform the therapist's therapeutic interventions and interpretations.

As discussed in previous chapters, many violent individuals, particularly those diagnosed with antisocial or borderline personality disorders, have poorly developed egos and defences inadequate to contain their impulses, and make excessive use of primitive defence mechanisms such as projection or splitting. They find it difficult to bear negative feelings such as anxiety, anger or aggression, and tend to discharge them into action, or project them into those around them. Such a patient may claim to be completely unaware of feelings of anxiety or anger, while the individuals they come into contact with not only experience these feelings but are unconsciously nudged into acting them out. This is often explained by the patient's use of the primitive defence mechanism projective identification. Here, the patient cannot bear to recognise their affects and object relationships as internal to themselves and therefore projects and attributes them to others. The person who has been invested with these unwanted aspects may unconsciously identify with what has been projected into them and may be unconsciously pressurised by the patient to act out.

Sandler's (1976) concept of 'role responsiveness' is helpful in further understanding this process. He described the interactions or 'intrapsychic role relationships' that unconsciously develop between patient and therapist in the therapeutic situation. At any particular time, the patient will unconsciously create a specific role relationship involving a role in which he casts himself, and a complementary role in which he casts the therapist. This role relationship, which may represent earlier or infantile relationships of the patient with significant objects, as well as later defensive relationships, is enacted by the patient in the transference. Sandler called this enactment 'actualisation', in other words, to put in action aspects of the patient's internal object relationships based on the unconscious wishful phantasy dominant at that time. Such actualisation involves manipulation of the therapist by the patient via rapid unconscious verbal and non-verbal signals. This subtle pressure from the patient to prod the therapist to behave in a particular way will provoke particular responses in the therapist, leading to countertransference experiences or enactments by the therapist.

A risk assessment was required on a 78-year-old man Mr M who had been admitted to a psychiatric ward following a violent assault on his wife whom he attempted to hit over the head with a hammer when she was asleep. Mr M claimed no recollection for the event. He had a history of heavy alcohol use and bipolar affective disorder, but it appeared that the offence was committed when he was sober and there was no indication that he was suffering a relapse of his mental illness. Tests showed no evidence of organic abnormality nor cognitive impairment. Mr M denied any animosity towards his wife and described their marriage in very positive terms, claiming that they never argued. Mrs M initially agreed with her husband when questioned but admitted that in the last year Mr M had become incontinent due to 'prostate troubles' and she had become more active in looking after him. Observation of the couple together revealed that she appeared bossy and critical towards her husband and seemed to be the more dominant partner in the relationship, whilst Mr M had a meek and submissive manner tending to agree with everything his wife said. Nursing staff on the ward reported that he was a model patient and considered him a 'sweet old man' of low risk, dismissing his offence as an accident that must have occurred when he was half-asleep.

The assessing psychiatrist, however, found herself feeling increasingly impatient with Mr M's repeated refusal to acknowledge any negative feelings towards his wife during their 40-year marriage, despite his mental illness and alcohol abuse. She found herself wanting to 'hammer these feelings out of him' and had to make an effort not to appear aggressive or rude in her interactions with the patient. Here we can see that her countertransference experience represented one side of the unconscious self-object role relationship that Mr M unconsciously sets up, in which a sado-masochistic relation is established between him and his objects. In his interaction with the psychiatrist Mr M denies his own anger and aggression, which are projected into the psychiatrist who then has to control the urge to act out her angry feelings towards him. A similar dynamic existed between Mr M and his wife and one can hypothesise that Mr M's (unconscious) anger and resentment of his wife's increased power over him, and feelings of humiliation due to incontinence and decreased virility led to his rage that erupted in the very violent attack on his wife. Consideration of the differing feelings that Mr M evoked in different members of the staff looking after Mr M led to an understanding how splitting was occurring within the team, into which Mr M was projecting different parts of his internal object relationships. The team agreed that the risk of Mr M becoming violent again towards his wife should not be underestimated and couple therapy was recommended to facilitate Mr M and his wife in acknowledging the unconscious tensions between them.

Inadequate analysis of the clinician's emotional responses to the patient can contribute to the subjective judgements that interfere with accurate evaluations of risk, as discussed above. Such faulty risk assessment may in itself increase risk. For example, a patient's actions may provoke anger, fear or disgust which may elicit unconscious punitive or sadistic responses in professionals, so that they overestimate the risk of the patient and institute inappropriate interventions such as prolonged incarceration or physical restraint. The patient's subsequent anger and resentment at feeling mistreated may lead to an increased risk of him behaving dangerously. Other offenders may elicit sympathy and present themselves as victims of circumstances of which they had no control. This may resonate with a clinician's 'rescue fantasies' in their desire to treat patients whom they perceive have been misunderstood and mistreated by other professionals, so that the risk here is underestimated.

Doctors and other clinicians are notoriously resistant to admitting that they have any feelings towards their patients at all. This is thought to be unprofessional or an admission of weakness, which could undermine the clinician's authority and respect from his colleagues. When these defensive attitudes of the clinician, however, mix with the primitive defences of violent or forensic patients, the resulting cocktail can be toxic. None of us is immune to emotional involvement with others, least of all the psychiatrist or mental health nurse looking after disturbed and dangerous patients. To prevent such defensive attitudes from becoming embedded, it is important to target trainees such as medical students, junior doctors or student nurses. Teaching communication skills should include awareness of their countertransference. This can be very effective through their participation in clinical discussion groups, sometimes known as Balint groups, after the psychoanalyst Michael Balint, who originally founded such groups for GPs to explore the doctor–patient relationship. In such groups, students are encouraged not to avoid, but to examine and discuss their feelings about the patients with whom they are in contact, as these may provide valuable information about the patient's state of mind, relationships with others and unconscious communications to those looking after him.

An experienced psychotherapist led a weekly discussion group for medical students in their first year of clinical contact with patients. A lively discussion developed about how doctors should deal with their emotions at work, triggered by the students' observations of their consultants' interactions with patients on the ward and in clinic. One male medical student proclaimed that it was 'best to leave one's emotions at home, as they will only interfere with clinical practice – for example how could a surgeon operate safely if he was feeling anxious about the patient?' A female student objected, saying that she had felt uncomfortable witnessing the very brief and emotionally distant contact of a male surgeon with a patient prior to an operation to remove a tumour, and said that afterwards the patient told her that he was very anxious, and asked her opinion about his prognosis, which made her feel guilty not being able to answer. Another male student agreed that this consultant was too abrupt in manner, and went on to describe a more friendly female oncologist, who was treating a cancer patient detained in custody charged with offences of violence and fraud. The student was shocked that the man, who had terminal lung cancer, was brought to the clinic in handcuffs, but also felt perturbed by the consultant who said she felt sorry for this man and had decided to prioritise his treatment over other patients who had been on the waiting list for longer.

The consultant psychotherapist drew attention to the apparent gender split that was emerging in the group's discussion, with the depiction of an emotionless male doctor versus a caring female doctor. Moreover, the male students in the group appeared to be more wary of emotional reactions, whilst the female students seemed to be advocating the importance of being in touch with their patients' and perhaps their own anxieties. The psychotherapist suggested that perhaps emotions were viewed as feminine and weak, detracting from or even having a corrupting influence on the clinical work, as illustrated by the female consultant who appeared to have been seduced by the male patient into putting him at the head of the waiting list. The psychotherapist added that instead of having no emotions, perhaps students or doctors were afraid of being controlled by their emotions, like being in handcuffs, and that to expose them would be a humiliating experience like the patient being publicly paraded as a prisoner in clinic. The students laughed with some embarrassment, but went on to talk about how other patients had made them feel unexpectedly upset or angry.

Patients evoke particular affective responses not only in individual clinicians looking after them, but also in the multi-disciplinary teams and institutions to which these clinicians belong. The impact that the dangerous and disturbed inhabitants have on the prisons and high-security hospitals that contain them, and the unhealthy ways in which these forensic institutions react, will be explored in Chapter 8.

Transference and the index offence

The violent or antisocial act committed by the offender that led to his incarceration in a secure institution is often known as the 'index offence'. Of course, prior to this event the individual may have been involved in many more minor criminal or delinquent activities, which may or may not have come to the attention of the authorities. In the criminal justice system, the emphasis is on punishment and incarceration, rather than understanding. But even when the offender is transferred to the mental health arena and becomes a patient, the shocking or shameful nature of his crime may cause both patient and practitioner to resist its exploration and instead focus on the patient's management and 'progress' in treatment. However, a thorough analysis of the index offence is crucial to elucidating the particular constellation of circumstances in which the patient is most at risk of future acts of violence. Such an analysis should incorporate the unconscious dimensions that influenced the offender's actions, in the light of the offender's history, and how his early object relations, primitive anxieties and defensive systems are repeated in the index offence.

Moreover, the index offence itself will be repeated, often in more subtle ways, in the transferential relationship that develops between the offender and others, including the professionals involved in his care. In psychoanalysis and psychoanalytic psychotherapy, examination and interpretation of the transference is the cornerstone of treatment and facilitates understanding of the patient. Like the concept of countertransference, Freud initially saw the transference as an impediment, but later regarded it as an indispensable vehicle to psychoanalytic work. The classic understanding of transference refers to the patient's experience of the analyst being distorted by his own previous experiences, due to him unconsciously transferring libidinally charged images and phantasies based on his significant early objects onto the analyst. As discussed earlier in this chapter, the transference could therefore be regarded as a repetition of the patient's past and could result in acting out involving the person of the analyst. As the patient is unaware of this, the role of the analyst was to interpret the past, restoring memory to the patient and facilitating his awareness of how his current perceptions were distorted by his previous traumas. With the growth of object relations theory, more emphasis was placed on how the patient's object relationships were repeated in the transference. More recently, some analysts, influenced by Kleinian and post-Kleinian theory, have narrowed their conceptualisation and use of the transference to focusing on the relationship between patient and analyst, proposing that classical genetic interpretations that attempt to reconstruct the past may be a defensive displacement by the analyst (Joseph, 1985; Malcolm, 1986). However, therapeutic work with violent patients continually reminds us of the perils of forgetting the past, and to do so means we risk colluding with our patients with dangerous consequences.

In offenders it is particularly important to see how their antisocial behaviour, and in particular their index offence, repeats itself in the transference. This way of looking at the offender should not be confined to the consulting room, but can be applied to the offender and his relationship with those involved in all aspects of his care and treatment, as will become clearer in the following chapters. Understanding these relationships, the feelings and anxieties in both offender and those around him, in the context of the patient's early history as well as offending behaviour, can facilitate a more accurate evaluation of the risk a person might pose. The following case was raised in a clinical case discussion group by a member of the team looking after the patient.

Mr J was a 60-year-old man transferred from prison to a medium secure unit whilst awaiting sentencing for killing his second wife. He had been married for 20 years to a woman with intractable health problems. Mr J had a history of depression himself and had been his wife's main carer, but denied that there had been any difficulties or tensions between them. Mr J claimed he had no recollection of the killing except afterwards finding himself covered in blood and ringing the police saying he had done something terrible. His wife had been stabbed in the chest many times. On the ward Mr J did not appear depressed and could offer no explanation for the killing. He acknowledged that he must have killed his wife as he was the only other person there, but did not appear to fully own responsibility for his actions. The nurses found him quiet and co-operative, and some described feeling sorry for him and wanting to look after him.

His past medical records, however, revealed that 25 years ago he had been convicted for a previous homicide – the murder of his first wife who had also had chronic health problems. This attack had also involved severe and frenzied violence. It was recorded that the charge of murder had been reduced to manslaughter on the basis of diminished responsibility, and Mr J was admitted to a low secure unit on a restricted order of the Mental Health Act (Section 37/41). He remained on the ward for several years and was described as a model patient. Significantly, he had no memory for this first killing either, and again described the relationship with his first wife as without conflict. He met his second wife whilst in hospital, and several years later he successfully applied for his restriction order to be rescinded.

When asked about his history, Mr J denied any difficulties in his relationships with his parents, but did admit to having spent long periods of his childhood in hospital due to a bone disorder requiring corrective surgery. His parents had been very protective of him and his childhood had been rather isolated with few friends and disrupted schooling, but he did not see these as an adverse experiences. He described himself as a quiet, peaceful man, perhaps prone to depression but not violence.

This clinical example shows how the patient's early history is enacted not once, but twice, in index offences of deadly aggression. The case illustrates how Mr J's early object relationships and primitive defence mechanisms of splitting and denial are repeated both in his pathological relationships with the women he killed, as well as in the transference-countertransference relationships with the staff who looked after him. Here we can see the extreme split between Mr J's conscious experience of himself as a man who avoided conflicts, and his murderous rage, which is split off from consciousness and enacted in his very violent behaviour. This rage is inaccessible to Mr J's conscious mind, and it seems was also not acknowledged by those responsible for his care and follow-up in the community after the original killing. There did not appear to be concern that Mr J was forming a relationship with a woman who had very similar characteristics to his first wife, in that both women had severe disabilities, and in both relationships Mr J was the main carer. In fact, instead of experiencing anxiety, the nurses described feeling caring and protective of him. Had these professionals been more aware of the discrepancy between their affective response or countertransference, which could be described as caring and even maternal, to the patient, and his history of lethal violence, a more accurate assessment of the patient's risk in the specific circumstances of his developing a 'caring relationship' with his wives, could have been formulated so that the second index offence could have been prevented.

It is also remarkable how similar both murderous acts were, despite being separated by a period of 25 years during which Mr J showed no violence, in fact behaved like a 'model citizen' to the point where he was considered of minimal risk. This is an example of Freud's compulsion to repeat in which the patient is obliged to repeat the repressed material as a contemporary experience or action instead of remembering it as something belonging to the past. One could speculate that Mr J's repressed rage from his infantile experiences of being hospitalised and overprotected by his parents is enacted in his violence towards a vulnerable hated deformed image of himself, that is projected into his disabled wives and has to be killed off. Anna Freud's defence mechanism of identification with the aggressor may also be apt here, in Mr J's identification with his parents in a conscious role as carer to his disabled wives, but one that conceals more unconscious control and aggression. He has again ended up as a long-term patient on a ward, as he was following his first offence, a repetition in the transference relationship to the nurses, of his childhood experience of prolonged in-patient admissions. Such an environment may be the one place in which he feels his violence can be contained.

Towards a psychoanalytic risk formulation and framework

Considerations of risk have been traditionally been subdivided into risk assessment, risk management and risk prevention. But clinical experience shows that the assessment of risk is an ongoing process that forms an integral part of the risk management of the patient. Current thinking on risk assessment and management is that it should be less concerned with overall risk prediction, which is notoriously unreliable, but should instead provide a comprehensive framework that would include a psychodynamic risk formulation tailored to each individual patient. The framework should be valid and reliable, and include relevant evidence-based risk factors, both clinical and actuarial. The most important message from the actuarial approach is that the best predictor of future behaviour is previous behaviour. But this historical pattern can only form a context in which current and future behaviour can be understood. Prediction of the triggers and timing of a violent act can be enhanced by an understanding of the complexity of unconscious communications of the violent patient, and how his reactions to the environment are influenced by unconscious processes determined by his history.

A psychoanalytic orientation and overview can help professionals involved in the day-to-day assessment and management of risk in constructing a psychodynamic formulation about individual patients. First, a thorough history should be taken, not only a detailed description of the offending behaviour, but as full an account of the childhood history as possible, with particular reference to the patient's history of attachment to his primary caregivers, experiences of trauma, loss, separations and abuse. Second, the patient's ego and superego functioning should be evaluated. This might include an assessment of the patient's defensive system, his ego strength and capacity for mentalization or psychological mindedness, with consideration given to the following questions. Is the patient capable of reflecting on painful experiences and tolerating unpleasant affects such as anger or sadness, or does he show a tendency to projection and evacuation of painful thoughts and feelings from his mind? The habitual utilisation of more primitive defence mechanisms such as projection, splitting, idealisation and denigration may increase the person's risk of violence. Even in patients whose ego and defensive system appear more mature and intact, it is important to identify the circumstances under which the patient might regress leading to primitive defences becoming more prominent. What are the patient's violent or sexual fantasies and do they show trends towards escalation of severity? What is the nature of his superego, both his attitude to authority and his own goals and standards of behaviour? Does he show evidence of a harsh superego in that he tends to be very self-critical and punishing, or does he tend to be more self-indulgent? Are there internal factors such as drug abuse or psychotic illness, or external factors such as unstable relationships, that will compromise ego functioning? Is the patient particularly susceptible to loss, perhaps because of early experiences of trauma and rejection, so that changes in key worker or therapist may be experienced as abandonment and trigger a defensive acting out? Is the patient hypersensitive to feelings of shame and humiliation that might precipitate a violent response?

The patient's internal object relational patterns should be evaluated, and how these are repeated in his relationships with others should be noted. Seemingly small violations within the therapeutic frame, either on the part of the clinician or institution, such as a key worker going on annual leave, or on the part of the patient, such as non-attendance at a therapeutic activity, may indicate increased risk.

As discussed above, analysis of the index offence and its unconscious symbolic meaning can help anticipate when the offender might be dangerous again. Identifying the type of violence and the underlying primitive phantasies and anxieties can also aid prediction of future violence. Does the violent act appear to be self-preservative or sado-masochistic in nature? More perverse acts of violence may be triggered by separation anxiety, whereas more overtly self-defensive violent responses may be triggered by anxieties of intrusion and feelings of paranoia (Hale, 2004). These two anxieties, that of abandonment, and that of being engulfed, intruded upon or annihilated, are, of course, the conflicting anxieties that constitute the defensive reactions and vicious circle of the core complex (Glasser, 1996a). The detection of prominent core complex anxieties may therefore alert the clinician that the patient may be more prone to violent reactions in interpersonal situations of intimacy. Cartwright (2002) suggests that evidence of an entrapping dyadic situation where little internal space is allocated to a 'third object', as well as the presence of precarious male identifications, may be linked to the risk of violence, especially in those offenders who have committed rage-type murder with no previous history of violence.

Finally, the external circumstances and factors that might influence risk should be recorded. This should include both potential triggers to future enactment, such as relationship breakdown or peer pressure to use drugs or alcohol, and protective factors, such as social, occupational or professional support. The patient's attitude to therapeutic interventions should be noted, as well as the clinician's reactions to the patient. Any pronounced countertransference feelings, such as fear, disgust, outrage or excessive positive feelings for the patient, should raise concern that the clinician's judgement may be distorted by his unconscious affective responses to the patient.

Overall, the formulation aims to provide a detailed individual psychodynamic portrayal of the patient that not only describes the circumstances in which the risk might increase for this particular individual and the reasons why, but also assists clinical thinking about whether, and under which clinical conditions, a psychological intervention could take place safely. Ideally, the information should be collected from several sources, including several meetings between assessor and offender to take a comprehensive history and collate countertransference impressions, as well as corroboration from other sources of information such as prison records, medico-legal reports, previous medical records, information from family members without betraying the patient's confidentiality and, very importantly, the impressions of other professionals such as nurses, who may be exposed to day-to-day contact with the patient.

As the offender or patient moves through the legal and care systems, he will be subject to numerous risk-influencing factors such as conviction and incarceration, relapse of a mental illness, changes in nurses or probation officers, movement between institutions and both engagement and disengagement in treatment. This chapter has highlighted the centrality of the role of clinical experience in the assessment of dangerousness. This experience comprises the unique encounters between patients and clinicians, in which the unconscious meaning of violent acts and feelings can be explored within the arenas of transference and countertransference in a safe therapeutic setting. But therapeutic interventions also carry risk. The following chapters will address the ongoing management of risk, a continual process informed by clinical contact with patients, and show how a psychoanalytic overview can ensure that different treatment approaches, of both patients and institution, can reduce re-offending. In the next chapter, the concept of containment will be introduced as an integral component of both the patient's treatment and the management of his risk in secure institutions. Chapters 9 and 10 will look at the risks and benefits of psychoanalytically orientated individual and group treatments for violent patients. In the final chapter we will explore how the tensions between the rights of the patient to maintain his confidentiality and the pressures for information sharing and disclosure can affect the risk management process.

Summary

- Risk assessment in mental health is traditionally divided into the actuarial approach, which measures static and historical factors associated with risk, and the clinical approach, which measures dynamic factors. Subjective responses can occur in both, arising from clinician's countertransference reactions.
- Awareness of the clinician's countertransference and role responsiveness can help understand the psychopathology of the offender and the risk that he poses. Reflective practice and case discussion groups are useful forums in which to explore how the dynamic relationship between the offender and others, and how the primitive defence mechanisms utilised in his communications influence the clinicians' emotional reactions towards him.
- The actuarial approach, reminding us that history is the best predictor, is consistent with Freud's repetition compulsion. The patient's early object relations, primitive anxieties and defensive systems are repeated in the index offence, and in the transference. Violence, in which action has replaced thinking, can be seen as a communication based on unconscious meaning in which the patient's past experiences are paramount.
- Risk assessment and management should be less concerned with prediction and more concerned with making a formulation about risk. A psychoanalytically based risk framework should take account of both clinical and actuarial evidence-based risk factors, should understand the meaning, including unconscious meaning, of the antisocial act to anticipate when the offender might be dangerous again and should be aware of the dynamic relationship between the offender and others. This will assist clinical thinking about whether and under what clinical conditions a psychological intervention can take place safely for a particular individual.

8

WORKING IN MEDIUM AND HIGH SECURITY SETTINGS

The most dangerous members of our society reside in locked institutions, forcibly removed from public life and mostly forgotten by that society, except for the courageous, or perhaps foolhardy, few who work in these institutions. A visitor to a secure forensic hospital or prison, once through the many security checks, thick walls and locked doors, may be pleasantly surprised by the apparent calm and orderliness within, the prison inmates quiet in their cells or the hospital patients settled on the wards, and wonder where the danger and anxiety has gone. This chapter will attempt to open a window into these secure forensic settings to observe and explore the experiences of those who live and work within, and to locate their anxieties, that have not disappeared, but have been re-distributed among the different parts of the institution to silently and insidiously corrode and distort its functioning. In describing these forensic settings, I will focus on the secure forensic hospital, but will finish by touching on some of the particular problems encountered in the environment of the prison.

Containment

Prisons, high and medium secure forensic hospitals, and more recently in-patient services for personality disorder and enhanced medium secure units for violent women, are all settings in which individuals who have been deemed to be a danger to the public are contained. But the verb 'to contain', broadly meaning 'to keep or hold something within', and the corresponding noun 'containment', can be used in very different ways. One meaning of containment is the action taken, or secure environment constructed, to restrict the movement, spread or force of something hostile such as an enemy, or something undesirable such as a disease. Prison inmates and forensic patients are certainly viewed by many as both dangerously alien and contagious and therefore to be controlled and segregated from the rest of society. But 'to contain' can also refer to holding things, emotions and feelings, within the mind. Within psychoanalysis, the concept of containment has acquired special status since it was originally introduced by Bion (1959, 1962). Bion extended Klein's concept of projective identification and proposed parallels between the analyst–patient relationship and the mother–baby relationship. The infant deals with unbearable feelings such as hunger by projecting them into his mother, who acts as a 'container' by being able to identify with these feelings, modify them and reflect them back to him in a form that is acceptable to him. Thus the baby has the experience of his intolerable feelings being projected into a containing object that can help him process these, facilitating normal emotional development and the capacity to think. Bion proposed that the analyst performed a similar task in accepting the patient's projections, containing and modifying them, and feeding them back in the form of interpretations that the patient can use. Similarly, around the same time Winnicott (1954) described the 'holding' function of the analyst and of the analytic situation in providing an atmosphere in which the patient can feel safe and contained even when severe regression has occurred.

The psychoanalytic concepts of containment and holding do not just apply to the therapist's consulting room, but extend to wider settings in which therapeutic tasks might take place. For forensic patients, the provision of such a containing therapeutic environment is essential for treatment to be effective, as well as for the ongoing management of risk. Risk can only be managed safely if the anxieties of patients, individual staff and the institutions in which they work are adequately contained. But as we have seen, many individuals with a history of violence, particularly those with a diagnosis of psychosis or personality disorder, lack the internal mental structures necessary to tolerate anxieties aroused by strong and conflicting emotions, and instead discharge them into action or project them into those around them, who are unwittingly forced to experience and act out these anxieties for them. In secure forensic institutions, the staff may feel physically safe because of the locked wards and high walls, but emotionally insecure, as they are the recipients of the projections of the dangerous and disturbed patients with whom they work, and they may need help to acknowledge and contain the anxieties provoked in them.

Minne (2003, 2008) has described the delicate and complicated task of the psychotherapist working within secure institutions of facilitating the patient to think about the meaning of his violence and to cultivate an awareness of how his dangerous behaviour resides in his mind, without such knowledge being experienced by the patient as a violent psychic assault. The patient unconsciously resists exploration of his mind by employing defence mechanisms such as denial, disavowal, minimisation or amnesia that may be very necessary for his psychic survival, for he fears that to 'know' about his crimes and what he has done means being overwhelmed with intolerable anxieties that may lead to psychotic breakdown or suicide. But the staff of the institution and other professionals involved in the patient's care may also unconsciously oppose examination of the patient's mind and how their own minds are affected, because of the massive anxieties that this might entail. For staff such as the ward nurses who are exposed to daily contact with these very disturbed patients, defending against these anxieties may seem as necessary for their own psychic survival as for the patients. Although a culture of bravado and camaraderie is rife, the reality that staff find it difficult to cope is reflected in the notoriously high rates of sickness, burnout and staff turnover in such secure institutions. This denial of anxiety does not produce the desired tranquillity, but instead, an atmosphere of emotional deadness, defending against a fear of nameless dread (Bion, 1959), and ultimately paralysing therapeutic functioning.

The sick and fragmented institution

Since Menzies-Lyth's (1959, 1988) classic study of the malfunctioning of a medical teaching hospital, a large literature has emerged on institutional dynamics and the small and large dynamic group processes that occur within institutions that hinder their effective functioning. Drawing on the concept of social defence systems (Jacques, 1955; Menzies-Lyth, 1959), Hinshelwood (1987) not only shows how individual clinicians struggle with their encounters with the patients' madness, but also shows how the staff group as a whole unconsciously employ organised group defences to protect themselves against the intense anxieties generated by working with highly disturbed patients. Ritualised work practices such as filling in forms or training in management techniques act to distance the staff from having any prolonged emotional contact with their patients so that anxiety is kept to a minimum or located elsewhere in the institution. Often the structure of such institutions is compartmentalised into separate functioning (or non-functioning) units composed of different professional groups, with their own very different trainings, sub-cultures and work practices. Thus, within a secure hospital, there might be separate departments or professional groupings of nursing, psychiatry, occupational therapy, psychology and psychotherapy, the representatives of each delivering their own treatment practices and programmes, often with minimal liaison with each other. Frequent managerial interference and re-structuring of departments and services can amplify this process of division and isolation further.

Such splintering of professional groups and the resulting fragmentation of the institution are often explained by the projection of the patients' own chaotic and fragmented minds into the institution as a whole, the reflection of the massive splitting and projective identificatory mechanisms of the patient and their early object relationships being unconsciously enacted by the staff. The nature of their severe psychological disturbance ensures that violent, antisocial and perverse patients will attack, corrupt and splinter objects around them, including the institutions in which they are detained. The shocking scandal involving Ashworth High Secure Hospital in the mid-1990s in which members of staff were caught smuggling children into the hospital to be abused by paedophile patients can be understood as an extreme example of the corrosive effect that such disturbed patients may have when incarcerated with each other and staff members for long periods of time with little involvement from management (Fallon Report, 1999). Another, less acute, example might be the patient with a narcissistic personality disorder who resists engagement in psychotherapy sessions to explore his own violent offending, yet ends up as the representative of the hospital's patients, becoming friendly with senior managers who allow him to attend board level management meetings that decide policy on restraint and control. Davies (2007) has eloquently described how professionals unwittingly become actors in an unconscious drama directed by the patient, with neither patient nor professionals being aware of the roles assigned to them.

However, these pathological defensive structures cannot solely be blamed on the patients, but belong to the institution itself and its component members, who form a collective pathological entity in need of treatment. Instead of being able to function healthily as a whole, the institution is rife with internal divisions, resentments and rivalries, serving to project anxiety and blame away from one professional group or department into another. Such hostilities and envious attacks are often rationalised by disputes over the different treatment approaches available for the patient that are advocated by different professions. Thus the psychologists may complain that the doctors are treating the patient with too high a dose of anti-psychotic medication so that he is over-sedated and cannot participate in the anger management group. Meanwhile, the nurses may complain that the patient is more disturbed following his sessions with the psychotherapist, and may consciously or unconsciously sabotage his attendance by scheduling a different activity for the patient, making the therapy room unavailable, or allowing the patient out on ground leave at the time of the therapy session.

Treating the institution

In contrast to the patient, with his array of available therapies and medications, personal therapy is rarely available or affordable to the clinicians who spend the most time with patients within the forensic hospital, such as the nurses, nursing assistants and auxiliary staff, who are exposed on the front line to the patients' projected fire. Even if such therapy was offered, and the associated stigma, disapproval or envy of colleagues withstood, this would be inadequate to address the ills of the institution in its entirety. Similarly, though individual supervision of nurses' and other therapists' cases can provide essential support and a rich training experience for that particular individual, something more is needed to tackle the wider institutional malaise and to halt the vicious cycle of patient–staff–managerial enactments and maladaptive solutions. Healing the fissures and splinters, taking back the projections, and understanding the emotional impact that patients have on staff, as well as how the staff interact with each other, requires integrative interventions aimed at restoring the healthy cohesion of the group – whether this group comprises the members of the ward, the multi-disciplinary team or the whole institution.

Here the role of the psychoanalytically informed forensic psychotherapist comes to the fore. The forensic psychotherapist can contribute to the therapeutic work in a variety of ways. She can assess patients to see if they might benefit from psychodynamic treatment, or provide a psychoanalytic formulation to assist in the patient's overall therapeutic and risk management plan. She can treat patients herself, in individual therapy and by running psychoanalytically orientated groups. She can supervise the work of other clinicians treating patients and be available to speak to individual nurses about their patients. She can regularly attend ward rounds and case conferences, to participate in the discussions about the treatment and progress of patients and to add her psychoanalytically informed opinions. But perhaps her most important role, with the aim of ministering to the institution's sickness, is to facilitate and promote reflective forums in which staff can come together in a non-threatening and creative way to think about their emotional reactions to patients and how these are enacted within the organisation.

Mr R was a 34-year-old man who had been a patient in a medium secure unit for a prolonged 5-year admission, following an index offence for the false imprisonment and assault of a girlfriend whom he accused of infidelity. Following his arrest and remand in custody, he was found to be psychotic with auditory hallucinations, and was diagnosed with paranoid schizophrenia characterised by morbid jealousy. After his transfer to hospital, for the first 2 years his symptoms were difficult to control, the most prominent being delusions of infidelity of past girlfriends whom he had thoughts of killing. Mr R was also violent to female staff on several occasions during this period. However, with a combination of high dose anti-psychotic medication and cognitive behavioural therapy focusing on his delusions, nurses described him as becoming gradually more settled, and his psychiatrist thought that his paranoid delusions had diminished. Although his aggression was mostly towards women, female staff in particular tended to describe him as charming and engaging and enjoyed reading the poetry that he wrote. Male staff found him more threatening, and were less enthusiastic about his progress. Nevertheless, he was being considered for discharge into the community.

His male social worker recommended that he should first go to a staffed hostel, as he had spent so much time in institutional care that he was not ready to be discharged straight into the community with no professional support. However, his female psychiatrist disagreed, arguing that he could cope with independent living, and should be discharged to a flat that his mother had managed to rent for him near to where she lived. Having not been in touch with her son for many years, his mother had become very involved in his care in the last year, successfully persuading the hospital managers to fund Mr R's treatment with a very expensive medication, and was considered by the psychiatrist as being very supportive. His mother had recently remarried and described herself as being happier and more stable than she had ever been. Mr R himself said he wanted to live near his mother. However, shortly before his CPA meeting when these discharge plans would be discussed and hopefully finalised, it was discovered that Mr R had been having a sexual relationship with a female patient from another ward in the same hospital, who herself was simultaneously having an affair with another male patient.

Mr R's ward benefited from a weekly reflective practice group that was run by an experienced forensic psychotherapist, and well attended by most members of the team, including Mr R's psychiatrist, social worker, psychologist, occupational therapist and nursing staff. Despite the disagreement between psychiatrist and social worker over Mr R's discharge plans that had created a tense atmosphere, both professionals were present at the meeting. The social worker presented Mr R's case, as he was concerned that Mr R's involvement in this new relationship would increase his risk of psychotic relapse and violence. The psychotherapist asked about Mr R's history. Although no specific therapeutic work had been carried out exploring his childhood experiences, it was known that his father had left his mother when he was a baby. From an early age, he became aware that his mother was a prostitute, who would entertain men in the bedroom, whilst he was left to his own devices in the room next door. His mother put him into local authority care on several occasions when she felt she could no longer cope with him.

The psychotherapist suggested that Mr R's diagnosis of pathological jealousy and delusions of infidelity had their basis in Mr R's real experience of being neglected, abandoned and betrayed by his mother as a child by his premature awareness that she was sexually active with other men. Unable to process this premature sexual psychic assault and consciously acknowledge anger at his mother, Mr R's rage was split off and repressed to later surface in his relationships with his girlfriends during his psychotic illness. On the ward, a split had developed between the female psychiatrist, supported by female nurses, promoting increased contact with his mother, and male staff advocating discharge to a staffed hostel. The therapist suggested that at an unconscious level Mr R might experience this as a divisive parental couple unable to come together to decide what was in Mr R's best interests. Discharge to the hostel where he knew no-one, felt like being abandoned yet again, replicating his original experiences of being left by father and then later mother to be placed in institutional care. The therapist suggested that Mr R had managed to seduce the female staff into believing that he was well enough to cope on his own, as he was made to feel by his mother expecting him to amuse himself whilst she was busy with other men. At the same time, both the hospital management and the clinical team were seduced by mother's efforts to help her son, seemingly forgetting her long history of neglect and indifference. Sanctioning the expensive medication may have been an enactment by both mother and professionals to allay unconscious guilt at not being able to bear the full intensity of emotional contact with Mr R who elicited fear at the same time as projecting intense neediness. Discharge now to the care of his mother, who was involved in yet another new *relationship, meant risking betrayal once again at her hands, as well as Mr R feeling betrayed by his psychiatrist whom he felt was pushing him out to focus on other patients. Mr R is unable to articulate any of this consciously, but enacts his internal drama once more by seducing a female patient, who in turn betrays him, with the risk that Mr R will respond violently as in the past. These pre-oedipal and oedipal scenarios that Mr R unconsciously recreates can be seen as a communication to the team about his fear of discharge, which will not mean independence, but abandonment and betrayal, and a wish to remain in hospital where he is looked after and kept in the minds of his team in a creative way.*

The provision of such groups aimed specifically at helping staff to consider and reflect upon their interactions with patients and each other, allowing them to admit to uncomfortable feelings about their work in the presence of each other, and to introduce them to psychoanalytic concepts such as the unconscious, countertransference and projection, can foster the development of a psychological atmosphere that will benefit both staff and patients, in which the capacity to think rather than act is promoted. However, although 'reflective practice' has been officially approved as being essential for good clinical work, many senior managers and practitioners only pay lip service to this, and it is often much more difficult to implement in any meaningful and sustained way into the hospital culture. Although staff malpractices were exposed in all three of the high secure hospitals in England in the 1990s (formerly known as 'Special' hospitals), and independent inquiries recommended radical changes, including a better understanding of patients' offending behaviour, more psychodynamic contributions to assessment and treatment and improvements in liaison between all staff groups including management (Fallon Report, 1999), such changes have been very difficult to put into practice. The institutional historical culture and collective memory about the workings of the hospital can prove very hard to shift. For example, in some of the older institutions, the staff – the security men, the cooks, the cleaners and some of the nurses – are comprised of successive generations of the same local families who are sustained by their own mythology of the patients' madness, cautionary tales and how best to survive.

Nevertheless, forensic psychotherapy has been introduced into the high secure hospitals, and in many of the medium secure hospitals that have been built in the last decade, with varying degrees of success. Gordon and Kirtchuk (2008) describe the application of reflective practice in forensic institutions based on the idea of countertransference as the staff member's basic relational potential. Because of the tensions between different professional groups, reflective practice groups may be introduced in a less threatening way if separate groups are held for each distinct profession, such as nurses, psychiatrists and occupational therapists. Reflective practice can also be offered to managers (Mercer, 2008). Once these clinicians feel more comfortable talking about their countertransferential feelings with other members of their own profession, they can be encouraged to participate in larger multi-disciplinary reflective practice meetings involving the wider staff group. The reflective practice group does not aim to be solely a supportive or therapeutic group for staff, but one in which its members engage in the challenging and at times threatening task of considering how other human minds and emotions can affect one's own.

The psychotherapist facilitating such groups must be prepared to withstand long periods of resistance from staff whose fear of emotional exposure is exhibited in a number of ways such as minimal attendance, scheduling other activities at the same time as the group or having 'more important or urgent' clinical work to carry out, which inevitably involves acting (injecting or secluding a patient, filling out forms) rather than thinking, which is derided as a waste of valuable time. The forensic psychotherapist who only attends the ward occasionally to consult or supervise risks resentment and denigration by ward staff who cannot believe that she really understands what it is like to care day in day out for patients capable of such dangerous violence. The therapist, by contrast, who has a sustained and visible presence on the ward, who is approachable and available, who is able to communicate effectively without psychological jargon and who also has substantial contact with patients, will be more likely to gain the respect of nursing staff and other members of the multi-disciplinary team.

However, the psychotherapist must also resist being seen as a saviour, who rescues and absolves the ward of its sins. Hinshelwood (1987) describes how all the longed for hope and life can be located in an idealised phantasy figure of the psychotherapist whose special insights and interventions are venerated and revered. This is of course the opposite extreme to the denigrated and devalued psychotherapist described above. But ultimately both of these exaggerated depictions of the therapist keep her at a distance so that her interventions are useless, as no creative link can be forged between the institution and a feared, hated or exalted figure (Gordon and Kirtchuk, 2008). The forensic psychotherapist needs to tread a delicate path between being the admired yet ultimately impotent outsider and being absorbed into the institution at the expense of being able to maintain independent mindfulness. This parallels the secure institution's fundamental task in being able to provide the right balance of both care and custody, without becoming either corrupted or destroyed (Hinshelwood, 2004). This can also be seen as the representation of a healthy parental couple, an institution that can provide and integrate both maternal and paternal functions, an experience which most of its patients did not experience from their primary caregivers. Indeed, reflective practice can be seen as being able to witness and experience, but without intruding – providing a third space from which object relationships can be observed, at the same time as a capacity to see ourselves in interaction with others and entertaining another point of view while retaining our own (Britton, 1998; Gordon and Kirtchuk, 2008).

Working in prisons

The therapeutic task is even more difficult in prisons, where the main aims for offenders are punishment, incarceration and deterrence, rather than understanding the origins of their criminality or treatment of their difficulties. The prison system in the UK has arguably been more adversely affected by political agendas and trends over the last half century than the health system. The 1960s and 1970s were characterised by an air of optimism, with the emergence of prisons run on therapeutic lines such as Grendon, the rebuilding of Holloway along a hospital design for women in recognition of their special needs and the emphasis on rehabilitating prisoners back into the community. However, this therapeutic era was replaced by a more authoritarian political agenda of crime and punishment in the 1980s, which promoted retribution over rehabilitation and continued during the 1990s to the present day with the growth of the public protection agenda. Re-organisations in prison management and commissioning, as well as continued cuts in funding, have disheartened already embittered staff who feel undervalued and forgotten.

The provision of health care to prison inmates has been beset with difficulties paralleling these political changes. The gradual process of introducing the National Health Service (NHS) into prisons, initially with a separate prison medical service, via partnership arrangements, to the current situation where most health care is provided via contracts with the NHS, has been problematic. Mental health services within prisons have had great difficulty in keeping up with a modernised NHS that is constantly evolving with new targets and initiatives (Grounds, 2000), leading to a sense of demoralisation and inferiority within prison health care. The problems are compounded by poor conditions and serious overcrowding within prisons as a result of recent sentencing policy that favours indeterminate sentencing, driven by the pressure for public protection. The rising rate of suicides within prisons spawns official inquiries and publicity more likely to attribute blame than generate compassionate curiosity as to what is really happening within these institutions, which become even more defensively closed and inward looking.

Enlightened prison governors attempting reform, or mental health professionals offering therapeutic assessment and treatment, face both overt and covert resistance. Mental health day hospitals are the first services to shut when there are staff shortages as security will always remain the priority in the prison service. Psychiatrists visiting a prisoner for a medico-legal assessment are often told by staff that the prisoner does not want to see them, when in fact he has not been asked at all. Anyone attempting to do therapeutic work within a prison has to confront a rigid hierarchy run on harsh patriarchal and punitive lines. Davies (2007) highlights particular difficulties facing the offender who is transferred from court, where he has been the centre of attention, to the pre-existing closed system of the prison, where all individuality is erased, and the prisoner becomes a number, stripped of personality and emotions. All his physical needs are treated as functions, and instead of being thought of as a whole person, he is divided into component parts that are separately catered for, such as being fed, transported, educated or controlled. A prisoner's life history is ignored and any attempt to acknowledge or explore this is strongly resisted, because of unconscious fears that the whole system would be overwhelmed by the terror, pain, grief and rage hidden within, which, therefore, need to remain buried at all cost. If any therapeutic contact can be established in the face of these oppositional forces, this is likely to be disrupted by the abrupt transfer of the prisoner to another prison, as part of the continuous turnover and over-spillage of inmates within a prison system unable to contain them. Davies draws our attention to how a prison regime that inherently supports a system of splits and treats its inmates as part objects rather than whole human beings replicates the deprived early histories and internal worlds of those who occupy it and repeats the cycle of abuse. Prisoners, as well as staff, unconsciously collude in perpetuating this state of affairs by their riots and hunger strikes, which, instead of effecting any real change, restore the equilibrium by provoking a reaction of greater control and restraint. This precarious equilibrium is one in which all despair, inferiority, impotence, madness and violence are located within the cells, and guarded against by collective staff defences of power, superiority, contempt and control. This is not to deny the existence of many humane and compassionate prison officers and other NHS and voluntary agency staff working within the prison service, but describes the unconscious pathological social defensive structures that can develop in institutions in which so much potential violence is restrained.

Hyatt-Williams (1998) defined some of the roles of the professionals who work with criminals, which he designated as 'guardians, care-givers and continuity figures'. The guardian figure, for example the prison officer, set boundaries and limits and contains anxieties. The caregiver, for example the prison doctor, deals with personal or group issues. The continuity figure provides a sense of ongoing involvement, as in a family. All three roles, when well articulated, lead to stability within the organisation, and security to the persons who reside within. Unfortunately, unlike the prisons in which Hyatt-Williams worked several decades ago, most prisons today lack the stability and retention of both staff and prisoners to make such continuity and co-ordination of care possible.

Despite the increasing availability of mostly cognitive behavioural treatment approaches for offenders, as well as the many dedicated individual clinicians and teams attempting therapeutic inroads into prisons, including the types of reflective practice groups for prison staff described earlier in this chapter, a co-ordinated therapeutic strategy aimed at the institution and one that addresses the unconscious factors at play is lacking. Fundamental organisational change is unlikely without central government authorisation, but this also remains a distant prospect until the society that has elected the government recognises that to punish violence with no attempt at understanding will only perpetuate violence.

Summary

- Bion's concept of 'containment' and Winnicott's concept of 'holding' are useful to understand how professional teams and institutions can form supportive frameworks that are essential in providing a safe environment for therapeutic work. Risk can only be managed safely if the anxieties of patients, individual staff and the institutions in which they work are adequately contained.

- Violent patients tend to project their anxieties into those around them, including health care professionals, who may unconsciously defend themselves against these projections in unhelpful ways. This may affect the functioning of the institution, which may become sick and fragmented as a result of the staff group unconsciously employing pathological group defences to protect themselves against the intense anxieties generated by working with highly disturbed patients.
- A key role of the forensic psychotherapist working in such institutions is to promote reflective practice and help the staff group think about how they are affected, both consciously and unconsciously, by the patients with whom they work.
- Prisons today tend to be harsh environments in which punishment and control are promoted over the welfare of individual inmates. Both prisoners and staff unconsciously collude in perpetuating a punitive regime that replicates the early abusive histories of many of its inmates. Effective therapeutic change is unlikely without central political involvement and a change in society's attitudes towards crime and punishment.

INDIVIDUAL PSYCHOANALYTIC PSYCHOTHERAPY FOR VIOLENT PATIENTS

Violence has always been considered to be one of the more serious contraindications for psychoanalytic treatment. Conventional psychoanalytic wisdom regarding suitability for psychoanalysis teaches that a patient who has a history of violence towards self or others indicates weak ego strength and primitive defences, and so is unlikely to be able to utilise psychoanalytic therapy, which in itself may increase the risk of the patient acting violently. However, the nature of human aggression is one of the most essential themes that has interested psychoanalysis since its inception, and in its investigation, eminent psychoanalysts on both sides of the Atlantic have treated violent patients. As we have seen in the preceding chapters, violence in itself has only achieved prominence in the psychoanalytic literature within the last few decades. However, earlier generations of analysts produced creative clinicians interested in expanding the boundaries of classical psychoanalysis, such as Menninger (1938, 1942, 1963, 1968) in the United States, who saw many very serious violent cases for treatment. In the UK, the Portman Clinic in London was founded in 1931 as the Psychopathic Clinic, the clinical arm of the then Institute for the Scientific Treatment of Delinquency, by Dr Grace Pailthorpe, a psychoanalyst and psychiatrist, who enlisted the interest and support of prominent psychoanalysts such as Edward Glover and Kate Friedlander. The Clinic's first formal patient seen in 1933 was 'a woman, 47 years of age, noted as having a violent temper, charged with assault on her woman employer' (Saville and Rumney, 1992).

Since then, the Portman Clinic has continued to treat violent, antisocial, delinquent and perverse patients with psychoanalytic psychotherapy, the clinical work inspired and research insights disseminated by psychoanalysts working there such as Glover, Glasser, Limentani and, more recently, Campbell, Dermen, Hale and Welldon. Meanwhile, other psychoanalysts have focused their interest on treating the most disturbed and violent patients held within psychiatric institutions, such as Cox, Sohn and Hyatt-Williams. These psychoanalysts working first hand with violent patients laid the foundations for the new field of forensic psychotherapy, which has rapidly expanded over the last 20 years to produce a multitude of clinicians from many different core professional backgrounds including psychiatry, psychology, social work, art and music therapy, nursing and probation, and who are treating violent individuals in psychoanalytically informed therapies in a variety of in- and outpatient settings. Parallel to and overlapping with the development of forensic psychotherapy is the recent interest in treatments and services for personality disordered patients, with the creation of specific therapies, some based on psychoanalytic concepts such as transference-focused psychotherapy (TFP) and mentalization-based treatment (MBT), for individuals with personality disorder, including those who have a propensity for violent behaviour.

In this chapter I will discuss the assessment process and treatment of violent patients with individual psychoanalytic psychotherapy, focusing in particular on some of the technical difficulties that can arise in the treatment of such patients. Following the clinical experience of other psychoanalysts I will advocate the necessity for the modification of more conventional psychoanalytic techniques in the therapeutic treatment of some of these individuals whose psychic structures and functioning are especially fragile or damaged. Although I will not be specifically discussing the psychoanalytically based therapies designed for the treatment of borderline personality disorder such as TFP and MBT, I will address some of the therapeutic strategies and techniques incorporated in these therapies that can also be usefully applied in the psychoanalytic psychotherapy of violent individuals. The discussion of the importance of attending to transference and countertransference phenomena in individual therapy is also very much of relevance in the psychoanalytic group treatment of violent patients, which will be reviewed in the next chapter.

Assessing the violent patient

There is a substantial literature on suitability for psychoanalysis (e.g. Baker, 1980; Freud, 1905b, 1912; Glover, 1954; Limentani, 1972; Shapiro, 1984) and assessment for psychoanalytic psychotherapy (e.g. Coltart, 1988a; Cooper and Alfille, 1998; Garelick, 1994; Hinshelwood, 1991), to which I will not pay full justice but will highlight the salient points relevant to assessment of the violent patient. Assessment is a multi-layered process with several functions, including diagnosis, forming a psychodynamic formulation about the patient, assessing the patient's suitability for psychoanalytic therapy and, of particular importance for the violent patient, consideration of issues regarding risk. The assessment interview may be the first exposure the patient has to a psychoanalytic way of thinking, which, for individuals who habitually act rather than think, may be a strange and threatening experience for them. How the therapist conducts these first meetings with the patient is critical for future engagement in therapy. Psychoanalytic assessment puts most emphasis on the clinical interview with the patient, rather than other methods of assessment, such as formal diagnostic psychological testing for personality traits, cognitive tests if there is suspicion of learning difficulty or structured risk assessment schedules such as the HCR-20 or PCL-R. Although these tests may be useful, the clinical meetings with the patient, attending in particular to the experience within the interviews and the nature of the relationship that emerges between patient and assessor, can yield the most meaningful information regarding the unconscious phantasies and functioning of the patient.

Selection for psychoanalytic psychotherapy traditionally aims to evaluate certain key aspects of the patient's psychological functioning and internal world, notably psychological mindedness, ego strength and defences, the capacity to form and sustain relationships and the nature of early object relations, superego factors, motivation for treatment, responses to previous therapeutic interventions and the extent of external support. However, many patients with violent tendencies will show serious deficits in these measures of psychic functioning, and the threshold for offering therapy may need to be lowered if sufficient expertise and support for the treatment is available. Coltart (1988b) enumerates the various components of psychological mindedness, which include an acknowledgement of the unconscious, awareness of emotionally significant historical events and capacity to recall memories with appropriate affect, use of imagination, capacity to dream, some signs of hope and self-esteem, curiosity about internal reality and capacity to tolerate internal anxiety, and ability to make links between past and present. Although many violent patients who have a diminished representational capacity and deficits in symbolic thinking would not score highly on many of these criteria, they may nevertheless have some awareness that their difficulties are influenced by unconscious internal factors. The assessment process aims to ascertain whether the patient's potential for curiosity in his internal world and ownership of his difficulties can be nurtured and developed.

Ideally, the assessor should arrange to see the patient on more than one occasion, at least two or three times, and more for complex cases and if resources are available. This allows the assessor the space and freedom to address the various factors that should be examined during the assessment process, as well as the adoption of different technical stances and observation of the patient's responses, including the effect of interpretations (Garelick, 1994). This might comprise offering an initial unstructured interview to observe how the patient responds to silences, his ability to free associate, and to assess the presence and quality of emotional contact within the session and degree of access to his internal world. A more accurate appraisal of the patient's ego strength, defences and motivation for therapy is facilitated by seeing the patient several times, to discover what the patient makes of the meetings, whether the patient is capable of reflection between sessions and whether he is able to tolerate the anxiety associated with the open-ended process of psychotherapy which offers an attempt at understanding rather than immediate cure. However, many violent patients may find such an unstructured situation very anxiety provoking and persecutory, and the assessor may need to intervene sooner than with a person whose ability to tolerate anxiety is greater. The strangeness of the analytic encounter should not be underestimated, and for many of these patients, who have never developed a capacity for reflection, or have constructed life-long defensive strategies to avoid thinking and feeling, being invited to talk about their difficulties may be experienced as extremely threatening. They are likely to know very little about psychotherapy and being referred is associated with shame, failure and stigma.

In subsequent interviews, the assessor can focus on more active history-taking. This should include a detailed account of the patient's offending behaviour, including an attempt to classify the type of violence that the patient has engaged in, and to determine its precipitants in relation to the patient's objects, both internal and external, and associated phantasies, both conscious and unconscious. The history should also give as comprehensive a picture as possible of the patient's object relations. Hinshelwood (1991) provides a useful framework for making a formulation about the patient's object relationships, by consideration of three areas – the patient's current life situation; the infantile object relations, as described in the patient's history or hypothesised from what is known; and the relationship that develops with the assessor, which is the beginning of a transference. Information from these three areas can help the assessor identify the patient's core object relationships, common themes in his object relations that run through all three areas of the patient's life.

Mr Y was referred to a specialist out-patient forensic psychotherapy clinic in another city as there were no appropriate services willing to treat him in his local area. He had spent 20 years in prison for the murder of a prostitute whilst intoxicated with alcohol. During the latter half of his sentence, Mr Y had impressed the Parole Board by his enthusiasm and motivation to engage in every therapeutic and occupational course available. At the time of his release, he had not touched alcohol for over a decade, alcohol having been pinpointed as one of the major risk factors implicated in his violence. However, his probation officer was concerned that although he had attended various anger management and victim empathy cognitive behavioural programmes, no therapeutic work had been done to address the roots of his aggression, nor had the sexual aspects been of the offence been explored, so he was referred for psychoanalytic psychotherapy specifically to reduce his risk living in the community.

The therapist met with Mr Y over several sessions during the course of an extended assessment. Mr Y appeared very motivated to receive more therapy and was very willing to talk about all aspects of his life, including his previous offending. However, the therapist was struck by the one-dimensional quality of his account. His description of his childhood was brief and he appeared unable to elaborate on or describe any emotional context to significant events. He had been physically abused by both parents and spent significant periods of time in care, where he had been sexually abused in one care home. Although acknowledging that it was not a happy childhood, he felt that he somehow deserved the abuse, because he was 'born bad', and he did not think he was affected by it in later life. He dismissed the therapist's suggestion that his previous alcoholism may have been connected to his unhappiness, saying that he was genetically predisposed to alcoholism. Since his release from prison he lived an isolated life in a staffed hostel, his only social contact being the people he saw at the Alcohol Anonymous (AA) groups he attended daily, to which he attributed his continued abstinence from alcohol. He had never had any close friends and had no contact with his family. Mr Y's account of his index offence was vague, saying he did not remember much because he was drunk, but had been angry with the prostitute because he felt she was mocking him, as he was unable to ejaculate. There had been no previous history of violence.

When the therapist tried to explore his relationship with his mother, and also when she asked him about his relationships with women, including his visiting prostitutes, she noted that Mr Y would tend to quickly change the subject. When she drew his attention to this, Mr Y appeared irritable, saying he did not think there was much to talk about, as he did not trust women and was not interested in seeing his mother again, and was very wary about starting a relationship with a woman. He added that he did not mean to cause any offence to her being a woman, as she was a professional. The therapist suggested that because she was a woman, he might feel uncomfortable and not trust her either, but Mr Y quickly dismissed this.

When the therapist saw him again, she asked whether he had had any thoughts about their last meeting. Mr Y said that if he had any thoughts he had pushed these out of his mind. The therapist enquired what these were. Mr Y admitted that thinking about his mother had upset him and she was not worth thinking about.

When the therapist saw him on the third occasion, Mr Y appeared more agitated and dishevelled. He admitted that for the first time in years he was 'desperate for a drink' and was worried he would relapse. The therapist suggested that the assessment process and discussing distressing subjects such as his mother had made him feel more disturbed. Mr Y categorically rejected this suggestion and insisted that he was upset because someone had moved into the room next door, who was noisy and rude.

On discussion of this case with other clinicians in the clinic, the therapist decided not to offer Mr Y psychodynamic psychotherapy. She thought that Mr Y did not have sufficient ego strength to withstand exploration into his internal world. It was apparent that Mr Y dealt with distressing thoughts and feelings by projection or actively pushing them out of his mind. Mr Y did not appear to be psychologically minded and was unable to make links between past experiences and present behaviour. He could not link his current anxiety to the therapist's attempts to open up his internal world, a transference experience in which the therapist was experienced as a rude and noisy intrusive object, like the neighbour, and his early experience of his mother. Any exploration of the index offence and its relation to Mr Y's rage towards his mother was impossible. In formulating his object relationships, we can see how information from each of the three areas of the patient's current life situation, the patient's description of his infantile object relations and the transferential relationship with the assessor concur to give a picture of Mr Y as having great difficulty in forming attachments at all, and how he distances himself from any emotional contact, particularly from a threatening maternal object. In view of this, the therapist concluded that Mr Y would find it difficult to form a secure enough attachment to the therapist in which 'as if' transference phenomena could be explored rather than Mr Y experiencing the relationship in a very concrete way. Moreover, in view of his limited internal capacities for mentalization, the unstructured and exploratory nature of psychodynamic psychotherapy would be likely to lead to intense persecutory anxieties that would increase his risk of alcoholic relapse and/or violence, and he would find it difficult to tolerate weekly out-patient psychotherapy and the travelling involved to get to the clinic. She suggested that the current external supportive network surrounding Mr Y, including his probation officer, staffed hostel and structured AA meetings, appeared to be containing his anxieties and should remain in place.

Throughout the assessment, the clinician should remain cautious about asking a patient to reveal very painful memories and open up traumatised areas of his inner world to a stranger whom he may only meet on a few occasions, but to whom he may form a rapid and intense transference that may complicate the transition to another clinician for therapy. The patient may be left in an emotionally vulnerable state following assessment sessions, and if therapy is thought appropriate but is not available in the near future, there is a danger that the patient's risk of acting out will be exacerbated or that his pathological defences will harden, and he will be less emotionally available once treatment is offered. It is therefore useful at the beginning of the assessment to make clear to the patient that the assessor will not necessarily be the patient's therapist, as well as having as clear an idea as is feasible about the availability of appropriate local services or therapists qualified to take on this specialised and challenging work.

Assessment of the psychopathic individual raises particular difficulties. The patient's veracity may be in doubt and his history confabulated. Multiple interviews can identify inconsistencies in his account, and emphasis should be placed on evaluating the relationship the patient establishes with the assessor and the latter's countertransferential responses, rather than the patient's account of his history. Meloy (1988) recommends that therapy will be of no benefit and should not be offered to psychopathic patients who manifest any of the following features: sadistic aggressive behaviour resulting in serious injury, complete absence of remorse or justification for such behaviour, very superior or mildly mentally impaired intelligence, a historical absence of capacity to form emotional attachments and unexpected 'atavistic' fear felt by the experienced clinician in the patient's presence.

The setting

The setting in which the patient is first seen has an important bearing on the assessment process. If the patient is an in-patient in a secure unit, his violence is already known about and is likely to be the reason for his incarceration, although a crucial part of the psychotherapeutic assessment is to gauge how much the patient can tolerate 'knowing about' his offence and its unconscious meaning. Considerations of risk will have already been raised about the patient, although again, not necessarily from a psychoanalytic perspective. However, people may also present for the first time to counsellors or psychotherapists in primary care or private practice, and reveal a history of or continued involvement in violent activities. Hasty decisions not to continue the assessment should be carefully examined to see how much these are determined by countertransferential responses in the clinician such as fear or repugnance, leading to premature conclusions about the patient's unsuitability for treatment, rather than those based on careful considerations about whether this person could use psychotherapy and what setting would be most appropriate. A person who has little external social or occupational support may find the gap between weekly sessions as an out-patient very difficult if he becomes more anxious or disturbed as a result of therapy, and may need extra external support, such as a community mental health team that could provide regular access to a psychiatrist, social worker or community psychiatric nurse. For patients who are still subject to probation, the probation officer who is monitoring the patient's risk of offending can also fulfil a helpful role in providing therapeutic support for a patient having out-patient psychotherapy. If issues regarding trust and confidentiality can be negotiated, the involvement of a third party in such cases can be felt by the patient to be a helpful parental couple working together in the patient's best interests, a novel experience for many of these patients that can be therapeutically mutative.

For a patient who is already detained in a secure hospital or prison without his consent, motivation for therapeutic treatment becomes more difficult to assess. The patient in a secure in-patient setting is less likely to request therapy himself, and unlike the out-patient, the therapist goes to see him, rather than the patient being able to come to the therapist for his sessions (Minne, 2008). The patient may believe that agreeing to have therapy will accelerate his progress and release into the community, rather than having any genuine wish to engage in a protracted and painful process of self-awareness. This may also be true for the convicted offender who receives a non-custodial sentence with a condition for treatment. In these cases it is advisable that psychotherapy is not one of the treatment conditions, as again, the offender may have no real interest in exploring the roots of his behaviour and may not see himself as a patient in need of therapy at all. Similarly, for individuals involved in medico-legal proceedings, assessment for and treatment with psychoanalytic therapy should wait until all such proceedings have terminated.

Engaging the patient

The assessment is the initial step in engaging the patient, but difficulties in the patient's ability to establish himself in a therapeutic process may persist for a long time after treatment has been offered, so that the therapist will need to adopt a technique that is flexible and sensitively attuned to the patient's manifest and unconscious anxieties. This will involve some modification of more conventional psychoanalytic technique that may be appropriate for less disturbed patients but proves ineffective or even counter-productive in violent patients. As Minne (2003) describes, one of the tasks that the therapist has to negotiate is how to introduce the patient to the unconscious contents of his mind, without either patient or therapist becoming overwhelmed by these contents, leading to states of unbearable anxiety, psychosis or suicidal despair. This requires careful timing and continuous titration of therapeutic interventions according to the patient's affective temperature. Long silences should be avoided, as these are often experienced as persecutory by the patient, because of the projection of his aggression onto the therapist who may be pushed into an unhelpful countertransferential defensive withdrawal of silence or passivity. Indeed, the unstructured therapeutic sessions may be experienced as so unbearable that the patient cannot tolerate the full analytic hour, and it may be advisable for very severely disturbed, particularly hospitalised psychotic patients, to initially limit the length of sessions to 30 minutes, and allow the patient to leave when he wishes, without interpretations that may sound punitive or retaliatory. Similarly, the therapist may need to withstand long periods of non-attendance of patients who are being treated as out-patients, or refusal to attend for the in-patient in therapy. The therapist's reliable availability, holding the patient in mind despite not meeting in body, may be a completely new and therapeutic experience for the patient whose body has been hijacked for violent purposes instead of being held in the mind of his original objects.

For patients with poor representational capacity and deficits in symbolic thinking, further modifications in therapeutic technique are necessary. These patient's communications are concrete and one-dimensional and they find it difficult or impossible to experience the 'as if' quality of the transference, instead identifying with the concrete content of interpretations, not their symbolic meaning (Davies, 1999). For these patients, their minds and other people's minds are experienced as concrete objects, and equated with physical reality (Fonagy, 1999). The lack of representational mediating process means that minds and bodies are experienced as equivalent, rather than having a symbolic relationship to each other, and communications can therefore only be via action rather than the symbolic activities of speech or thought. Interpretations of unconscious conflicts and phantasies are therefore not understood by the patient, and should be avoided at this stage. Instead, it is more constructive for the therapist to provide brief simple descriptive comments about the patient's state of mind (Bateman, 1999; Fonagy, 1999). This will include the therapist naming affects, putting words to the patient's concrete thoughts and feelings, and using basic metaphors to introduce him to symbolic thinking. Rather than making the unconscious conscious, the aim here is to establish and maintain emotional contact with the patient by giving the patient a clear and coherent picture of their own mind in the analyst's mind (Fonagy, 1999). This again is a novel experience for the patient whose nascent mind was not held and nurtured in the mind of his early caregivers.

Mr V was a 35-year-old man referred for psychotherapy due to severe anxiety and panic attacks that he had suffered in the past few years and which prevented him from working. He had a history of involvement in serious violent activities as a teenager and young man and had spent time in prison for armed robbery. Mr V telephoned at his appointment time saying he was lost, and eventually arrived 40 minutes late with a friend whom he wanted to bring into the assessment interview. The therapist suggested that his friend stay in the waiting room and she would see him briefly on his own. In the room, Mr V could barely speak due to anxiety. The therapist simply commented that Mr V appeared very anxious about coming to be assessed but that he now knew the way here and she could see him again in 2 weeks time. Mr V said he thought he would be less anxious the next time. The following appointment he again arrived with the friend, but was on time and more able to talk.

This brief vignette shows how the therapist simply verbalises Mr V's affective state by commenting that he is anxious. Although it is not at all clear yet what Mr V's anxiety is about, simply naming his manifest affect appears to have been helpful as Mr V is then able to attend on time at the next appointment. The therapist's non-verbal adherence to boundaries – that she does not let the initial session over-run due to Mr V's lateness, and does not accede to his request to be seen with his friend – are communicated in a clear but non-persecutory way, to convey the experience of a containing space in which Mr V can begin to find his way.

The internalisation of a stable figure of a therapist who is consistent and boundaried, empathic and non-judgemental, but able to consider different points of view, is an important therapeutic factor. This opens up a space within the patient's mind where difference can begin to be tolerated rather than feared, an area of psychic experimentation and playfulness from which the patient can begin his journey towards mentalization. This is akin to Winnicott's transitional space (1951), which he believed was a pre-requisite for the child to develop a capacity to play, relate and be. Many of these patients exhibit profound difficulties in separation and separateness, because of their early experiences of not being conceived of as separate individuals with their own individual needs, but instead were intruded upon or treated as the narcissistic extensions of their parents. Fonagy (1999) describes the therapeutic paradox in patients who use violence to distance themselves from their objects, yet at the same time show considerable dependency on those objects, including the therapist, with difficulties tolerating breaks in therapy and expressing fears of losing their therapist. The patient needs the continuous physical presence of the object so that their internal states do not become overwhelming. Winnicott (1967) described how the caregiver needs to accept, contain and metabolise the infant's anxieties, re-introduce them in a bearable form and mirror the self-state to facilitate the development of the representation of his own internal states, rather than prematurely internalising an intrusive object that undermines the developing self and ultimately experienced as an alien being within his self-representation. The therapist must be prepared to be used in this way, as an auxiliary ego (Freud, A., 1965), for a considerable length of time before the patient's own mind feels safe enough to rely on. The therapist will need to contain affects that are too painful for the patient to bear, as well as being used as an object that will tolerate the patient's aggressive impulses without retaliation.

For these patients whose sense of self is so precarious, and for whom the world is experienced as menacing and punitive, premature interpretations of the negative transference or attacks on the therapist will be perceived by the patient as critical, retaliatory and confirmation that the world consists of only bad objects, the therapist being no exception. In her experience of analysing a violent patient, Davies (1999) describes how it is a technical error for the therapist to attempt to return projected parts of the patient prematurely via interpretations, and that the patient needs to use the therapist as a vehicle for his projections to deny the object's separateness. The gradual awareness by the patient of the therapist's struggle with his projected hatred, and interpretation of the affect behind the patient's attacks, rather than interpretation of the manifest attack itself, are the mutative factors. The patient's expectation of the therapist's hostile reaction is not fulfiled, and the resulting dissonance between expectation and experience can lead to a change in the patient's perception.

Several authors (e.g. Bateman, 1999; Davies, 1999; Cartwright, 2002; Christie, 2006) recommend the use of 'analyst-centred interpretations' (Steiner, 1994) with violent patients. An analyst-centred interpretation is one in which the therapist attempts to clarify the patient's perception of what is going on in the therapist's mind, such as saying 'You are afraid that I am angry with you.' This conveys a sense of being understood by the therapist, which can be more containing for very anxious patients, rather than patient-centred interpretations about their own conflicts that can make the patient feel blamed. Again, being invited to observe what might be going on in the therapist's mind, which may not be what the patient fears, initiates a process of triangulation, potentially opening up a third space for thinking (Britton, 1989).

Mr V, introduced above, attended his second assessment session on time, and although less anxious, he appeared sullen, withdrawn and reluctant to talk. With prompting from the therapist, he gave an account of how he felt unfairly blamed and treated by social workers and other professionals who did not believe he was safe to be on his own with his partner's children, due to his history of violence. The therapist suggested that he was very anxious that she will be another one of the professionals who blames him and disapproves, rather than try to understand what his violence is all about. Mr V did not directly reply to this but went on to tell her about his anxiety and how he had a panic attack when he first held his partner's new baby. Later he spoke of his father's violence towards him as a child.

In this assessment session, the therapist limits herself to making an analyst-centred interpretation about Mr V's fears that she disapproves, an attitude he expects from all professionals. The therapist's articulation of this fear in itself is a surprise for Mr V, who expects a punitive response, and the resulting dissonance between his expectation and actual response opens up a space in which Mr V is able to associate to his anxiety about holding a new-born baby. At this stage the therapist does not interpret underlying unconscious conflicts and it is only much later when Mr V is established within individual therapy that his anxiety can be linked to fears of his own aggression, and that the therapist will be unable to hold him, like the baby, and instead will attack him, as did his father. The therapist also does not interpret his lateness, wanting to bring a friend into the sessions, and his reluctance to speak, as Mr V's pre-emptive attacks on the therapeutic setting and its boundaries, but instead simply comments on his underlying anxiety.

The fostering of a positive treatment alliance, including the acknowledgement and validation by the therapist of the reality of the adversities experienced by the patient in the external world, also draws on classical psychoanalytic technique in the recognition of the real relationship that exists between patient and therapist. Both Anna Freud (1954) and Greenson (1967) proposed that the full analytic relationship was an intermingling of three levels: the transference relationship, the therapeutic relationship and the real relationship. Greenson believed that a trusting relationship with an analyst who showed ordinary human responses was essential to the development and interpretation of the transference. If the therapist can initially ally himself with more healthy aspects of the patient's ego that can be identified and nurtured, these can be used to strengthen the ego and contribute to a good working alliance or therapeutic relationship with the therapist, that will form the foundation from which insights can emerge, and that can moderate the patient's aggressive attacks on both therapist and himself, with corresponding diminution in the harshness of his superego. In his treatment of rage-offenders, Cartwright (2002) endorses some of the technical procedures advocated by Kohut (1978) by the therapist's empathic mirroring of the patient to consolidate a workable therapeutic alliance in the initial stages of treatment. Cartwright warns that if the offender's idealised self is not initially recognised, or is prematurely challenged, interpretations of defensive structures will be unsuccessful and lead to increased defensiveness or depressive collapse.

Transference and countertransference

The therapist's attentive awareness and monitoring of the vicissitudes in transference and countertransference phenomena form an essential part of the analytic work with the violent patient, although the therapist may have to wait for some considerable time before such phenomena can be safely interpreted to the patient. The violent patient with a borderline personality organisation whose psychic world is populated by polarised extremes and who operates via primitive defence mechanisms such as splitting and projection will shape the transference into an intense experience of rapidly oscillating perspectives of the therapist between an idealised and denigrated object. Initial idealisation of the therapist may be abruptly reversed by any slight indication of perceived abandonment by the therapist, leading to catastrophic reactions in the patient and raised potential for violence. Cartwright (2002) links this with Shengold's (1989) concept of 'soul murder', in which the infant's self is smothered by his narcissistic mother's idealisations, which, once removed, leave the infant bereft and without identity, having been promised an ideal world. Again, the anxieties underlying and motivating the patient's behaviour towards the therapist and his fears of what is in the therapist's mind should be explored with the patient before interpretation about what the patient is 'doing to' the therapist.

Perelberg (1999b) distinguishes between maternal and paternal functions that co-exist and alternate within the transference. She conceptualises violence as a defence against a terrifying object, and an attempt to create a distance from which they feel neither too close and overwhelmed, nor too far away and separate. In her experience of the analysis of such patients, the analyst's interpretations, independent of their content, can be seen as introducing differentiation and separations into the interpersonal experience of the patient that is previously undifferentiated and chaotic. Thus the analyst's formulations fulfil a paternal function of intervening in and disrupting a phantasy of maternal fusion. Here again we see the process of triangulation as creating a new space within the patient's mind and in the patient–therapist dyad in which the patient can begin to symbolise his aggressive and sexual impulses through articulation of his thoughts and feelings, instead of violent discharge in an attempt to separate from an intrusive object. This also links to Glasser's (1996a) concept of the core complex and its associated anxieties. Identification and interpretation of their emergence in the transference can help the patient understand the interpersonal triggers to his violence.

Mr R was an intelligent young man who was referred for psychotherapy due to violence towards his parents and siblings. His father had died when he was young and his mother remarried a man who was violent to her, the patient and his siblings. He felt aware of his mother's unhappiness from an early age. Mr R was bullied at school, which he felt unable to tell anyone about, but instead coped by focusing on his studies, doing well academically. When he became a teenager he realised that he was bigger than his stepfather and started to become violent towards him. His family tolerated this and sought no external intervention due to their guilt and shame, until Mr R himself requested therapy whilst at university. He was still living at home.

Mr R initially assumed an intellectually superior and contemptuous attitude towards the therapist, denigrating her qualifications and asserting that therapy was 'psychobabble pseudoscience'. Whenever the therapist tried to make an interpretation, Mr R would interrupt, his voice would become louder and he would talk over the therapist. The therapist eventually understood Mr R's behaviour as a self-preservative defensive reaction to her as a maternal transferential object experienced as intrusive and overwhelming, which he had to distance himself from by not listening to and disparaging the therapist. At the same time, Mr R could not bear to hear another point of view in the therapist's interpretation (here serving a paternal function) that might be different from his own, and would disrupt his unconscious phantasy of idealised fusion with his mother. Towards the end of sessions Mr R's narrative would accelerate so that the therapist would be forced to interrupt him to announce that it was time to finish. Thus we see exhibited in Mr R's transferential relationship with the therapist both sides of the core complex – fear of being overwhelmed and annihilated, and fear of abandonment, and how his aggressive response in his verbal attacks on the therapist is the enactment of self-preservative violence.

As the therapy progressed, the fluidity and confusion of Mr R's identificatory processes, in particular between male and female identifications (Perelberg, 1999b), became clearer. Understanding and empathy offered by the therapist were felt to be a dangerous seduction by an all-powerful preoedipal maternal therapist to whom Mr R was forced to adopt a feminised homosexual position. Mr R would defend himself against this by articulating a view of the world in which he did not care about or need anyone else and that to succeed one had to ruthlessly and even violently use other people,

*in the way that his step-father had behaved. During the first break, before
which erotic feelings appeared to be emerging towards the therapist, but
which could not yet be verbalised, Mr R beat up his step-father for 'not sort-
ing everything out'. Much later this violence against his step-father, whilst
gratifying fantasies that avenged his father's previous violence towards him,
could also be understood as protecting him from the murderous rage he felt
towards his therapist/mother for not protecting him and using him for her
own narcissistic needs.*

Modern psychoanalytic technique places great emphasis on the
transference–countertransference paradigm, the current interplay
between analyst and patient, the interpretation of the transference
and the centrality of the countertransference as an analytic tool. Analysis of countertransference is of no less importance for therapists
working with violent patients, but the complex concept of countertransference is in danger of becoming simplified and misused as
a therapeutic technique. As explained in Chapter 7, understanding
of countertransference has shifted from Freud's original view that
it was an impediment to treatment, to an awareness of how the
patient's pathology actively affects the analyst's countertransference,
the examination of which can provide clues to the patient's unconscious and internal world. However, this can lead to the mistaken
belief that all of the therapist's feelings are caused by the patient's
projections. This may unconsciously influence the therapist to inap-
propriately skew the affective tone of her interpretations so that
they are experienced by the patient as persecutory and disapprov-
ing, and neglects the original understanding of countertransference
as the analyst's distorted and inappropriate responses to the patient
derived from her own unresolved unconscious past conflicts. For
example, feelings of boredom or sleepiness in the therapist may
be a response to the one-dimensional quality to the patient whose
capacity for representation is limited. However, such a countertransferential response may also be the therapist's defensive reaction
to unbearable thoughts of violence, and if this is not recognised
and attended to, the offender's unconscious belief that bad parts
of the self need to be split off and disowned will be reinforced
(Cartwright, 2002).

It may be more salutary to think of a countertransferential
response as an unconscious reaction in the therapist to the patient's
unconscious communications of affect, defence, or internal object
relations, but one which inevitably resonates with the therapist's

own unconscious configurations. Therapists who work with violent patients need to be aware of their own potential for violence and be able to tolerate their own aggressive and sexual impulses without fearing them or becoming overwhelmed. In working with violent and perverse patients the therapist may experience a range of distressing and intense countertransferential feelings such as dread, disgust, rage, terror and sexual excitement, as well as psychosomatic responses such as dissociative experiences or even temporary paralysis. It is unadvisable for clinicians to undertake intensive long-term psychotherapeutic work with such disturbed patients without having had their own experience of psychotherapy, which is of course a pre-requisite of psychoanalytic or psychotherapy training. If personal psychotherapy is unavailable, the role of supervision, consultation and reflective practice groups as discussed in previous chapters becomes essential.

In framing interpretations, the therapist can convey to the patient the idea that she may also struggle with problematical impulses and feelings, without resorting to actual self-disclosure. Again, analyst-centred interpretations such as 'You must be very worried that I may become too anxious to treat you, but if I am not anxious, you are afraid I do not understand or care about you' can be experienced as less persecutory to the patient as they acknowledge that the therapist also experiences difficult emotions and conflicts, but can tolerate and articulate them, without resorting to action such as rejection or seduction of the patient. In this way, the therapist is restored as a container, as ego rather than superego or id (Lloyd-Owen, 2007). This facilitates the strengthening of the patient's own ego, and allows him to feel that his impulses might be more acceptable (by his superego) and able to be psychically processed or mentalized, rather than discharged through violence (id-impulses).

Countertransference does not encompass the totality of the therapist's emotional reactions to the patient, as this would negate the importance of the real relationship and therapeutic alliance. However, the real relationship can be very difficult to discriminate in more psychopathic or perverse individuals who unconsciously subvert all their object-relationships. Such individuals invariably have a disturbed relationship to their superegos, which they externalise onto the relationships with their objects, including that with the therapist. It is very easy for the therapist to become unwittingly drawn into a sado-masochistic transference–countertransference enactment, which can only be recognised, understood and explored with the patient after it has occurred. Sandler's (1976) concept of role respon-siveness is again helpful in elucidating and negotiating these techni-cal dilemmas.

Mr R, introduced in the previous clinical vignette, despite making consid-erable therapeutic progress, could still fill sessions with verbal attacks on the therapist's credentials and psychoanalysis as a discipline in general, and often threatened not to come as the therapy was so useless. At times, the therapist found herself explaining and defending psychoanalytic theory, and 'forgot' to tell the patient about her annual leave until a week before she was due to be away. Here, we can see how the therapist is drawn into enacting both sides of the patient's unconscious sado-masochistic role rela-tionship in which one person is the abuser, the other the abused. Bullied by the patient, she tries to defend herself by entering into an intellectualising argument with him, and then unconsciously retaliates by omitting to warn him of her break, subjecting him to painful feelings of abandonment in her wish to get rid of him. With the help of supervision, the therapist was able to recognise and interpret the underlying fear of dependence that the patient was increasingly aware of, which he defended himself against by becoming the one who is abusive and threatens to leave. The patient was then able to admit how worried he was about losing control when he became violent and the excitement he felt whilst recently beating up his step-father – here we can see how his self-preservative violence becomes sado-masochistic, which is also exhibited in his relationship with the therapist.

The countertransference tends to be thought about when the therapist becomes aware of unusual or negative thoughts and affects towards the patient, whereas more positive feelings are often neglected or ignored. While feelings of enthusiasm, hope, warmth and concern about the patient may be a reflection of the real relation-ship and therapeutic progress, these feelings may also indicate an unconscious countertransferential response to an idealising transfer-ence. Patients with fragile narcissistic pathology who need to eject all bad self- and object-parts from their experience may unconsciously invite the therapist to collude in the formation of an idealised rela-tionship where patient and therapist are united in blissful union, but in which real therapeutic work, involving separation and differ-ence, cannot take place. Cartwright (2002) warns against the ther-apist becoming caught up in the rage-offender's defensive system, and unconsciously imitating the patient's defensive style. Clinicians should be alert to this possibility if therapy appears to be progressing with no apparent hurdles or conflicts.

Mourning and working through

The patient and therapist who embark upon a psychotherapeutic journey together may be unprepared for its obstacles and duration. Introducing the patient to the contents of his mind, facilitating his awareness of previously repressed thoughts and feelings, encouraging him to take back projected parts of himself and exploring his unconscious phantasies comprise a huge therapeutic undertaking that may take many years to negotiate, if the task is achievable at all. The therapist may oscillate between therapeutic nihilism and therapeutic zeal, and with patients who are so seriously psychically damaged, therapeutic aims should be realistically limited to effecting small shifts in their internal world. The painful paradox that a patient has to confront in therapy is that becoming more knowledgeable about his internal world brings with it, at least temporarily, more psychic distress and anguish. If the process of self-awareness is too rapid, the patient will avert becoming overwhelmed by intolerable feelings by regressing to previous pathological but familiar and safer states of mind. Minne (2008) reminds us of the multiple traumas that these patients have to endure – the trauma of their abusive childhoods, the trauma of their offence and the trauma of discovering that their minds are disordered. She proposes that therapy can lead to the development of a post-traumatic stress-type of disorder, caused by increased awareness and understanding, which should be seen as a positive prognostic indicator. In practice, during the course of therapy, patient and therapist will need to endure many cycles of apparent progress and insight, followed by negative therapeutic reactions and regression to withdrawn, depressive states or manic, impulsive behaviour, both of which serve to obliterate self-knowledge and reflection with its associated psychic pain. The empathy and insight achieved in one session will be subverted and attacked in the next. In Kleinian terms, these cycles represent oscillation by the patient between paranoid schizoid and depressive states of mind (Bion, 1984). The former characterises the patient's familiar pathological configuration in which primitive defence mechanisms operate to keep objects split and bad parts of the self projected. If therapy is successful, the patient will gradually move towards occupying a more depressive position, in which conflictual feelings can become more integrated and directed towards the same object, ambivalence can become more tolerable, loss can be acknowledged, concern and guilt predominate over grievance and a process of mourning initiated.

However, this raises the seemingly insoluble paradox of how to mourn the loss of an object that the patient has himself destroyed, not in phantasy, but in reality. When the index offence has been extreme violence or even killing, particularly if the victim was some-one close to the patient, the realisation of the consequences of the patient's actions may fill him with such despair that the only option may appear to be suicide. In the therapy of such individuals, the patient's suicide risk may be increased for long periods, and the intervention and co-operative support of other members of the multi-disciplinary team in caring for the patient during these times are paramount. Such a severe depressive state should not be confused with the patient reaching the depressive position. In suicidal states of mind, the patient remains in a paranoid schizoid state, his aggression unable to be digested psychically, but now directed towards himself. True mourning, reparation and genuine acceptance of the loss and damage he has caused may take many years and remain an incom-plete process. Hyatt-Williams (1998) suggests that for pre-meditated murderous crimes, mourning has to be life-long. Like others, he underscores the necessity of the development in therapy of a men-tal apparatus in the patient capable of containment and reflection rather than evacuation, the growth of a psychic function that enables a detoxification process to take place in the mind.

The therapist should be wary of a 'pseudo-mourning' process that can occur in the place of true mourning. Segal (1957) refers to 'manic reparation', a glib process that evades the pain of genuine mourn-ing and lacks the authenticity of true reparation. Cartwright (2002) warns that the therapist should not be taken in by the patient's 'pseudo-digestive' capacities, demonstrated by the patient talking about the index offence for a couple of sessions, in which appar-ent remorse is verbalised, but then not referred to again. Glasser (1986) describes the problems with deception in these patients, which are unconscious and not the same as malingering. He describes the defensive process of simulation that develops in some individuals, in which the person appears to comply with the demands others place upon him, but this compliance is false, albeit unconscious. Such a process, which is caused by severe early abnormalities in identificatory processes, has become part of his life-long defensive make-up and characterises his way of relating to others in general. This is akin to Winnicott's (1960) notion of the 'false self' person-ality and Gaddini's (1969) description of imitation as a defence. Lloyd-Owen (2007) describes patients who adopt what she calls a 'sado-masochistic compliant-defiant transference', which defends against any real contact or relationship with their objects, which is so feared. Glasser cautions that such simulative processes may be very subtle, and often only detected via an intuitive sense that something about the offender, who appears to be making behavioural progress, does not ring quite true.

The process of mourning and working through may also be aided by certain technical interventions by the therapist. Although psycho-analytic sessions are not usually structured by the analyst but guided by the free associations of the patient which are received by the free-floating attention of the analyst, therapeutic work with offenders may need to be more directive at times. Cartwright (2002) recom-mends that for patients who have killed, actively bringing them back to the homicide or crime and reworking the murder scene can serve two important functions. First, this facilitates a narrative process in which the patient can locate himself at the crime scene and recognise and take responsibility for the 'bad' violent and murderous parts of himself that he has previously split off. Second, this can address the traumatisation of the offender by their offence, to begin to process the flashbacks and nightmares of their crime which these patients often suffer from. If these symptoms are not addressed and recur in unsymbolised form, this reinforces the patient's unconscious belief that such bad experiences need to remain split off and projected.

This brings us to reconstruction, a psychoanalytic technique that has been somewhat neglected or even discredited as an agent of therapeutic change in recent years with the shift towards priori-tising the transference–countertransference paradigm and attention to the 'here and now'. Although entering into a historical dialogue with violent patients may be a therapeutic pitfall which can draw the therapist's attention away from addressing the patient–therapist interactions in the heat of the transference, I believe that an explo-ration of the patient's history is not always defensive, but forms an essential part of the therapy of the violent and perverse patient. Lloyd-Owen (2007), in her experience of treating female offenders, emphasises the importance of information-gathering and history-taking in understanding the roots of their defences, given the severe early, often pre-verbal, traumas these patients have sustained. Such history-taking should not be limited to the assessment process, but can be continued in a collaborative way as part of the flow of ongoing therapeutic work. Patients will often present with disrupted narra-tives of their early lives, and the reconstruction of a more coherent narrative, aided by the re-working of memories within the trans-ference, forms a vital part of the restructuring of the patient's mind and strengthening of his ego. In-depth understanding of the unconscious meaning of the patient's index offence is incomplete without understanding its antecedents in the patient's early object relationships, which includes ongoing appraisal and acknowledgement of the external reality of the abusive and neglectful childhoods that many of these patients have been subjected to. Such work does not ignore the inevitable distortions that the patient will apply because of his own unconscious phantasies and wishes, which are continually addressed within the transferential relationship to the therapist, but the therapy is one-dimensional and limited if it occurs in a vacuum of no historical context. As Blum (2005) writes: '... reconstruction is not only reciprocal to transference interpretation in the present, but it is a complementary agent which guides and integrates interpretations and reorganizes and restores the continuity of the personality.'

Finally, the long-term nature of the therapeutic work with violent offenders should be recognised. This is unfashionable in the current era of time-limited and brief therapeutic interventions that are easier to research and market as more cost-effective than psychoanalytic therapies. However, genuine and lasting intrapsychic change, if possible at all, is likely to take years rather than weeks or months. Minne has pioneered the long-term treatment of patients through different levels of security, seeing patients initially in a high secure hospital and continuing their therapy as they progress through medium security until they can be seen as out-patients in the community. Obviously such long-term work requires not only committed and experienced clinicians, but the understanding and support of the commissioners who fund such treatment and whose opinions increasingly influence clinical decisions. I should also underline that I am not advocating individual psychoanalytic psychotherapy for all violent patients, nor that it should be their only treatment, but that for some carefully assessed individuals it will be beneficial, often in conjunction with other types of therapy and/or medication. The next chapter addresses group psychotherapy, which may be a more appropriate modality for many patients with violent tendencies. Glasser (1996b) advocates a meeting ground for psychodynamic and more structured supportive approaches in that while the former explores the roots of violence including its triggers, the latter aims to protect the patient from coming into contact with these triggers until he can be unaffected by it. Judicious time-limited use of anti-psychotic medication can also be useful in patients, who are not overtly psychotic but in whom psychotherapy raises intense psychotic anxieties (Minne, 2008). Lastly, this intensive psychotherapeutic work should not be carried out alone. The involvement of other professionals, whether these are members of the multi-disciplinary mental health team, the probation officer, social worker or external supervisor or consultant, forms a supportive network around both patient and therapist, reducing risk and contributing essential boundaries to the containing space in which the patient's mind can begin to prosper.

Summary

- Many violent patients do not fulfil conventional suitability criteria for psychoanalytic psychotherapy such as psychological mindedness and ego strength, so the normal threshold for offering therapy may need to be lowered. Assessment should occur in a non-threatening manner and aim to ascertain whether the patient's curiosity in his inner world can be nurtured.
- The forensic psychotherapist treating violent patients should have sufficient expertise, support and supervision. The setting in which the patient is seen forms an integral part of the treatment in providing adequate containment in which the therapy can take place safely.
- Engaging very anxious patients may involve some modification of technique to foster the therapeutic alliance, such as initially giving shorter sessions, avoiding long periods of silence, using supportive techniques to build ego strength such as naming affects and using analyst-centred interpretations.
- Transference interpretations, especially those addressing the negative transference, should be avoided too early in therapy, particularly with more paranoid patients. Monitoring of the therapist's countertransference is essential to avoid being drawn into collusions or enactments with the patient.
- The therapist's expectations of therapy should be limited given the severe psychopathology of many violent patients. Therapy aims to foster the development of a psychic function in the patient's mind that can begin to experience and tolerate loss, remorse, concern and empathy. However, repeated regressions to more primitive states of mind should be expected during the long course of therapy.

10
GROUP-ANALYTIC PSYCHOTHERAPY FOR VIOLENCE

For many individuals with a history of violent behaviour, group psychotherapy may be the treatment of choice. In a group setting, the violent person may feel safer and more contained than in individual therapy where the intensity of the relationship with the therapist may feel overwhelming. The triggers to potential violent behaviour may also be more easily recognised and confronted than in an individual treatment. Violent individuals may prove to be valuable group members, particularly in facilitating other members of the group in acknowledging their own anger and potential aggression, which may be an unrecognised but important component of their pathology. Many people who resort to violence have grown up in dysfunctional families in which anger and violence characterised the communication between family members. Such individuals inevitably have difficulty in forming intimate adult relationships based on mutual respect and trust. The group can act as a socio-familial microcosm in which the violent person's interactions with other group members can be understood as reflecting the pathological dynamics of their original familial experiences. The group experience may offer the opportunity of learning more healthy and mature ways of relating to others.

Different group treatments for people with mental health and psychological problems have proliferated over recent years in an array of settings, including the forensic field. Regular group therapy was started in Broadmoor High Secure Hospital in 1970 (Cox, 1976), and since then there have been comprehensive group programmes running in the high secure psychiatric hospitals and many medium secure psychiatric units in the UK. In this chapter I will focus on group-analytic psychotherapy – the clinical application of group analysis – and why this specific group approach may be particularly suitable to violent individuals. This raises a striking paradox of the therapeutic group for deviant or dangerous individuals – that instead of violent or antisocial behaviour being potentiated by meeting with other violent members of a group such as a prison or gang sub-culture, engaging in a therapeutic group and seeing one's own difficulties reflected in others acts to attenuate such behaviour and bring about therapeutic change (Schlapobersky, 1996).

Selection for group-analytic psychotherapy

Careful psychodynamic assessment of the violent patient, as described in the previous chapter, is an essential pre-requisite to the decision to offer group-analytic psychotherapy. Certain characteristics of the patient and his history may indicate group therapy rather than individual as the treatment of choice. Patients who have had authoritarian parents or have been subjected to an intense overprotective relationship with one parent, for example, an over-possessive mother, may benefit from being in a group in which they can be encouraged by other members to express anti-authoritarian feelings that they previously considered forbidden (Welldon, 1996). Such individuals with difficulties in separating from parental authority and lacking self-confidence and assertiveness, and who lead relatively isolated lives with difficulties in forming age-appropriate peer relationships, may flourish in group therapy if they can overcome the initial anxiety of being with others in a group. By contrast, individuals who come from large and chaotic families with many siblings, or who have a history of fostering or adoption, may feel lost and neglected in a group, which replicates their original early familial experience.

Many violent individuals, as we have learnt, have deficits in their capacity to reflect on feelings and thoughts, and find it difficult to tolerate internal anxiety, tending to discharge it in action or project it into those around them. For these patients who lack psychological mindedness and insight, who exhibit concrete and schizoid modes of thinking and functioning and whose capacity for mentalization is rudimentary, group therapy may be more effective than individual. Here the group can act both as container of the patient's projections and as a collective auxiliary ego that can think and reflect on behalf of the patient, very gradually promoting more healthy ego functioning in the individual. Other group processes are also important, such as modelling of more appropriate behaviour and interpersonal inter-actions, which can be eventually adopted and internalised by the patient.

Patients whose capacity to distinguish internal from external real-ity is limited may also do better in group therapy, as in individual therapy they will tend to form an intense transference relationship with the therapist that may develop erotic and/or psychotic dimen-sions. In group therapy the transference relationships are multiple, and the intensity of feeling diluted and distributed among the dif-ferent members of the group. Indeed, this is one of the possible reasons why violence may be best contained and understood within a group setting (Welldon, 1996). Many violent patients are terrified of their own aggressive impulses, and the multiple transferences that a group provides offer the patient more than one target for their aggression which they find reassuring.

Group psychotherapy rather than individual will often be the treatment of choice for patients whose violent activities involve secretiveness and deception, such as perpetrators of sexual abuse. Here, a group can more effectively challenge and penetrate the pervasive patterns of deception, often not entirely conscious, that characterise the person's way of relating to himself and others.

Certain pathologies, professions and living circumstances may preclude someone from being able to engage and benefit from group-analytic psychotherapy. Individuals who have a diagnosis of voyeurism or exhibitionism may use the group sessions for the concrete acting out of these perversions to the captive audience of the other group members (Welldon, 1996). Other behaviours, such as murder or paedophilia, may evoke such disgust and outrage in group members that the individual concerned is scapegoated and eventually ejected from the group. Indeed, this has led to the forma-tion of special groups for specific conditions, such as groups for peo-ple who have killed (Adshead et al., 2008) or groups for paedophiles. Patients with severe narcissistic pathology may also dominate ses-sions with their stories that are acted out in the group at the expense of any significant internal change, leaving other group members feeling marginalised and diminishing their trust in others. Certain occupations may also encounter difficulties – members of the med-ical profession tend to become 'co-therapists', and policemen and probation officers may not feel able to maintain the confidentiality of other members if they are still involved in criminal activities.

The patient with a history of violence is likely to be very anx-ious at the prospect of being with others with whom there might be conflict, which he imagines can only be resolved through violence or rejection. Careful preparation by the group therapist meeting individually with the patient on several occasions prior to starting in the group may be essential. This will facilitate the patient in developing a sense of trust, commitment and toleration of anxiety between sessions that can hopefully be transferred to the group. The patient may need help in coping with a sense of specialness and subsequent betrayal by the therapist when he is confronted with having to share her with other group members.

The group process

Group-analytic therapy differs from other modalities of group therapy in that it tends to be long term (lasting for years rather than weeks or months), does not have a pre-determined focus, task or structure, is concerned with unconscious group processes and aims for long-standing personality change rather than just symptom relief. Up to eight patients meet regularly, usually weekly, for 75 or 90 minutes, in a room with a therapist. The latter, often known as the group conductor, fulfils a dual, and sometimes ambiguous, role of both leader, and member of the group (Foulkes, 1964). Although some analytic groups have two 'co-therapists', which has the advantage of both providing continuity if one therapist is absent and providing another professional perspective, many very disturbed violent or perverse patients who are functioning for the most part at a pre-oedipal level find it difficult to tolerate the presence of a professional pair who, in the patient's mind, assumes the role of an oedipal couple that must be attacked and split apart.

There is no overt structure or direction for each group session and the group members are encouraged to talk as freely as possible about whatever comes to mind. This forms the group's 'free-floating discussion', the group analytic equivalent of free association (Foulkes, 1975; Schlapobersky, 1996). The therapist contributes to the discussion by highlighting common themes, being particularly alert to the unconscious processes that unfold and develop within the group. Such an open and unstructured invitation to talk in front of a group of strangers, however, may initially be experienced by the violent person as highly anxiety-provoking, as he will anticipate moral judgement from the other members, rather than his deviant behaviour being understood in the context of history and experience. Group therapy may, however, allow the very anxious patient to move more easily at his own pace, and to feel less pressure to reveal himself prematurely than in individual psychotherapy where he is the sole focus of the therapist's attention.

The various dialogues within the group are multi-layered and interact to form a complex matrix from which shared experience and therapeutic change can emerge. As described in Chapter 6, Bion (1961) proposed that therapeutic groups could operate via two different methods. The first, which he described as 'work groups', involved the group working together consciously on a task. However, this conscious work could be blocked by a second, more unconscious way in which the group functioned, which he called 'basic assumption groups'. These are latent defensive group cultures that develop which block the more conscious and manifest work of the group. These cultures include 'dependency' – the assumption that solutions are provided by the leader, 'fight-flight' – the assumption of a threat to the group, and 'pairing' – the assumption that a new leader will arise. These ideas will become clearer in the clinical examples given a little later in this chapter.

All therapeutic groups promote change in individual members via a variety of curative factors, including interpersonal learning, catharsis, group cohesiveness, insight, development of socialising techniques, existential awareness, the realisation that others suffer from similar difficulties (universality), the instillation of hope, imitative behaviour and the corrective recapitulation of the primary family group (Yalom, 1970). The group aimed at the treatment of violent, antisocial and criminal behaviours, however, presents a further therapeutic challenge in that it hopes to reduce such deviant behaviour rather than amplify it, as might be expected by the pooling of extreme human deviation (Schlapobersky, 1996). Groups and organisations such as an army or criminal gang actively perpetuate violence as described in Chapter 6, rather than contain and reduce aggressive action. A process of positive change, rather than further deviation and destruction, can occur in the therapeutic group by drawing on the underlying humanity and hope that has pushed each individual member to risk embarking upon the group journey. Freud (1916) believed that the process of identification within a group worked to promote positive feelings and limit aggressiveness as the person with whom one is identified tends to be protected from more negative and hostile feelings. The group is encouraged to create its own therapeutic culture, which recognises that in every perpetrator there is a victim, and in every victim there is a perpetrator. Such a healing atmosphere is very different from the moral code which may be initially created by the group which represents an excessively harsh group superego, the collective projection of the punitive superegos of individual members. How the group negotiates its rules and boundaries forms an important part of the group therapeutic task.

The setting, group 'rules' and boundaries

Most therapeutic groups for violent offenders and forensic patients will take place within the institution in which they are detained – the prison or secure hospital – and any understanding of the dynamics within the small therapeutic group must include those within the wider institutional context. Effective liaison and communication with other staff involved in the potential group members' care, and anticipation of both the anxieties that running a psychoanalytic group might induce and the organisational defensive responses to these anxieties, as explored in Chapter 8, are essential to the group's survival. Such attention to external boundaries is no less important for the out-patient group for violent and antisocial patients, but may be easier to negotiate as there are fewer institutional staff involved. However, here as well, the other professionals involved in the community care of the patient, such as the probation officer or community psychiatrist, may act to provide an essential supportive structure that enables the patient to engage in weekly group therapy.

If the group is embedded in a secure external setting, it can begin to develop its own internal rules and boundaries, which contribute to a therapeutic sense of containment. This presents another paradox for the offender patient, of how to develop a sense of responsibility and awareness of appropriate boundaries when his early caregivers did not respect his most basic body boundaries, and his adult life has been characterised by breaking society's laws and rebelling against authority. The group therapist will initially be seen as the leader who must set the group rules in order for the group to feel safe, as well as representing a parental authority figure against whom the group can rebel. Group members are often informed by the therapist before starting therapy about the necessity for certain 'rules' to be respected, such as confidentiality, a commitment to attend the group for a certain period of time, a certain minimum number of patients needed for each group session to proceed, discharge after a certain period of non-attendance and a prohibition against meeting other group members between groups. The latter recommendation is to discourage the formation of sub-groups and cliques that will affect alliances within the group, but may not be sustainable for the in-patient group whose patients inevitably will be meeting daily in other forums.

The delinquent and antisocial person will inevitably react against whatever rules he feels are imposed upon him, and the group must permit the expression of anti-authoritarian attitudes without these becoming destructive to the group. The group therapist promotes an atmosphere of concerned inquiry, rather than condemnation, and encourages the group to develop their own capacity for curiosity and concern for themselves and others, at the same time fostering a collective sense of containment and responsibility for appropriate boundaries necessary for the group to function effectively. In this way, group members begin to develop their own parenting for themselves and the other members – both the 'mothering' aspects of nurture and empathy, and the 'fathering' aspects of setting consistent limits (Schlapobersky, 1996) – and begin to recognise and own the psychic changes and psychological maturation occurring in each individual member and the group as a whole. A sense of group togetherness and commitment to common goals is advanced by encouraging the sharing and discussion of all information and communications pertaining to the group, including correspondence about particular members sent to the therapist outside of the group, group members' non-attendance and late arrivals or departures (Foulkes, 1975).

Gordon, a relative newcomer to an out-patient group for violent men, had not attended or contacted the group for 3 weeks. Another group member, Nick, asked the therapist whether he would be writing a letter to Gordon. The therapist wondered what was stopping the group writing to Gordon themselves. Howard, another patient, said that he felt angry with the therapist for not intervening sufficiently in an argument which had ensued between Howard and Gordon at the last session Gordon had been present. Howard had felt unfairly attacked by Gordon, who had accused him of being more interested in himself than his children. Howard had had a violent and acrimonious relationship with his wife and separated from her when his children were small. After many years of no contact, Howard had recently made contact with his now teenage son, and had been telling the group about feeling rejected by his son's reluctance to have anything to do with him.

The therapist suggested that the group wished him to be like a caring parent who would intervene in the fights between the children, and would take control when one of the children went missing. The group feared that their aggression had led to Gordon being rejected from the group, as Howard felt he had rejected his children. However, at the same time, the group felt like neglected children themselves who could not tolerate having to share another member/sibling with the therapist.

Following this interpretation, another patient, Steve, who had come into the group at the same time as Gordon, said that he felt resentful towards Gordon, as he (Steve) had made a huge effort to attend every session, whereas Gordon 'clearly wasn't interested'. This prompted a discussion in the group about whether Gordon was rejecting the group or in fact too anxious to attend and reveal his vulnerabilities. The group decided to write a letter to him, expressing concern at his non-attendance and hoping he would return. Towards the end of the group, Howard admitted that he was worried that he was addicted to cannabis, which he took to feel calmer. He acknowledged that when his cannabis use had previously been discussed in the group he had felt that the therapist had exaggerated its seriousness and that his individual rights were being undermined. However, he now realised it was a problem and he wanted to get professional help. Another group member, Colin, pointed out that Howard could get help in this group, and perhaps he used cannabis to damp down angry feelings which he was afraid of expressing as they might erupt in violence.

Here we can see how the therapist's interpretation of their infantile fears of conflict and rejection, and wish for an exclusive relationship with an ideal parent, allowed the group to express their conflicts with each other without fear that the group would disintegrate. We can also understand the group's wish for the therapist to take the decision to write to the absent member as an example of Bion's first basic assumption of dependency – the assumption that the leader will provide solutions for the group. The therapist's interpretations led to a more collective sense of care, responsibility and faith that they could create their own solutions, for example deciding themselves to jointly write to Gordon to encourage his return. This also facilitated Howard to think about his addiction to cannabis as a problematic behaviour that needed to be addressed and understood, rather than as a righteous act of rebellion against unreasonable authority.

Transference and defence

One of the reasons why violent individuals may be better contained and treated within a group setting rather than in individual therapy is that the multiple transferences within the group provide patients with more than one target for their aggression (Welldon, 1996), so that the intensity of aggressive feelings can be diluted and absorbed by the other group members. This principle also applies to the expression of sexual feelings, which may cause as much anxiety to the violent person as his aggressive impulses. The group process dilutes the homosexual panic that may be experienced by violent men who are not used to intimacy with other men (Madden and Lion, 1978). In the group, the transference and countertransference relationships are complex, existing not only between each individual patient and therapist, but between one patient and another, each representing objects from the other's childhood. Thus patients may be experienced by each other as competitive siblings, punitive parents or sadistic teachers. In addition, the group as a whole may become a transference object for each patient, a repetition of their earlier familial and institutional relationships. The therapist must be sensitive to this complex relational matrix within the group and able to interpret the different levels and directions of communication. Thus analysis does not just occur *in* the group (treatment of the individual within the group), but is also *of* the group (Bion, 1961), with the therapist interpreting the transference relationship of the whole group (e.g. pointing out how the group perceives the therapist as a sadistic parent). Foulkes (1964) advocated analysis *through* and *of* the group, allowing for interpretation of individual member's, as well as collective feelings and experiences.

This out-patient weekly group meeting for eight men with a history of violence occurred 2 weeks before a long summer break when the group would not be meeting for 4 weeks due to the therapist's annual leave. One group member had sent his apologies, and others had not yet arrived. Christopher, Harry, John and David were on time. Christopher started by reporting that he felt very angry towards people he met on the bus coming here, who were rude and disrespectful. As he spoke, two other group members, Ben and Richard, arrived. The therapist suggested that Christopher, who rarely missed a session and was always punctual, might be feeling that absent and late members were disrespectful to the members who were on time, as well as feeling annoyed at the therapist, who would shortly be absent for 4 weeks. Christopher denied this but mentioned that his mother had never been on time and he had painful memories of being left waiting at school worried that something terrible had happened to her. The therapist wondered whether the group as a whole were frightened of openly expressing anger with each other in case something terrible happened. Harry, who was the most recent member to join the group, said that he was annoyed that people came late, and 'hid behind masks' by not being open. John suggested that those members, like himself, who had been in the group the longest, were perhaps at a more advanced stage than Harry who had 'joined us at Chapter 15', and that much had already been discussed which Harry had missed out on. Richard, another recent member, apologised for missing sessions recently, and for perhaps not been as open as he could be. By contrast, Ben, another group member who had been in the group from the beginning, appeared irritated and told Harry that he had spoken of personal matters and would 'tell things the way I want to'. Ben then angrily turned to the therapist and told him that for the first time he felt furious with him for 'deliberately provoking this situation'.

The therapist suggested that Ben perhaps felt accused by him for being late, and was afraid that he did not appreciate the effort he put into coming to the group. The therapist went on to say that the group as a whole appeared to be afraid that he (the therapist) would not be able to contain, and perhaps even enjoyed (if he was felt to deliberately start fights) the intense and angry feelings that were being aroused in the group both by having new members join the group and being expected to cope for themselves over the summer break. The therapist suggested that the group were afraid that if anger was expressed within the group it would lead to violence, and so it was best to locate their aggression outside of the group, in the people on the bus. Ben said that his father did enjoy provoking conflicts and would get pleasure out of watching Ben and his brother fighting when they were children. Harry said it was not the therapist's fault and admitted that he deliberately pro-voked fights to 'raise the emotional temperature'. John suggested that was because Harry liked being the centre of attention. David said that everyone seemed to be making a lot of noise, but this was obscuring the 'truth'.

In this group session, the therapist directs his interventions at individ-ual members, for example interpreting Christopher and Ben's individual transferential experiences of the therapist and other group members, but also interprets what he believes are the collective anxieties and defensive mech-anisms of the group, again both in relation to the transference relationship to himself, as well as to each other. The group's interactions in this ses-sion also illustrate Bion's second basic assumption of 'fight/flight', in which the group feel they can only defend themselves by either fighting or fleeing against a perceived threat (in this case the introduction of new members and the therapist's forthcoming absence).

Bion's basic assumptions describe unconscious defensive manoeu-vres of the group, which defend against primitive anxieties of depen-dence, aggression and sexuality. These anxieties are present in all of us, but may be overwhelming in violent patients, and exacerbated by experiences of separation, such as the therapist's holidays. The group may be left feeling neglected and abandoned, as they were by their original caregivers. Individual and group defences are mobilised against these separation anxieties, which can cause dangerous acting out both outside of and within the group. Welldon (1996) describes two specific ways in which the group can defend itself from such infantile oral anxieties. The first is where a violent threat is used as a defence. Here, an angry patient both terrorises and excites the group by the use of aggressive language, and although there is no overt violence in the group, such behaviour represents a repetition of actual violent acting out within the group. The second defence is erotisation of the group. Here the group starts acting in an excited, manic way by unconsciously promoting one of its members to talk about sexually perverse material in an often provocative and repetitive manner. Although this initially may appear as if the patient is opening up to the group by trusting them, it becomes apparent that the patient is using the therapeutic situation, the group session, as an audience or partner to his perversion. The group is cast as the voyeur to the patient's exhibitionist behaviour, with the patient trying to seduce and excite the other members. Such situations can be very difficult to handle. If the therapist intervenes she may be seen by the group as a prohibitive authority figure who forbids any sexual pleasure, but if she remains silent she will be experienced as colluding, or being seduced and corrupted herself by group forces beyond her control. Carefully timed and worded interpretation of the underlying anxieties of loss, rejection, abandonment and psychic fragmentation may allow the excitement to subside sufficiently for the group to regain a sense of containment and understanding of what is being repeated.

This psychodynamic group, in a medium secure unit, was run by two therapists – an experienced male psychotherapist, and a younger female psychologist, who had only recently joined as co-therapist. The five patients who attended this session – Simon, Mark, Tony, Matt and Rowan – were all detained under the Mental Health Act, having 'dual diagnoses' of mental illness and personality disorder, and a history of violence. Simon often found it difficult to attend the group regularly due to feelings of aggression and wanting to self-harm. He had a history of childhood sexual abuse from an older female cousin, and had been admitted following the sexual assault of his wife and then attempting suicide, in the context of a psychotic illness. This was the first group he had attended with the female psychologist.

Simon started by relating a dream in which he had been having sex with his sister-in-law. He related the dream in graphic detail, using explicit language, and appeared visibly excited, giggling and making lewd gestures. He said that his wife and her sister had visited him recently on the ward, but his wife refused to have sex with him as he was violent, so he might try to seduce her sister when he is discharged. Mark asked Simon why he wanted to do this, and said that he still had fantasies of wanting to have sex with his

· *mother, but had to accept these. Other members of the group looked uncomfortable but animated. Tony said that his mother used to undress in front of him and sleep in his bed as a child. Matt asked if Simon was angry with his wife. Simon denied this but said he was going to have sex with her sister anyway. Rowan said that his wife had lost interest in sex after having children, which had led to him having an affair.*

The male therapist pointed out that the group appeared to be in an excited state, and linked this to the excitement and anxiety of having a new female therapist. He suggested that Simon's dream contained the anxieties of the group regarding women, mothers and wives who were being seen as either dangerous sexual predators, or rejecting and hostile. The mood in the group became more sombre and a discussion ensued about whether women could be trusted. For the first time, Simon told the group that the cousin who had abused him had later committed suicide, and he wondered whether she had been sexually abused herself.

A group that contains both patients who have been referred for the treatment of perverse sexual behaviour and those with violent behaviour, such as is offered at the Portman Clinic, can facilitate understanding of the complex relationship between sexual and violent impulses. Many perverse patients present as quiet, passive individuals, who are unaware of their repressed and split-off anger and aggression, which has been defended against by sexualisation resulting in perverse behaviour, as discussed in Chapter 4. Violent patients, whose aggressive impulses are exhibited more openly within the group, may facilitate the identification and expression of angry and aggressive feelings in other members. The risk is that the violence of all the group members is located in one individual, who is scapegoated and ejected from the group in an unconscious attempt to rid the group of terrifying and unacceptable aggressive impulses. Such a group defence can also occur with the projection of intolerable sexual anxieties into one person, who becomes the scapegoat and is made to leave by defensive group manoeuvres. For this reason, paedophiles and murderers are rarely tolerated in groups for patients with mixed psychopathologies and behaviours, and may need to be treated in selective groups for people who have committed similar offences.

Endings and beginnings

Most psychoanalytic groups are open-ended, sometimes described as 'slow open groups', in which members who leave the group are replaced by new people. Thus the group as an entity in itself has a history that is continually evolving, and that can survive the symbolic births and deaths of its individual members, both patients and therapists. This can provide an essential sense of continuity and containment that underpins the group's therapeutic endeavour.

This gradual overlapping and exchange of individuals as the group progresses is not, of course, a seamless process, but one in which strong emotions are aroused as attachments are formed and then disrupted, awakening previous experiences of loss and rejection. Often group members leave the group prematurely, dropping out of treatment because they cannot tolerate exposing their vulnerabilities to others whom they cannot trust, or feeling persecuted and scapegoated by accepting the projections of other members who unconsciously wish to engineer the unwelcome person's expulsion from the group. The subsequent disappearance of group members can leave the remaining group participants in a vulnerable state of unprocessed affect and understanding, and active interpretations by the therapist may be necessary to prevent ongoing damage and low morale.

Planned endings of group patients may also, however, be difficult to negotiate. Evaluating whether someone is ready to leave the group, as in any therapy, will always be a relative and subjective process. Other members may consciously and unconsciously oppose people leaving, because of feelings of envy, anger, rejection and inadequacy. Members may be tempted to leave the group quickly, rather than allowing the group to explore their reasons for leaving and the impact on the remaining patients during a planned period of time. The fragility of such moments during the group's life marked by people leaving or entering may be strengthened by someone bringing a dream, in which the collective unconscious fears of the group are crystallised. Exploring these anxieties when the group is vulnerable, yet receptive, may constitute transformative periods in the group's progression, facilitating the recognition and acceptance that someone may be ready to leave – that this person has, through confrontation of himself through others, begun to understand and forgive himself for his violent misdeeds, and has internalised sufficient insight and more healthy modes of relating from the group to think of re-entering the world without needing to retreat to violent solutions. The members who remain know that they will live on in the mind of the departing individual, and are given hope that they too may change, and also eventually graduate from the group by becoming able to utilise their aggression in the direction of healthy development and independence, rather than towards a violent end.

Summary

- Group therapy may be the treatment of choice for violent patients, who may feel more contained in a group setting where the multiple transferences offer more than one target for their aggressive and sexual impulses. Engaging in a therapeutic group and seeing one's own difficulties reflected in others can reduce antisocial behaviour and bring about therapeutic change.
- Patients who may do better in group therapy rather than individual therapy include those who have difficulties in mentalization and differentiating reality from fantasy, patients whose activities involve secretiveness and patients who have problems with authority figures. Contraindications include adopted patients or those from large families, narcissistic psychopathology, certain professions concerned with confidentiality, patients with exhibitionism/voyeurism and patients who may become scapegoated, such as paedophiles and murderers, who do better in specific groups.
- Group-analytic therapy is concerned with unconscious group processes, and aims for long-standing personality change rather than symptom relief. The therapist is alert to the underlying unconscious phantasies and enactments of the group that defend against primitive anxieties of dependence, aggression and sexuality, and impede psychic change.
- Common group defences employed against separation anxieties that may be provoked during breaks in therapy are violent threats towards the group and/or erotisation of the group, in which the group is both frightened and excited by a particular member's aggressive or sexualised behaviour.
- One of the important therapeutic tasks in group therapy is how the group negotiates its rules and boundaries. This is particularly important for individuals who have experienced inappropriate boundaries from their original caregivers.

11

WORKING WITH THE WIDER PROFESSIONAL NETWORK

Violent individuals, by the nature of their antisocial behaviour, are more likely to come into contact with other institutions within our society than those concerned with health, most obviously the criminal justice agencies (police, probation and the courts), but also services such as housing, social services and education. The concerns over risk and public safety, broadcast by the media and resulting in an era of public protection policies and legislation, have influenced the way society deals with offenders by prioritising punishment and public protection, rather than focusing on the welfare of the offender. Where each professional agency locates itself on this spectrum will determine its attitude towards management of the violent person, but all agencies risk being pushed, by the overt pressure of government policies, and the more insidious influence of public opinion, towards undermining the rights of the individual offender in favour of the protection of society as a whole.

The psychotherapist working with violent patients is not immune from being influenced by such concerns. There will always be three key parties involved in the therapy of the offender patient – the patient, the therapist and the criminal justice system, each coming with distinct and sometimes opposing agendas, creating inherent tensions that must be recognised and negotiated within the clinical situation. This chapter will explore how forensic psychotherapists can work constructively with the other professional services involved with the violent person, both at the level of the individual concerned such as acting as expert witnesses in the courts, or attending multi-disciplinary meetings such as multi-agency public protection panels (MAPPPs), but also as consultants to provide an overview of how institutions can work with each other and how the offender's pathology is acted out within the system. The therapist must be vigilant to how much she is being unconsciously drawn into colluding with decisions that may not be in the best interest of the patient, and be aware of some of the ethical dilemmas that may be encountered, such as confidentiality and capacity to consent to treatment.

Confidentiality

All doctors and other health professionals in the UK owe a duty to treat communications with their patients as confidential (Department of Health, 2003). This is both a statutory duty as defined in law and an ethical duty as enshrined in the relevant professional regulatory bodies' codes of conduct and ethical guidelines. The latter for doctors is the age-old physician's Hippocratic oath, the most recent interpretation set out by the General Medical Council (GMC, 2004), and amplified by guidance from the British Medical Association (BMA, 1999, 2002) and the Royal College of Psychiatrists (RCPsych, 2006). In law, both the European Convention on Human Rights and the Data Protection Act 1998 stipulate duties that apply to patients, in the right to respect for privacy and family life (Article 8, European Convention on Human Rights, 1998) and the duty to only disclose patient-identifying information with the prior consent of the patient, unless certain conditions are satisfied (Data Protection Act, 1998). The recently amended Mental Health Act (2007) also includes references to confidentiality and information sharing regarding patients detained under the Act.

For the psychotherapist, it could be argued that the need for confidentiality is even greater than for other professionals working with patients. For a patient to engage in a therapeutic process he needs to feel that he can trust the therapist with thoughts, fantasies and feelings that he may be ashamed or terrified of admitting to himself, let alone others. This is facilitated by the therapist creating a safe and containing environment within the boundaries of the therapeutic relationship, which include the concrete reliability of the physical environment in which the therapy takes place, but also the interpersonal boundaries between patient and therapist, in which the therapist minimises self-disclosure as well as the disclosure of the contents of the therapy to others. This has led some (e.g. Bollas and Sundelson, 1995), following very restrictive legislative control of psychotherapists in the United States in favour of disclosure, to argue that confidentiality in the therapeutic situation should be preserved unconditionally, with the therapist never disclosing information about the patient, whatever the risk to others. In the UK, the decision to disclose remains up to the individual clinician, and most would take a more pragmatic view that disclosure of information to other parties is necessary under special circumstances where there is risk of serious harm to the patient or others.

Psychoanalytic and psychotherapy organisations worldwide have become more concerned about confidentiality in the last 15 years, establishing ethical codes, guidelines and committees in attempts to address this (O'Neil, 2007). However, there are often discrepancies between psychoanalytic codes of ethics and those of other professions such as psychology (Bollas, 2003), as well as significant conflicts between psychoanalytic and legal processes, which vary between countries. This is reflected in the International Psychoanalytic Association (IPA) and British Institute of International and Comparative Law project (Garvey and Layton, 2004) which reviewed the extent to which psychoanalytic patients were protected by the law in seven jurisdictions: Argentina, Brazil, Canada, England and Wales, Germany, Italy and the United States. None of the psychoanalytic codes of ethics reviewed specifically addressed potential conflicts of maintaining patient confidentiality versus protection of another individual such as in child abuse, or protection of the public if there was a threat of spread of AIDS or other communicable disease, whereas in many jurisdictions these are binding in law.

Psychotherapists working with offenders in forensic institutions cannot afford to ignore these potential conflicts as they face a complex setting in which competing interests and expectations of medical and criminal justice agencies co-exist. Whereas the generic psychotherapist may be clear about her duty of care to her individual patients, in forensic psychotherapy it could be argued that their duty of care and responsibilities should be as much to the State as their employers in the service of public protection, as to the patient (Stone, 1997). Whether the therapist works within an out-patient clinic, a medium or high secure hospital, she will be working with other professionals involved in the patient's overall treatment who provide essential back-up and support for the therapeutic work. The respective roles of the different members of the team and the degree of communication between them need to be carefully defined to create a therapeutic framework that can maintain enough privacy in the therapeutic relationship, while allowing other professionals involved with the patient to have sufficient knowledge of his progress or risk to provide appropriate containment.

Disclosure may not always be detrimental to the patient, and in fact in some cases, a decision not to disclose may be more damaging. The patient may feel more understood and contained by a therapist who takes his fantasies and the fears that he will enact these seriously. In these cases disclosure may actually decrease risk. If the therapist decides not to disclose worrying fantasies or behaviour that have emerged in the therapy, the patient may feel as if he has fooled the therapist, or the therapist is colluding in something dangerous, and therefore cannot be trusted. If the risk of dangerous enactment appears high, this should be explored with the patient who should be encouraged to make any disclosures himself, so that he feels a greater sense of responsibility for his actions. Disclosure may, in the first instance, be to another mental health professional, who may provide another perspective or intervention such as medication that may reduce anxiety and decrease risk. This introduction of a third object into the patient–therapist dyad can create a triangular situation in which a different point of view can be considered, and the patient himself can feel understood and contained by a more healthy parental couple, a new experience for the offender who never had adequate parental guidance or supervision.

Mr F, a 25-year-old man, had been having out-patient individual psychotherapy with a middle-aged female psychotherapist following a conviction for ABH involving an assault on his father. Although he was under probation supervision in the community, his attendance at therapy was voluntary. Psychotherapy had been recommended by the psychiatrist who had assessed him for a pre-sentence report, to explore the links between childhood sexual abuse by his father and his violence as an adult. Although Mr F initially appeared to engage well in the therapy, his attendance started to become more erratic, and when he did come to sessions the psychotherapist became increasingly concerned by Mr F's expressions of rage against his father and his wishes to kill him, which appeared to be intensifying. Mr F eventually told her that therapy was not helping and the only way he could prevent himself from killing his father was to kill himself. The therapist, concerned about these suicidal and homicidal feelings, referred him to be seen urgently by a male psychiatric colleague in the same clinic. Mr F admitted to this psychiatrist that he was finding psychotherapy increasingly difficult as he had been having sexual fantasies about the therapist, who reminded him of his mother, and these both disgusted and frightened him. The psychiatrist suggested that such sexual fantasies might protect him from feeling angry with the female therapist, as he might feel angry towards his mother, for not protecting him against abuse, and that his murderous rage was not only directed at his father. Mr F found this consultation very helpful, and was able to resume sessions with the psychotherapist and explore these disturbing feelings about her, with a corresponding diminution in his violent thoughts.

In this case example, the therapist is rightly concerned about Mr F's increased risk of violence, both to his father and to himself, but instead of immediately informing his probation officer, she discusses her concerns with the patient and suggests it might be helpful for him to see a clinical colleague. She rightly suspects that there may be transferential issues contributing to Mr F's resistance and the impasse in therapy, and that these may be easier for him to talk about with a male clinician. In the UK, clinicians do not have a legal duty to warn specific third parties who are at risk of being potential victims of violence from a patient, as in the United States following the case of *Tarasoff* in 1969, when a student at the University of California killed a young woman, Tatiana Tarasoff, after having told his therapist he wished to harm her (Stone, 1994). By contrast, in the above case of Mr F, instead of being obliged to break clinical confidentiality and inform the probation officer, who might have felt it necessary to warn Mr F's father about the threat to him from his son which would risk seriously disrupting or terminating the therapy, the therapist manages to contain the situation within the clinical setting by involving her colleague. Although clinicians in the UK are still allowed to use their clinical judgement in determining the threshold of harm at which it may become necessary to disclose confidential information about a patient to third parties, the trend towards multi-disciplinary working with offenders, exemplified by the formation of MAPPA (see below), is increasingly creating complex situations in which therapists' duties of care and confidentiality may be eroded, if not clearly defined.

Multi-Agency Public Protection Arrangements

Since 2000 (Criminal Justice and Court Services Act), there has been a statutory obligation in the UK for the police, prison and probation services to formally liaise in the management of violent and dangerous offenders, resulting in the creation of Multi-Agency Public Protection Arrangements (MAPPA). These arrangements developed in the 1990s against a background of increasing social and political concern about violent and sexual offenders, which called for closer working relationships between these three services to minimise the risk to the general public posed by high-risk offenders known to be living in the community. The Criminal Justice Act 2003 established the police, probation and prison services as the 'Responsible Authority' to oversee these statutory arrangements for public protection by the identification of high-risk offenders, the assessment and management of their risk and the sharing of relevant information among the agencies involved. This act also introduced a 'Duty to Co-operate' clause stipulating that certain other agencies, including social services, youth offending teams, housing authorities and health services, in particular mental health NHS trusts, should also be involved to enhance multi-agency work by the co-ordination of the different agencies in assessing and managing risk. Monthly meetings known as 'MAPPPs' are held in each borough to discuss high-risk offenders, at which permanent representation of the core agencies of the police, probation and prison services is mandatory, supplemented by representatives of other involved agencies where needed. The small group of offenders who are considered as posing the most serious risk (known as the 'critical few') is also discussed at emergency meetings.

However, since their inception, many have argued that psychiatrists and other mental health professionals should have nothing to do with MAPPA, as such involvement constitutes a further erosion of the boundaries between mental health and the criminal justice system. Although recent MAPPA guidance on effective strategies does include cognitive behavioural programmes to address the causes of offending behaviour (Home Office, 2007), most of the work is focused on changing external circumstances or limiting the behaviour of offenders rather than aimed at more fundamental internal change. Furthermore, there are concerns that information sharing undermines patient confidentiality, and that pre-occupation with risk and dangerousness damages the therapeutic relationship with patients. Mental health workers are being asked to become agents of social control, a role incompatible with a duty of care. There has been much debate about the exact meaning of the Duty to Co-operate, the most vigorous being whether 'co-operation' implies a duty to disclose information about patients. Medical confidentiality may be considered to be different and more restrictive than the codes of the other duty to co-operate agencies, being a common law duty which is closely defined in professional guidelines, the breaking of which may leave the doctor open to court action and GMC sanctions. Psychotherapists, whether or not they are also members of the medical profession, may be even more cautious about revealing confidential information about patients. Clinicians who participate in the MAPPA process may be unprepared for the subtle pressures placed upon them to disclose information in the context of an organisation committed to public protection rather than patient care. At the other extreme, the prospect of having to engage with MAPPA may pressurise some doctors or therapists to become overly cautious or defensive in their clinical practice, restricting their written documentation and correspondence about patients in case it might be divulged to other non-clinical parties at a later date.

In my personal experience of attending MAPPA meetings, each offender's case was discussed sensitively and at length by police and probation officers, with much consideration and compassion given to the rights of the offender, as well as to those of potential victims. However, although MAPPA originally envisaged potential roles for psychiatrists and other relevant mental health professionals in the MAPPA process such as the identification of relevant MAPPA cases, participation in MAPPA meetings and the provision of information, in my view the psychotherapist should resist participating in these ways for patients directly involved in her care. If a patient receiving psychotherapy is also subject to MAPPA proceedings, another health professional, such as the case-coordinator, should be designated to liaise with MAPPA, thus safeguarding the privacy of the therapeutic relationship, which should only be breached if the psychotherapist has very serious concerns regarding the dangerousness of her patient. In practice, it is enough for the MAPPP to know that the patient is engaged in psychotherapeutic treatment, without the need to disclose further content of the psychotherapy sessions.

The psychoanalytically minded clinician may usefully participate in the MAPPA process in other ways, not just in specific MAPPA cases by giving their expertise on assessment and management, but also offering an important educative and advisory role in shaping MAPPA policy on key issues such as confidentiality. The effective communication of psychodynamic insights, in language that avoids jargon, into how the internal world of the offender is being played out in the system may facilitate the involved professionals in understanding his behaviour in novel ways, and in formulating his overall management. Thus an awareness of how the police or probation may be experienced by the offender as persecutory and punitive parental objects, or how the disagreements and impasses in inter-agency working may be experienced by him as an all too familiar pattern of parental conflict, may cause professionals to reflect on how their own behaviour towards the offender may be perceived as retaliatory and perpetuating the cycle of abuse. Such splitting between agencies may be a reflection of the projections of the offender, but may also represent our own projections as professionals anxious to defend our individual identities and suspicious of different attitudes and ways of working that can seem alien and threatening. Such anxieties exist in all institutions and may be useful in fostering rivalry and competition necessary for survival and growth. However, when such anxieties become tinged with paranoia, relationships may break down and effective functioning is stifled or prevented. If the wish to denigrate, or even deny the existence of the other predominates, independent agencies may end up working in isolated and precarious ways. By contrast, if different agencies and the professionals working within them can relate to each other in more healthy and less paranoid ways, the capacity for genuine growth and understanding can be enhanced.

Whether we like it or not, MAPPA will not go away, but is an evolving process to which we may contribute by promoting the interests of our patients while being mindful of the rights of others. My own experience is that meeting the different professionals involved in MAPPA work in person can go a long way to allay anxieties on both sides about incompatible attitudes and conflicts of interest. Thoughtful involvement and discussion with each other can lead to helpful compromises, solutions or sometimes the acceptance of difference. In recent years the police and other criminal justice agencies have developed more sophisticated attitudes to the understanding of mental illness, and are more interested in psychological theories of criminal behaviour than biological explanations (Irving, 1996), which has enhanced their attitudes to working with offenders and therapeutic institutions. The police are also more aware of the traumatic impact of their work on themselves, which has led to the introduction of counselling services within forces to combat more traditional and defensive ways of coping with occupational stress such as alcohol, smoking or medical retirement (including the closure of the private policemen's bar at New Scotland Yard, the Headquarters of the Metropolitan Police!). Reflective practice work groups, as described in Chapter 7, may also be welcomed by police, prison and probation officers, to provide a neutral space in which to discuss cases, and avoid the stigma of personal therapy. Such groups can be therapeutic for the professionals themselves involved in such difficult work, offering containment and helping them recognise their own (often unconscious) responses to the offenders they work with, ultimately promoting a more integrated and understanding approach to their clients, which in itself helps reduce the risk of future violence.

Working with the courts

At first glance, the purposes and functions of the legal system, with its adversarial approach based on contest, conflict and confrontation, may seem at variance with the process of psychoanalytic psychotherapy that seeks understanding and healing rather than blame. Timescales and pace of work may also differ considerably between each of these different fields, with court deadlines and an urgency to make decisions regarding the sentencing of an offender, or the placement of a child in care proceedings, interfering with the much slower and more gradual development of insight and change in psychotherapy. Even language can be ambiguous, exposing crucial differences in meaning and articulation, and difficulties in translating unconscious insights into the precise definitions of legal 'facts' or criteria acceptable to the court.

The psychotherapist is likely to come into contact with the legal system in one of two ways: if her patients become involved in legal proceedings during the course of therapy, and as an expert witness providing specialised assessments and evidence for the criminal or family courts. This underscores a potential confusion between the assessment/reporting and treatment roles of the psychotherapist. In the UK, unlike the United States, it is common for forensic psychiatrists to both prepare court reports and give testimony on the patients who are under their care (Grounds, 1996). However, for the psychotherapist, the request to evaluate her patient's progress and disclose this to an external agency such as a court of law may fatally undermine the therapeutic process. As discussed in Chapter 9, if a patient believes that his liberty and independence, or his freedom to see his children, are dependent on his progress in therapy, this will affect his motivation for treatment and may cause him to be less than honest about his true thoughts and feelings in order to create a positive impression with his therapist. If he knows that the therapist is reporting details of the contents of sessions to criminal justice agencies that he fears may punish him for his transgressions, he will hesitate before revealing aggressive feelings and thoughts that, if not explored, may hinder his therapeutic progress. The risks of damaging confidentiality and the therapeutic alliance mean that stipulating psychotherapy as a condition of treatment attached to a community rehabilitation (probation) order, or as mandated treatment so that patients can have access to their children, is rarely successful.

Dr J, a Consultant Psychiatrist in Psychotherapy, had assessed Ms A, a 23-year-old woman, to prepare a medico-legal report addressing Ms A's parenting skills and ability to protect her children from harm, in the context of care proceedings involving Ms A's children initiated by Ms A's Local Authority social services. Ms A was a vulnerable young woman who, when she was 13, had discovered her father sexually abusing her younger sister, and when her mother refused to believe her she went to social services herself which resulted in her father eventually being convicted and her mother blaming her for splitting up the family. She was put into care herself following this, and became involved with a violent young man, with whom she had two children by the time she was 19. Social services became involved again following episodes of violence between Ms A's partner and herself and concern that the children had not only witnessed this violence but had also been hit by their father. The children were removed on an interim care order and placed in foster care whilst further assessment of the family proceeded. Ms A had by this time separated from her partner and wanted to be considered as a sole carer for her children.

Dr J found Ms A to be surprisingly insightful about her difficulties, and observed emotional warmth and sensitivity towards her children during contact sessions. She recommended that Ms A be offered psychological therapy in which to explore how she became involved in this violent relationship and her failure to protect her children, and how this related to her own childhood history of sexual and emotional abuse. Dr J advised that Ms A should be re-assessed by her in 6 months time to ascertain whether she was able to use the therapy and demonstrate capacity for change. This time scale was thought to be a compromise between allowing enough time for Ms A to engage in therapy, whilst not being too long a period of uncertainty for the children who did not know whether they would be rehabilitated to the care of their mother.

Ms A started individual psychotherapy with Dr P, a psychotherapist who worked in the same clinic as Dr J. From the start, Ms A's solicitor insisted that Dr P have no access to Dr J's report as this might influence Dr P's view of Ms A and bias the therapeutic relationship. Although Ms A was aware of the stipulation that her sessions with Dr P were confidential and Dr P would not be reporting to social services, for the first few weeks she remained wary of Dr P, reporting her daily activities in superficial detail and appearing reluctant to address underlying issues. She expressed her suspicions that Dr P and Dr J did in fact communicate with each other to discuss her progress behind her back.

The therapist gradually realised that Ms A not only feared that her therapist was breaking confidentiality to talk to her colleague, but that she also wanted her to do so: this represented both a fear that the parental object was not to be trusted, but also a wish that a parental couple could come together in a constructive way to promote Ms A's best interests. The therapist interpreted this and linked this to Ms A's experience of discovering shameful secrets within the family that were going on behind her back, and the catastrophic events that happen when confidentiality is broken, as when Ms A disclosed her father's abusive behaviour leading to her being ostracised by the family. This led Ms A to become more open in the therapeutic sessions, admitting both her disgust at her father's behaviour, but also her jealousy of her sister, who was 'favoured' by receiving her father's sexual attentions, rather than herself. She also began to examine how her relationship with her abusive partner represented an attempt to get close to an (abusive) father figure, and how in doing so she had unconsciously recreated her own early family configuration of an abusive father, neglectful mother and damaged children.

Dr J met her again for a re-assessment interview 6 months after starting therapy, in which she was reflective and able to talk about her difficulties with more insight. Dr J concluded that she was well engaged in psychotherapy where she had begun to acknowledge and explore her difficulties, and because contact with the children was also going well, she recommended that the children be rehabilitated with their mother. Ms A continued with psychotherapy for 2 years after all care proceedings had been concluded and the children had been returned to her care, during which time she felt freer to explore her uncertainties in being a mother, in the safety of a therapeutic relationship no longer under scrutiny.

This case illustrates the benefits of separating the roles of assessment and treatment, with the therapist free to focus on the therapeutic work and not compelled to provide reports of the patient's progress, while any evaluation of her patient is carried out by an independent person. Unfortunately, it can be hard to convince other professionals of the reasons behind maintaining such a distinction between therapy and appraisal, so it is advisable to clarify the framework for treatment at the outset with patients involved in a legal process, to avoid misunderstandings and resentments by other professionals who may perceive the therapist as being obstructive. Ideally, an assessment for psychotherapy should occur after all legal proceedings have terminated, to determine whether a person is really motivated to change in the absence of short-term external reward. However, this may be impossible in child care proceedings, where it is often recommended that parents be offered therapy to see if their parenting capacity can be enhanced in the timescales appropriate to the child's developmental needs. The assessment of motivation for treatment must also include consideration of a patient's capacity to consent. Many violent patients, especially those detained in secure institutions, are vulnerable, and may agree to having psychotherapy because of subtle coercion from the treatment team, or again because the patient believes it will accelerate his discharge, and may be unaware that they are likely to feel more distressed during the process of therapy unless this is explained to them. The recent Mental Capacity Act (2005) sets out a framework and safeguards to ensure that vulnerable people are not subjected to treatments that they do not understand.

Over the last 30 years all branches of the legal system have become increasingly open to considering expert advice about the causes of human behaviour. The greater appreciation of the role of mental illness in causing criminal behaviour has led to the development of court diversion schemes in the UK where pre-sentence offenders who are thought to be mentally ill are diverted into the psychiatric system. In the last 10 years 'Mental Health Courts' and 'Therapeutic Courts' have been pioneered in the United States, where prosecution and defence, along with other court room participants, collaborate to not only try and resolve the criminal case, but also address the issues underlying the criminal behaviour, which may include mental illness. One of the major benefits of such courts is that they encourage problem solving in what is otherwise a very adversarial system, resulting in both decreased recidivism and treatment for the offender (Finkle, 2007).

In the UK, forensic psychotherapists, as well as psychodynamically trained child and adolescent psychiatrists and psychotherapists, are progressively becoming more involved in writing legal reports and appearing as expert witnesses in both the criminal and family courts. Many of the lawyers and judges who request such expert opinions are correspondingly welcoming more sophisticated psychological explanations of the violent and antisocial behaviour of offenders, often wanting more than a terse conclusion such as 'no mental disorder' or 'fit for any punishment the Court may decide' common to some traditional psychiatric reports, which are of little help to the client or the courts. Detailing problematic personality traits that contribute to poor impulse control or poor parenting skills, even if these do not constitute a full-blown diagnosis of personality disorder, can be helpful in fleshing out a more comprehensive profile

of the offender and his treatability. Offering a preliminary understanding of his crimes in the context of a traumatic childhood history
can influence judges to consider therapeutic, as well as penal, issues
in their final judgements. However, working at the interface between
psychotherapy and the law is not for the faint-hearted, and interested clinicians should educate themselves about the basic tenets of
the legal system and be robustly prepared for the traumas of cross-
examination, ideally through apprenticeship-type learning with a
senior colleague, or via specific expert witness-skills training courses.
Concepts concerning unconscious mechanisms, if thought relevant
to the offence, for example in a case of apparent malingering, must be
conveyed in terminology comprehensible to a layman. It can be difficult to convey conceptualisations to do with emotions and feelings
in a legal arena demanding evidence and facts (Kennedy, 2005).

This chapter has aimed to provide a brief overview of some of
the issues and difficulties encountered when psychotherapists accept
instructions to prepare an expert legal report, or enter the court
room. The interested reader can find further detail about forensic
psychotherapy assessments and the legal system (e.g. Welldon and
Van Velsen, 1997), psychotherapists as expert witnesses in the family courts (e.g. Kennedy, 2005) and guidelines about being an expert
witness, giving evidence and cross examination (e.g. Wall, 2000), in
other texts. Finally, in a triumph for the preservation of the confidential privilege between psychotherapist and patient, as well as
the effective communication of an important psychoanalytic concept to a lawyer, Minne (Personal communication, 2004) successfully
argued against having to release her confidential notes on one of
her detained forensic psychotherapy patients when ordered to by
a tribunal. She contended that such information, which concerned
the patient's unconscious thoughts and feelings of which he was
unaware and knowledge of which at this point was likely to be
premature and do him harm, constituted information from a third
party (the unconscious) to which the patient had no right of access.
This argument was accepted, testimony to the increasing respect
that psychoanalysts and psychotherapists can generate because of
their fruitful collaboration with professionals who may be from other
fields, but whose common purpose is in addressing violence.

Summary

- Forensic psychotherapy always involves three parties: the patient,
  the therapist and the criminal justice system. Negotiating this

triangular situation successfully by managing the competing demands of confidentiality, risk and containment parallels the way in which a good parental couple will promote the best interests of their child, an experience many offenders never had.

- The protection of confidentiality is essential to facilitate offenders to engage in treatment. In the UK, clinicians may use their clinical judgement to determine the threshold of harm where it may be necessary to disclose confidential information about a patient to third parties. When therapy takes place in a forensic setting, the lines of communication and duties of care of different members of the team should be clearly defined.

- MAPPA are statutory arrangements for public protection where the police, probation and prison services oversee the identification of high-risk offenders in the community, the assessment and management of their risk and the sharing of relevant information among the agencies involved. Psychotherapists and other mental health clinicians treating offenders who are involved with MAPPA must be careful to protect the patient's confidentiality, while maintaining a helpful dialogue with these external agencies so that they can provide background supportive containment for the patient without needing to know all the details of the patient's therapy sessions.

- The psychotherapist may become involved with the legal system if her patients become involved in legal proceedings during the course of therapy, or as an independent expert witness providing specialised assessments and evidence for the courts. It is important to separate the assessment/reporting and treatment roles of the psychotherapist, to avoid confusion regarding a patient's motivation for therapy, as well as protecting the confidential nature of the therapeutic process.

GLOSSARY

Affect

In psychiatry, affect refers to the observed expression of emotion, which may be inconsistent with the patient's description. In psychoanalysis, the term is used more generally to denote any emotional state, whether painful or pleasant, vague or well-defined. Freud believed that each instinct expressed itself by both affects and ideas. The affect was the expression of the amount of energy the instinct possessed. Affects may not always be conscious, but may be unconscious, such as an unconscious sense of guilt.

Anal stage

The anal stage of personality development, according to Freud, occurs between the ages of 1 and 3 years. The child gains pleasure by control over defecation. The anal period is one of striving for independence and separation from the parents.

Attachment

Attachment is the normal tendency of a young child to seek close proximity to its primary caregivers, usually initially the mother, and to feel secure in their presence. Bonding describes the initial intense emotional relationship a mother develops with her baby, whereas attachment is the relationship the baby develops with its mother and other caregivers in the first year of life. Based on the work of John Bowlby, and expanded by researchers such as Mary Ainsworth and Mary Main, **attachment theory** proposes that the human need for significant relationships is universal and established at a psychobiological level. Early disruptions in attachment caused by separation, trauma or loss can produce long-term pathological effects giving rise to mental illness and character abnormalities in adult life.

Containment (Container/contained)

Containment is a concept introduced by Bion (1959, 1962) to describe the mother's function in dealing with her baby's unbearable anxieties via a process of projective identification. The infant projects unbearable feelings such as hunger into his mother, who acts as a 'container' by being able to identify with these feelings, modify them and reflect them back to him in a form that is acceptable to him (and is then 'contained'). Bion proposed that the analyst performed a similar task in accepting the patient's projections, containing and modifying them, and feeding them back in the form of interpretations that the patient can use. The concept of containment has been extended to include the ways in which not only the patients' anxieties, but those of the staff and institution can be managed, so as to create a safe and therapeutic environment in which treatment can occur.

Core complex

The core complex (Glasser, 1996a) is a constellation of interrelated feelings, ideas and attitudes in which there is a conflict between the longing to merge with the object (originally the mother) and a fear that the object will be overwhelming and obliterating. The person therefore oscillates between desire for contact and union with the object and flight from the object, with concomitant feelings of emotional isolation and abandonment leading to desire for contact once more. The fear of being overwhelmed by the object and loss of separate existence provokes an aggressive response in the subject towards the object. Glasser proposes that in the perversions, this aggression is sexualised in order to preserve the object.

Countertransference

Countertransference describes the feelings and emotional reactions that the therapist has towards the patient. This affective response of the therapist is not always conscious, and is a result of both unresolved conflicts in the therapist and the projections of the patient. Freud originally saw countertransference as a resistance to treatment, but later analysts see it as a source of useful information about the patient, in that the therapist's response to the patient might reflect how other people respond to the patient and so may provide some information about the patient's internal object relations.

Death instinct

In Freud's final theory of the instincts (*Beyond the Pleasure Principle*, 1920) he proposed two opposing instincts – the life instinct and the death instinct (referred to as Eros and Thanatos). The latter strived towards the reduction of tension to zero, to convert living matter to an inorganic state. Initially aimed at self-destruction, the death instinct is later turned against the outside world and underlies aggression.

Denial

Denial is a defence mechanism in which the awareness of a painful aspect of reality is avoided by negating sensory data. Denial exists in both normal and pathological states.

Developmental stages

Freud believed that children are influenced by sexual drives and proposed a developmental trajectory in which the early manifestations of infantile sexuality were associated with bodily functions such as feeding and bowel control. Psychosexual development consists of libidinal energy shifting from oral to anal to phallic to genital erotogenic zones respectively, where each corresponding stage of development is characterised by particular functions and objectives (see glossary entries for each developmental stage), but builds upon and subsumes the accomplishments of the preceding stage.

Depressive position

The depressive position is a stage of development in the infant described by Melanie Klein (1935), in which conflictual feelings can become more integrated and directed towards the same object; there is tolerance of ambivalence and loss, concern and guilt for the object and mourning. Post-Kleinian analysts no longer propose that the infant definitively achieves the depressive position in the first few months of life, but that there is continuous oscillation in states of mind throughout life between the more primitive paranoid schizoid position (see below) and the more mature depressive position.

Disavowal

Disavowal is a defence mechanism in which the person fails to recognise the reality of a traumatic perception, most notably the perception that a woman does not have a penis. Freud suggested that pathological states such as psychosis and fetishism involved this defence mechanism.

Drive

See 'instinct'.

Ego

In Freud's second theory of the mind, the structural model, the psychical apparatus is divided into three structures – id, ego and superego. The ego mediates between the conflicting demands of id, superego and reality. It is the executive organ of the psyche, controlling motility, perception and contact with reality, and via the defence mechanisms, which are located in the unconscious part, the ego modulates the drives coming from the id.

Ego-ideal

The ego-ideal is a term proposed by Freud to describe a psychical agency which constituted a model to which the person aspired. It is a narcissistic structure formed from an identification with the assumed ideals of the parents and idealisation of the ego. Freud later made the ego-ideal a part of the superego. Failure to achieve the standards of the ego-ideal gives rise to feelings of low self-esteem and shame.

Ego psychology

The cornerstone of ego psychology is Freud's structural model of the mind, the three separate structures – id, ego and superego – having distinct functions. Ego psychology was developed in the United States by psychoanalysts such as Heinz Hartmann, following on from the influence of Anna Freud. It focuses on the functions and properties of the ego, including defence mechanisms, the regulation of instinctual drives, relation to reality and object relationships. Hartmann described autonomous ego functions, which are primary, and develop independent of conflict, and include perception, learning, intelligence, language, thinking and motility.

Erotogenic zone

In Freud's developmental theory of the stages of personality development (oral, anal, phallic and genital stages), the erotogenic zone refers to the particular area of the body on which the pleasure-seeking id focuses and the activities of which provide the child with gratification. In the oral stage, the erotogenic zone includes the mouth, lips and tongue; for the anal stage it encompasses the anal sphincters; and in the phallic phase erotogenic activity is focused on the genital region.

Fantasy

See 'phantasy' (below).

Fetish

A fetish is an object, usually closely associated with the human body (such as shoe, glove or foot) that is not usually thought of as a sexual object, but becomes the focus of sexual activity in certain individuals.

Frotteurism

Frotteurism is a sexual perversion characterised by a man rubbing himself against another clothed person to achieve orgasm, or by rubbing his hands against an unsuspecting victim. This offence usually occurs in crowded places.

Genital stage

Following the period of latency, the genital stage of psychosexual development, according to Freud, occurs between the onset of adolescence and young adulthood. This phase is triggered by the biological hormonal changes occurring at adolescence which reawaken the sexual drives. The objectives of this period are to achieve separation from dependence on the parents and to establish mature sexual relationships.

Holding

Winnicott (1954) described the 'holding' function of the analyst and of the analytic situation in providing an atmosphere in which the patient can feel safe and contained even when severe regression has occurred. This is also a function of the 'good-enough' mother in being able to provide a 'facilitating maternal environment' necessary for normal infant development.

Id

In Freud's structural model of the mind (1923), the id refers to a reservoir of unconscious unorganised instinctual drives, which operate according to primary processes under the domination of the pleasure principle.

Individuation

See 'separation-individuation'.

Instinct

Instinct refers to a hereditary pattern of behaviour, specific to a species, that unfolds in a predetermined fashion during development and is resistant to change. Freud took this biological concept ('trieb', sometimes translated as 'drive') to embed his psychological theory of the mind in biology with his theory of the instincts or drives. For Freud, all instincts had a *source* in a part of the body or bodily stimulus; an *aim*, to eliminate the state of tension deriving from the source; and an *object* (often another person), which was the target of the aim.

Introjection

Introjection describes the process of internalising the qualities of an object. Introjection is essential to normal early development, but can also be a primitive defence mechanism in which the distinction between subject and object is blurred.

Libido

Freud described libido as 'the force by which the sexual instinct is represented in the mind'. The association with sexuality is misleading, as Freud considered libido to include the notion of pleasure as a whole.

Libidinization

Libidinization describes the process whereby an object or another function is invested with libido. This can be used as a defensive process to neutralise the aggressive instinct. Glasser proposed that in the perversions aggression was libidinized to cause sadism.

Mentalization

Mentalizing is an essential human capacity underpinning interpersonal relations that develops in the first few years of life in the context of safe and secure child–caregiver relationships, in which the infant finds its mind represented in the mind of the other. This facilitates the development of a sense of self, the ability to differentiate and represent affect states and the regulation of impulse control. This developmental process can be disrupted by experiences of childhood neglect or abuse, where inadequate mirroring and disorganised attachment undermine the capacity to mentalize, so that internal states remain confusing, unsymbolised and difficult to regulate. Mentalization-based treatment (MBT) has been developed in the UK by Bateman and Fonagy (2004) for patients with borderline personality disorder, who have an unstable or reduced capacity to mentalize.

Object

An object refers to a significant person in the individual's environment, the first significant object usually being the mother.

Object relation(ship)

This denotes the person's mode of relation to the world. Object relations theory, developed by psychoanalytic theorists such as Klein, Winnicott and Fairbairn, proposes that the child's experience, perceptions and phantasies about their relationships with significant caregivers become incorporated in the mind at an early stage of development to become prototypical mental constructs which will influence the person's mode of relating to others in adulthood.

Oedipus complex

Freud named the Oedipus complex after the Greek tragedy in which Oedipus unknowingly killed his father and married his mother. Freud proposed that the Oedipus complex was a normal stage of development occurring between the ages of 3 and 5 years, where the boy is attracted to his mother and develops feelings of rivalry and jealousy for his father. The equivalent constellation in the little girl is called the **Electra complex**. Castration anxiety refers to the boy's fear that his father will castrate him for his desire for the mother. Resolution of the Oedipus complex results in the formation of the superego.

Oral stage

The oral stage, according to Freud, is the first stage of personality development, occurring in the first 18 months of life, when the infant's needs are centred on sucking, and other activities involving the mouth and associated organs. The early part of the oral stage consists of more libidinal oral needs (oral erotism) whereas in the later part of the oral stage these are mixed with more aggressive needs (oral sadism). In normal development the infant gradually learns to develop a trusting dependence on his objects via the gratification of oral needs. Excess oral gratifications or deprivations can lead to pathological traits, such as pathological narcissism and excessive dependence on others.

Paranoid schizoid position

The paranoid schizoid position is an early stage of development in the infant described by Melanie Klein (1946), where persecutory anxieties of annihilation and immature defence mechanisms such as splitting and projection predominate. The baby is unable to integrate conflicting experiences, and manages his aggression by splitting the object and attributing all negative and hostile feelings and phantasies to the 'bad breast' and all the warm and loving experiences to the 'good breast'.

Phallic stage

The phallic stage of personality development, according to Freud, occurs between the ages of about 3 and 5 years. Urination is the source of erotic activity, which, in boys, is the preliminary stage leading to adult genital sexuality.

Freud proposed that in boys, the penis is the erotogenic zone in this stage of development, but proposed that in girls, erotogenic activity shifted to the clitoris from the vagina after puberty. This view has subsequently been challenged. This stage coincides with the Oedipus complex and is characterised by unconscious phantasies of sexual desire for the opposite-sex parent and corresponding anxieties of castration in boys, and penis-envy in girls. Conflicts arising from the phallic stage may lead to later confusion in sexual identity.

Phantasy or Fantasy

This is an imaginary scene in which the subject represents the fulfilment of a wish in a way that is distorted by defensive processes to a greater or lesser degree. In this book where this is a conscious activity, such as day-dreaming, I refer to this as 'fantasy' and where it is unconscious, as 'phantasy'. A 'primal phantasy' such as that of the 'primal scene' (see below) is prototypical universal unconscious phantasy structure that is responsible for organising phantasy life.

Pleasure Principle

Freud (1911b) described two modes of mental functioning. The pleasure principle is the inborn tendency of the organism to avoid pain and seek pleasure via the release of tension. The reality principle is only learnt later with the maturation of the ego, and acts to modify the pleasure principle by delaying gratification.

Pre-oedipal

Pre-oedipal refers to the early period of a child's psychosexual development, which occurs before the onset of the Oedipal phase, that is, from birth until 3 to 4 years. During this period the attachment to the mother predominates in both sexes.

Primal scene

This is a primal unconscious phantasy of sexual intercourse between the parents, which is normally interpreted by the child as an act of violence on the part of the father.

Projection

Projection is a primitive defence mechanism in which unacceptable aspects of the self are expelled and attributed to someone or something else.

Projection occurs in pathological states such as paranoia, but also in 'normal' modes of thought such as superstition.

Projective identification

This is a term introduced by Melanie Klein to describe a primitive defence mechanism in which the subject inserts an aspect of himself into the object in order to possess and control it. This mechanism is associated with the paranoid depressive position.

Reaction formation

Reaction formation is a neurotic defence mechanism in which an unacceptable impulse is transformed into its opposite. Reaction formation is characteristic of obsessional neurosis or may become a more permanent character trait in obsessional personalities.

Reconstruction (or construction)

Construction is a term introduced by Freud (1937) to designate a therapeutic intervention where the analyst aims to reconstitute part of the subject's childhood, history, both real and phantasised, and how this influences the person's thoughts, feelings and behaviour.

Repetition compulsion

This is a person's unconscious tendency to repeat past traumatic behaviour. Freud explained this as a manifestation of the death instinct.

Repression

Repression is a neurotic defence mechanism where unacceptable thoughts and feelings are expelled or withheld from consciousness, in order to avoid conflict.

Reverie

Reverie is a term introduced by Bion (1959, 1962) in describing the concept of 'containment'. Reverie is the mother's capacity to understand her baby via empathic identification, bear his intolerable anxieties, moderate them and feed them back in a form which the baby can tolerate, which promotes healthy mental and physical development.

Self-psychology

This is a school of psychoanalysis developed in the United States by Heinz Kohut and his followers. This school prioritises narcissism and the roles of self-esteem and self-cohesion over those of sexuality or aggression in the development of the self.

Separation–individuation

A term coined by Margaret Mahler (1975) to describe the phase of development in the very young child in which he gradually moves from total dependence on his mother towards tolerating periods of separation and developing an independent sense of self as an individual in his own right. This normal process takes place against a background of safety and secure attachment.

Sexualisation

Sexualisation is a defence mechanism in which an object or function is endowed with sexual significance that it did not previously have to ward off more primitive anxieties concerned with aggression, dependence and loss.

Splitting

Splitting is a primitive defence mechanism. Freud (1927, 1940) used this term to specifically describe splitting of the ego in psychoses and fetishism where the subject simultaneously recognises reality and disavows it. Klein (1946) described splitting of the object as the most primitive defence against anxiety, in which the infant deals with the conflict between his erotic and destructive impulses by splitting the object into 'good' and 'bad'.

Structural model

This is Freud's second model of the mind (1923) (the first being the topographical model), in which the psychical apparatus is divided into three parts: id, ego and superego.

Sublimation

Sublimation is a more mature defence mechanism whereby unacceptable sexual impulses are channelled into more socially sanctioned activities and behaviour.

Superego

The superego is the third component of Freud's tripartite structural model of the mind (1923). He saw the superego as the heir to the Oedipus complex with the internalisation by the child of parental standards and goals to establish the individual's moral conscience. Failure to achieve these moral standards gives rise to feelings of guilt.

Transference

Freud (1912) described the transference as the wishes and feelings that the patient develops towards the analyst, which reflect childhood conflicts, and may serve as a resistance to the process of free association. The transference has been subsequently conceptualised as the externalisation and manifestation of the patient's internal object relations in the relationship with the analyst, the interpretation of which forms an essential part of contemporary psychoanalytic technique.

REFERENCES

Adshead, G. (1997) 'Written on the body: deliberate self-harm and violence', in Welldon, E.V. and Van Velsen, C. (eds), *A Practical Guide to Forensic Psychotherapy* (London: Jessica Kingsley).

Adshead, G., Bose, S. and Cartwright, J. (2008) 'Life after death: a group for people who have killed', in Doctor, R. (ed.), *Murder – A Psychotherapeutic Investigation* (London: Karnac Books).

Aichorn, A. (1925) *Wayward Youth* (New York: Viking).

Alexander, F. (1923) *Psychoanalysis of the Total Personality* English Translation. (New York: Nervous and Mental Disease Publications, 1930).

Alexander, F. (1930) 'The neurotic character', *International Journal of Psycho-Analysis*, 11, 292–313.

Alexander, F. (1935) *Roots of Crime* (New York: Knopf).

Altman, N. (2000) 'Black and white thinking: a psychoanalyst reconsiders race', *Psychoanalytic Dialogues*, 10, 589–605.

Alwin, N., Blackburn, R., Davidson, K., Hilton, M., Logan, C. and Shine, J. (2006) *Understanding Personality Disorder: A Report by the British Psychological Society* (Leicester: The British Psychological Society).

American Psychiatric Association (APA) (1994) *Diagnostic and Statistical Manual of Mental Disorders; Fourth Edition, Text Revision* (Washington, DC: American Psychiatric Association, 2000).

Arendt, H. (1951) *The Origins of Totalitarianism* (New York: Harcourt Brace Jovanovich).

Arlow, J. (1971) 'Character perversion', in Marcus, I. (ed.), *Currents in Psychoanalysis* (New York: International Universities Press).

Baker, R. (1980) 'The finding of "not suitable" in the selection of supervised cases', *International Review of Psycho-Analysis*, 7, 353–364.

Baldassare, M. (1994) *The Los Angeles Riots: Lessons for the Urban Future* (Boulder, CO: Westview Press).

Barry, C.T., Frick, P.J., DeShazo, T.M., McCoy, M.G., Ellis, M. and Loney, B.R. (2000) 'The importance of callous-unemotional traits for expanding the concept of psychopathy to children', *Journal of Abnormal Psychology*, 109, 335–340.

Bateman, A. (1999) 'Narcissism and its relation to violence and suicide', in Perelberg, R. (ed.), *Psychoanalytic Understanding of Violence and Suicide* (London: Routledge).

Bateman, A. and Fonagy, P. (2004) *Psychotherapy for Borderline Personality Disorder: Mentalization-based Treatment* (Oxford: Oxford University Press).

Bhui, K. and Morgan, N. (2007) 'Effective psychotherapy in a racially and culturally diverse society', *Advances in Psychiatric Treatment*, 13, 187–193.

Bion, W.R. (1957) 'Differentiation of the psychotic and non-psychotic personalities', *International Journal of Psycho-Analysis*, 35, 266–275.

Bion, W.R. (1959) 'Attacks on linking', *International Journal of Psycho-Analysis*, 40, 308–315.

Bion, W.R. (1961) *Experiences in Groups* (New York: Basic Books).

Bion, W.R. (1962) *Learning from Experience* (London: Heinemann. Reprinted London: Karnac Books, 1984).

Bion, W.R. (1970) *Attention and Interpretation* (London: Karnac Books).

Bion, W.R. (1984) *Second Thoughts: Selected Papers on Psychoanalysis* (London: Karnac Books).

Blackburn, R. (1993) 'Clinical programmes with psychopaths', in Howell, K. and Hollin, C.R. (eds), *Clinical Approaches to the Mentally Disordered Offender* (Chichester: Wiley).

Blum, H. (2005) 'Psychoanalytic reconstruction and reintegration', paper read to the Contemporary Freudian Group meeting of the British Psychoanalytic Society, 1 November, 2005.

Blumenthal, S., Huckle, C., Czornj, Roman, Craissati, J. and Richardson, P. (2009) 'Clinical and actuarial approaches to assessing risk', *Journal of Mental Health* (accepted for publication).

Bollas, C. (2003) 'Confidentiality and professionalism', in Levin, C., Furlong, A. and O'Neil, M.K. (eds), *Confidentiality, Ethical Perspectives and Clinical Dilemmas* (Northvale, NJ: The Analytic Press).

Bollas, C. and Sundelson, D. (1995) *The New Informants: Betrayal of Confidentiality in Psychoanalysis and Psychotherapy* (London: Karnac Books).

Bowlby, J. (1944) 'Forty-four juvenile thieves: their characters and home life', *International Journal of Psycho-Analysis*, 25, 1–57, 207–228.

Bowlby, J. (1969) *Attachment and Loss, vol. 1, Attachment* (New York: Basic Books).

British Medical Association (BMA) (1999) *Confidentiality and Disclosure of Health Information* (London: British Medical Association).

British Medical Association (BMA) (2002) *Patient Confidentiality – Guidelines* (London: British Medical Association).

Britton, R. (1989) 'The missing link: parental sexuality in the Oedipus complex', in Steiner, J. (ed.), *The Oedipus Complex Today* (London: Karnac Books).

Britton, R. (1992) 'The Oedipus solution and the depressive position', in Anderson, R. (ed.), *Clinical Lectures on Klein and Bion* (London: Routledge).

Britton, R. (1998) *Belief and Imagination: Explorations in Psychoanalysis* (London: Routledge).

Buchanan, A. (1999) 'Risk and dangerousness', *Psychological Medicine*, 29, 465–473.

Campbell, D. (1999) 'The role of the father in a pre-suicide state', in Perelberg, R. (ed.), *Psychoanalytic Understanding of Violence and Suicide* (London: Routledge).

Campbell, D. and Hale, R. (1991) 'Suicidal acts', in Holmes, J. (ed.), *Textbook of Psychotherapy in Psychiatric Practice* (London: Churchill Livingstone).

Canetti, E. (1960) *Masse and Macht* (Frankfurt am Main: Fischer Taschenbuch Verlag).

Carlson, E. and Sroufe, L.A. (1995) 'Contribution of attachment theory to developmental psychopathology', in Cicchetti, D. and Cohen, D.J. (eds), *Developmental Psychopathology. Vol. 1: Theory and Methods* (New York: Wiley).

Cartwright, D. (2002) *Psychoanalysis, Violence and Rage-type Murder* (Hove and New York: Brunner-Routledge).

Chasseguet-Smirgel, J. (1984) *Creativity and Perversion* (New York: W.W. Norton).

Chasseguet-Smirgel, J. (1990) 'Reflections of a psychoanalyst upon the Nazi biocracy and genocide', *International Review of Psycho-Analysis*, 17, 167–176.

Christie, R. (2006) 'On a hiding to nothing? Work with women affected by violence', in Harding, C. (ed.), *Aggression and Destructiveness: Psychoanalytic Perspectives* (London and New York: Routledge).

Cleckley, H. (1941) *The Mask of Sanity* (St. Louis, MO: C.V. Mosby).

Coltart, N. (1988a) 'Diagnosis and assessment of suitability for psychoanalytic psychotherapy', *British Journal of Psychotherapy*, 4, 127–134.

Coltart, N. (1988b) 'The assessment of psychological-mindedness in the diagnostic interview', *British Journal of Psychiatry*, 153, 819–820.

Cooper, A.M. (1991) 'The unconscious core of perversion', in Fogel, G.I. and Myers, W.A. (eds), *Perversions and Near-Perversions in Clinical Practice: New Psychoanalytic Perspectives* (New Haven and London: Yale University Press).

Cooper, J. and Alfille, H. (eds) (1998) *Assessment in Psychotherapy* (London: Karnac Books).

Cox, M. (1976) 'Group psychotherapy in a secure setting', *Proceedings of the Royal Society of Medicine*, 69, 215–220.

Dalal, F. (2002) *Race, Colour and the Processes of Racialization* (Hove: Brunner Routledge).

Dalal, F. (2006) 'Against the celebration of diversity', *British Journal of Psychotherapy*, 24, 4–19.

Darre, W. (1930) *La Race, Nouvelle Noblesse du Sang et du Sol* (Paris: Sorlot, 1939).

Davids, M.F. (1992) 'The cutting edge of racism: an object relations view', *Bulletin of the British Psychoanalytic Society*, 28(11), 19–29.

Davids, M.F. (1998) 'The Lionel Monteith Lecture'. Lincoln Centre and Clinic for Psychotherapy (unpublished).

Davies, R. (1999) 'Technique in the interpretation of the manifest attack on the analyst', in Perelberg, R. (ed.), *Psychoanalytic Understanding of Violence and Suicide* (London: Routledge).

Davies, R. (2007) 'The forensic network and the internal world of the offender: thoughts from consulting work in the forensic sector', in Morgan, D. and Ruszczynski, S. (eds), *Lectures on Violence, Perversion and Delinquency: The Portman Papers* (London: Karnac Books).

DeMause, L. (1990) 'The history of child assault', *Journal of Psychohistory*, 18, 1–29.

Department of Health (2003) *Confidentiality: NHS Code of Practice* (London: Department of Health).

Department of Health (2004) *The Children Act 2004* (London: HMSO).

De Zulueta, F. (2006) *From Pain to Violence*, 2nd Edition (London: Wiley).

Doctor, R. (2008) 'The history of murder', in Doctor, R. (ed.), *Murder – A Psychotherapeutic Investigation* (London: Karnac Books).

d'Orban, P.T. (1979) 'Women who kill their children', *British Journal of Psychiatry*, 134, 560–571.

Elmendorf, S.S. and Ruskin, R. (2004) 'Trauma, terrorism: man's inhumanity to man', *International Journal of Psycho-Analysis*, 85, 983–986.

Fairbairn, W.R.D. (1952) *Psychoanalytic Studies of the Personality* (London: Tavistock).

Fallon Report (1999) *Ashworth Special Hospital: Report of the Committee of Inquiry*.

Fanon, F. (1986) *Black Skin, White Masks* (London: Pluto Press).

Fenichel, O. (1931) 'The pre-genital antecedents of the Oedipus complex', *International Journal of Psycho-Analysis*, 12, 412–430.

Fenichel, O. (1945) *The Psychoanalytic Theory of Neurosis* (New York: Norton).

Finkle, M. (2007) 'Behavioral health: commitment based on mental illness', in Thomas, I. (ed. Ch. 4C), *Washington Health Law Manual* 3rd Edition (Washington: Washington State Society of Healthcare Attorneys).

Fonagy, P. (1999) 'Final remarks', in Perelberg, R. (ed.), *Psychoanalytic Understanding of Violence and Suicide* (London: Routledge).

Fonagy, P., Steele, M., Steele, H., Moran, G.S. and Higgit, A.C. (1991a) 'The capacity for understanding mental states: the reflective self in parent and child and its significance for security of attachment', *Infant Mental Health Journal*, 12, 201–218.

Fonagy, P., Steele, M. and Steele, H. (1991b) 'Maternal representations of attachment during pregnancy predict the organisation of infant-mother attachment at one year of age', *Child Development*, 62, 891–905.

Fonagy, P., Moran, G. and Target, M. (1993) 'Aggression and the psychological self', *International Journal of Psycho-Analysis*, 74, 471–486.

Fonagy, P., Steele, M., Steele, H., Leigh, T., Kennedy, R., Mattoon, G. and Target, M. (1995) 'The predictive validity of Mary Main's adult attachment interview: a psychoanalytic and developmental perspective on the transgenerational transmission of attachment and borderline states', in Goldberg, S., Muir, R. and Kerr, J. (eds), *Attachment Theory: Social Developmental and Clinical Perspectives* (Hillsdale, NJ: Analytic Press).

Fonagy, P. and Target, M. (1995) 'Understanding the violent patient: the use of the body and the role of the father', *International Journal of Psycho-Analysis*, 76, 487–501.

Foulkes, S.H. (1964) *Therapeutic Group Analysis* (London: George Allen and Unwin).

Foulkes, S.H. (1975) *Group-Analytic Psychotherapy, Methods and Principles* (London: Gordon and Breach).

Freud, A. (1936) *The Ego and the Mechanisms of Defence* (London: Hogarth Press).

Freud, A. (1954) 'The widening scope of indications for psycho-analysis', *Journal of the American Psychoanalytic Association*, 2, 607–620.

Freud, A. (1965) *Normality and Pathology in Childhood: Assessments of Development. Writings of Anna Freud*, vol. 4 (London: Hogarth Press, 1969).

Freud, S. (1905a) 'Three essays on the theory of sexuality', in Strachey, J. (ed.), *The Standard Edition of the Complete Psychological Works of Sigmund Freud*, vol. 7 (London: Hogarth Press and the Institute of Psychoanalysis).

Freud, S. (1905b) 'On psychotherapy', in Strachey, J. (ed.), *The Standard Edition of the Complete Psychological Works of Sigmund Freud*, vol. 7 (London: Hogarth Press and the Institute of Psychoanalysis).

Freud, S. (1910) 'The future prospects of psychoanalytic therapy', in Strachey, J. (ed.), *The Standard Edition of the Complete Psychological Works of Sigmund Freud*, vol. 11 (London: Hogarth Press and the Institute of Psychoanalysis).

Freud, S. (1911a) 'Psychoanalytic notes on an autobiographical account of a case of paranoia (dementia paranoides)', in Strachey, J. (ed.), *The Standard Edition of the Complete Psychological Works of Sigmund Freud*, vol. 12 (London: Hogarth Press and the Institute of Psychoanalysis).

Freud, S. (1911b) 'Formulations on the two principles of mental functioning', in Strachey, J. (ed.), *The Standard Edition of the Complete Psychological Works of Sigmund Freud*, vol. 12 (London: Hogarth Press and the Institute of Psychoanalysis).

Freud, S. (1912) 'Recommendations to physicians practicing psychoanalysis', in Strachey, J. (ed.), *The Standard Edition of the Complete Psychological Works of Sigmund Freud*, vol. 12 (London: Hogarth Press and the Institute of Psychoanalysis).

Freud, S. (1914) 'Remembering, repeating and working through', in Strachey, J. (ed.), *The Standard Edition of the Complete Psychological Works of Sigmund Freud*, vol. 12 (London: Hogarth Press and the Institute of Psychoanalysis).

Freud, S. (1915) 'Instincts and their vicissitudes', in Strachey, J. (ed.), *The Standard Edition of the Complete Psychological Works of Sigmund Freud*, vol. 15 (London: Hogarth Press and the Institute of Psychoanalysis).

Freud, S. (1916) 'Some character-types met with in psycho-analytic work: III Criminals from a sense of guilt', in Strachey, J. (ed.), *The Standard Edition of the Complete Psychological Works of Sigmund Freud*, vol. 14 (London: Hogarth Press and the Institute of Psychoanalysis).

Freud, S. (1917) 'Mourning and melancholia', in Strachey, J. (ed.), *The Standard Edition of the Complete Psychological Works of Sigmund Freud*, vol. 14 (London: Hogarth Press and the Institute of Psychoanalysis).

Freud, S. (1919) 'A child is being beaten', in Strachey, J. (ed.), *The Standard Edition of the Complete Psychological Works of Sigmund Freud*, vol. 17 (London: Hogarth Press and the Institute of Psychoanalysis).

Freud, S. (1920) 'Beyond the pleasure principle', in Strachey, J. (ed.), *The Standard Edition of the Complete Psychological Works of Sigmund Freud*, vol. 18 (London: Hogarth Press and the Institute of Psychoanalysis).

Freud, S. (1921) 'Group psychology and the analysis of the ego', in Strachey, J. (ed.), *The Standard Edition of the Complete Psychological Works of Sigmund Freud*, vol. 18 (London: Hogarth Press and the Institute of Psychoanalysis).

Freud, S. (1923) 'The ego and the id', in Strachey, J. (ed.), *The Standard Edition of the Complete Psychological Works of Sigmund Freud*, vol. 19 (London: Hogarth Press and the Institute of Psychoanalysis).

Freud, S. (1924) 'Neurosis and psychosis', in Strachey, J. (ed.), *The Standard Edition of the Complete Psychological Works of Sigmund Freud*, vol. 19 (London: Hogarth Press and the Institute of Psychoanalysis).

Freud, S. (1927) 'Fetishism', in Strachey, J. (ed.), *The Standard Edition of the Complete Psychological Works of Sigmund Freud*, vol. 21 (London: Hogarth Press and the Institute of Psychoanalysis).

Freud, S. (1937) 'Constructions in analysis', in Strachey, J. (ed.), *The Standard Edition of the Complete Psychological Works of Sigmund Freud*, vol. 23 (London: Hogarth Press and the Institute of Psychoanalysis).

Freud, S. (1940 [1938]) 'An Outline of Psychoanalysis', in Strachey, J. (ed.), *The Standard Edition of the Complete Psychological Works of Sigmund Freud*, vol. 23 (London: Hogarth Press and the Institute of Psychoanalysis).

Friedlander, K. (1945) 'Formation of the antisocial character', *Psychoanalytic Study of the Child*, 1, 189–203.

Gaddini, E. (1969) 'On imitation', *International Journal of Psycho-Analysis*, 50, 475–484.

Gaddini, E. (1992) *A Psychoanalytic Theory of Infantile Experience* (London, Routledge).

Garelick, A. (1994) 'Psychotherapy assessment: theory and practice', *Psychoanalytic Psychotherapy*, 8(2), 101–116.

Garvey, P. and Layton, A. (2004) *Comparative Confidentiality in Psychoanalysis* (London: IPA & British Institute of International and Comparative Law).

General Medical Council (2004) *Confidentiality: Protecting and Providing Information* (London: GMC Publications).

Gilligan, J. (1996) *Violence: Our Deadliest Epidemic and Its Causes* (New York: Grosset/Putnam).

Glasser, M. (1978) 'The role of the superego in exhibitionism', *International Journal of Psychoanalytic Psychotherapy*, 7, 333–352.

Glasser, M. (1985) 'Aspects of violence', paper given to the Applied Section of the British Psychoanalytic Society.

Glasser, M. (1986) 'Identification and its vicissitudes as observed in the perversions', *International Journal of Psycho-Analysis*, 67, 9–17.

Glasser, M. (1996a) 'Aggression and sadism in the perversions', in Rosen, I. (ed.), *Sexual Deviation* 3rd edition (Oxford: Oxford University Press).

Glasser, M. (1996b) 'The assessment and management of dangerousness: the psychoanalytic contribution', *The Journal of Forensic Psychiatry*, 7(2), 272–283.

Glasser, M. (1997) 'Problems in the psychoanalysis of certain narcissistic disorders', *Psycho-analytic Psychotherapy in South Africa*, 5, 35–49.

Glasser, M. (1998) 'On violence: a preliminary communication', *International Journal of Psycho-Analysis*, 79, 887–902.

Glover, E. (1933) 'The relation of perversion-formation to the development of a reality sense', *International Journal of Psycho-Analysis*, 14, 486–504.

Glover, E. (1954) 'The indications for psychoanalysis', *Journal of Mental Science*, 100, 393–401.

Gordon, J. and Kirtchuk, G. (eds) (2008) *Psychic Assaults and Frightened Clinicians: Countertransference in Forensic Settings* (London: Karnac Books).

Green, A. (1993) *Le Travail du Negative* (Paris: Les Editions de Minuit).

Greenacre, P. (1945) 'Conscience in the psychopath', *American Journal of Orthopsychiatry*, 14, 495–509.

Greenacre, P. (1958) 'The imposter', *Psychoanalytic Quarterly*, 27, 359–383.

Greenson, R. (1967) *The Technique and Practice of Psychoanalysis*, vol. 1 (London: Hogarth Press).

Grotstein, J. (1980) 'A proposed revision of the psychoanalytic concept of primitive mental states', *Contemporary Psychoanalysis*, 16, 479–546.

Grotstein, J. (1982) 'Newer perspectives in object relations theory', *Contemporary Psychoanalysis*, 18, 43–91.

Grounds, A. (1996) 'Expectations and ethics', in Cordess, C. and Cox, M. (eds), *Forensic Psychotherapy: Crime, Psychodynamics and the Offender Patient* (London and Philadelphia: Jessica Kingsley).

Grounds, A. (2000) 'The future of prison health care', *The Journal of Forensic Psychiatry and Psychology*, 11, 260–267.

Grunberger, B. (1985) 'Outline for a study of female sexuality', in Chasseguet-Smirgel, J. (ed.), *Female Sexuality* (London: Karnac Books).

Gurr, T.R. (1970) *Why Men Rebel* (Princeton, NJ: Princeton University Press).

Hale, R. (2004) Personal communication.

Hale, R. and Dhar, R. (2008) 'Flying a kite – observations on dual (and triple) diagnosis', *Criminal Behaviour and Mental Health*, 18, 145–152.

Hare, R. (1991) *Manual of the Revised Psychopathy Checklist* (Toronto: Multi Health Systems).

Hart, S.D., Michie, C. and Cooke, D.J. (2007) 'Precision of actuarial assessment instruments', *British Journal of Psychiatry*, 190(suppl. 49), 60–65.

Heidensohn, F. (1991) 'Women and crime in Europe', in Heidensohn, F. and Farrell, M. (eds), *Crime in Europe* (London: Routledge).

Heimann, P. (1950) 'On countertransference', *International Journal of Psycho-Analysis*, 31, 81–84.

Hinshelwood, R.D. (1987) 'The psychotherapist's role in a large psychiatric institution', *Psychoanalytic Psychotherapy*, 2, 207–215.

Hinshelwood, R.D. (1991) 'Psychodynamic formulation in assessment for psychoanalytic psychotherapy', *British Journal of Psychotherapy*, 8(2), 166–174.

Hinshelwood, R.D. (2004) *Suffering Insanity* (London: Brunner Routledge).

Hodgins, S. (2007) 'Persistent violent offending: what do we know?', *British Journal of Psychiatry*, 190(suppl. 49), s12–s14.

Hollin, C.R. (1989) *Psychology and Crime: An Introduction to Criminological Psychology* (London: Routledge).

Home Office (2004) *Violent Crime in England and Wales* (London: Home Office, Research, Development and Statistics Directorate).

Home Office (2006) *Violent Crime Overview, Homicide and Gun Crime, 2004/2005* (London: Home Office, Research, Development and Statistics Directorate).

Home Office (2007) *MAPPA Guidance* www.probation.homeoffice.gov.uk/files/pdf/MAPPA%20Guidance%202007%20.

Horney, K. (1945) *Our Inner Conflicts* (New York: Norton).

Hough, G. (2004) 'Does psychoanalysis have anything to offer an understanding of terrorism?', *Journal of the American Psychoanalytic Association*, 52, 813–828.

Hyatt-Williams, A. (1998) *Cruelty, Violence and Murder: Understanding the Criminal Mind* (London: Jason Aronson).

Irving, B. (1996) 'A police perspective', in Cordess, C. and Cox, M. (eds), *Forensic Psychotherapy: Crime, Psychodynamics and the Offender Patient* (London and Philadelphia: Jessica Kingsley).

Jacques, E. (1955) 'Social systems as a defence against persecutory and depressive anxiety', in Klein, M., Heimann, P. and Money-Kyrle, R. (eds), *New Directions in Psycho-Analysis* (London: Tavistock).

Jaspers, K. (1959) *General Psychopathology* (Berlin, Heidelberg: Springer-Verlag).

Joseph, B. (1985) 'Transference: the total situation', *International Journal of Psycho-Analysis*, 66, 447–454.

Kennedy, R. (2005) *Psychotherapists as Expert Witnesses* (London: Karnac Books).

Kernberg, O.F. (1975) *Borderline Conditions and Pathological Narcissism* (New York: Jason Aronson).

Kernberg, O.F. (1976) *Object Relations Theory and Clinical Psychoanalysis* (New York: Jason Aronson).

Kernberg, O.F. (1984) *Severe Personality Disorders* (New Haven and London: Yale University Press).

Kernberg, O.F. (1992) *Aggression in Personality Disorders and Perversions* (New Haven and London: Yale University Press).

Kernberg, O.F. (1998) *Ideology, Conflict and Leadership in Groups and Organizations* (New Haven and London: Yale University Press).

Kernberg, O.F. (2003a) 'Sanctioned social violence: a psychoanalytic view: Part I', *International Journal of Psycho-Analysis*, 84, 683–698.

Kernberg, O.F. (2003b) 'Sanctioned social violence: a psychoanalytic view: Part II', *International Journal of Psycho-Analysis*, 84, 953–968.

Keval, N. (2005) 'Racist states of mind: an attack on thinking and curiosity', in Bower, M. (ed.), *Psychoanalytic Theory for Social Work Practice* (London: Routledge).

Klein, M. (1927) 'Criminal tendencies in normal children', *British Journal of Medical Psychology*, 7, 177–192.

Klein, M. (1932) *The Psychoanalysis of Children* (London: Hogarth Press).

Klein, M. (1935) 'A contribution to the psychogenesis of manic depressive states', in Klein, M. (ed.), *Love, Guilt, Reparation and Other Works 1921–1945* (London: Hogarth Press).

Klein, M. (1946) 'Notes on some schizoid mechanisms', in Klein, M. (ed.), *Envy and Gratitude and Other Works* (London: Hogarth Press, 1975).

Klein, M. (1952) 'The origins of transference', in Klein, M. (ed.), *Envy and Gratitude and Other Works* (London: Hogarth Press, 1975).

Koch, J.L. (1891) *Die Psychopathischen Minderwertigkeiten* (Ravensburg, Germany: Maier).

Kohut, H. (1972) 'Thoughts on narcissism and narcissistic rage', in Ornstein, P. (ed.), *The Search of the Self* (London: International University Press).

Kohut, H. (1978) *The Search for the Self* (New York: International University Press).

Kohut, H. (1985) *Self Psychology and the Humanities: Reflections on a New Psychoanalytic Approach* (New York and London: W.W. Norton).

Kovel, J. (1988) *White Racism: A Psychohistory* (London: Free Association Books).

Kraepelin, E. (1887) *Psychiatrie: Ein Lehrbuch* 2nd Edition (Leipzig: Abel).

Kraepelin, E. (1889) *Psychiatrie: Ein Lehrbuch* 3rd Edition (Leipzig: Barth).

Kraepelin, E. (1896) *Psychiatrie: Ein Lehrbuch* 5th Edition (Leipzig: Barth).

Kraepelin, E. (1903–1904) *Psychiatrie: Ein Lehrbuch* 7th Edition (Leipzig: Barth).

Kraepelin, E. (1915) *Psychiatrie: Ein Lehrbuch* 8th Edition (Leipzig: Barth).

Lacan, J. (1966) *Ecrits* (Paris: Seuil) *Ecrits: A Selection* (Sheridan, A. trans.) (London and New York: Routledge).

Laming, H. (2003) *The Victoria Climbie Inquiry: Report of an Inquiry by Lord Laming* (London: The Stationary Office).

Laplanche, J. and Pontalis, J.-B. (1973) *The Language of Psychoanalysis* (London: Hogarth Press. Original publication in French, 1967).

Le Bon, G. (1952) *The Crowd* (London: Ernest Benn. First published 1895).

Lecours, S. and Bouchard, M. (1997) 'Dimensions of mentalization: outlining levels of psychic transformation', *International Journal of Psycho-Analysis*, 78, 855–875.

Link, B.G. and Stueve, C.A. (1994) 'Psychotic symptoms and the violent/illegal behaviour of mental patients compared to community controls', in Monahan, J. and Steadman, H. (eds), *Violence and Mental Disorder: Developments in Risk Assessment* (Chicago: University of Chicago Press).

Limentani, A. (1972) 'The assessment of analysability: a major hazard in selection for psychoanalysis', in Limentani, A. (ed.), *Between Freud and Klein* (London: Karnac Books).

Limentani, A. (1991) 'Neglected fathers in the aetiology and treatment of sexual deviations', *International Journal of Psycho-Analysis*, 72, 573–584.

Lloyd-Owen, D. (2007) 'Perverse female: their unique psychopathology', in Morgan, D. and Ruszczynski, S. (eds), *Lectures on Violence, Perversion and Delinquency: The Portman Papers* (London: Karnac Books).

Lord's Hansard text of Lord Howe's speech, 5 February 2003 (http://www.parliament.the-stationery-office.co.uk/pa/ld200203/ldhansrd/vo030205/text/30205-10.htm#column_316).

Lucas, R. (2003) 'Risk assessment in general psychiatry: a psychoanalytic perspective', in Doctor, R. (ed.), *Dangerous Patients: A Psychodynamic Approach to Risk Assessment and Management* (London: Karnac Books).

Lynam, D.R. and Gudonis, L. (2005) 'The development of psychopathy', *Annual Review of Clinical Psychopathy*, 1, 381–407.

Madden, D.J. and Lion, J. (1978) 'Treating the violent offender', in Kutash, I.L., Kutash, S.B. and Schlesinger, L.B. (eds), *Violence: Perspectives on Murder and Aggression* (San Francisco and London: Jossey-Bass).

Mahler, M.S., Pine, F. and Bergman, A. (1975) *The Psychological Birth of the Human Infant: Symbiosis and Individuation* (New York: Basic Books).

Malcolm, R.R. (1986) 'Interpretation: the past in the present', *International Review of Psycho-Analysis*, 13, 433–443.

McDougall, J. (1985) *Theatres of the Mind: Illusion and Truth on the Psychoanalytic Stage* (New York: Basic Books).

Meadow, R. (1977) 'Munchausen syndrome by proxy: the hinterland of child abuse', *Lancet*, 2, 343–345.

Meloy, J.R. (1988) *The Psychopathic Mind: Origins, Dynamics and Treatment* (Northvale, NJ: Jason Aronson).

Meloy, J.R. (1992) *Violent Attachments* (Northvale, NJ: Jason Aronson).

Menninger, K.A. (1938) *Man Against Himself* (New York: Harcourt Brace).

Menninger, K.A. (1942) *Love Against Hate* (New York: Harcourt Brace).

Menninger, K.A. (1963) *The Vital Balance: The Life Process in Mental Health and Illness* (New York: Viking).

Menninger, K.A. (1968) *The Crime of Punishment* (New York: Viking).

Menzies-Lyth, I. (1988) 'The Functioning of social systems as a defence against anxiety', in Menzies-Lyth, I. (ed.), *Containing Anxiety in Institutions: Selected Essays*, vol. 1 (London: Free Association Books. First published 1959 in *Human Relations*).

Mercer, M. (2008) 'Bearable or unbearable? Unconscious communication in management', in Gordon, J. and Kirtchuk, G. (eds), *Psychic Assaults and Frightened Clinicians: Countertransference in Forensic Settings* (London: Karnac Books).

Meyer, A. (1904) 'A review of recent problems of psychiatry', in Church, A. and Peterson, F. (eds), *Nervous and Mental Diseases* 4th Edition (Baltimore: Williams and Wilkins).

Millon, T., Davis, R. and Millon, C. (1994) *Manual for the Millon Clinical Multiaxial Inventory – III (MCMI-III)* (Minneapolis, MN: National Computer Systems).

Ministry of Justice (2008) *Arrests for Recorded Crime (Notifiable Offences) and the Operation of Certain Police Powers under PACE England and Wales 2006/07* http://www.justice.gov.uk/docs/arrests-recorded-crime-engl-wales-2006–07.pdf.

Minne, C. (2003) 'Psychoanalytic aspects to the risk containment of dangerous patients treated in high-security hospital', in Doctor, R. (ed.), *Dangerous Patients: A Psychodynamic Approach to Risk Assessment and Management* (London: Karnac Books).

Minne, C. (2004) Personal communication.

Minne, C. (2008) 'The dreaded and dreading patient and therapist', in Gordon, J. and Kirtchuk, G. (eds), *Psychic Assaults and Frightened Clinicians: Countertransference in Forensic Settings* (London: Karnac Books).

Mizen, R. and Morris, M. (2007) *On Aggression and Violence: An Analytic Perspective* (London: Palgrave Macmillan).

Monahan, J., Steadman, H.J., Silver, E., Appelbaum, P.S., Robbins, P.C., Mulvey, E.P., Roth, L.H., Grisso, T. and Banks, S. (2001) *Rethinking Risk Assessment: The MacArthur Study of Mental Disorder and Violence* (Oxford: Oxford University Press).

Money-Kyrle, R. (1971) 'The aims of psychoanalysis', in Meltzer, D. and O'Shaughnessy, E. (eds), *The Collected Papers of Roger Money-Kyrle* (Strath-Tay: Cluney Press).

Morgan, H. (2007) 'Issues of "race" in psychoanalytic psychotherapy: whose problem is it anyway?', *British Journal of Psychotherapy*, 24, 34–49.

Motz, A. (2008) *The Psychology of Female Violence: Crimes Against the Body* 2nd Edition (London and New York: Routledge).

O'Neil, M.K. (2007) 'Confidentiality, privacy and the facilitating role of psychoanalytic organizations', *International Journal of Psycho-Analysis*, 88, 691–711.

O'Shaughnessy, E. (1981) 'A clinical study of a defensive organization', *International Journal of Psycho-Analysis*, 62, 359–369.

Parens, H. (1993) 'Rage towards self and others in early childhood', in Glick, R.A. and Roose, S.P. (eds), *Rage, Power and Aggression* (New Haven and London: Yale University Press).

Perelberg, R. (1995) 'A core phantasy of violence', *International Journal of Psycho-Analysis*, 76, 1215–1231.

Perelberg, R. (1997) 'Introduction to Part 1', in Raphael-Leff, J. and Perelberg, R. (eds), *Female Experience: Three Generations of British Women Psychoanalysts on Work with Women* (London and New York: Routledge).

Perelberg, R. (1999a) 'Psychoanalytic understanding of violence and suicide: a review of the literature and some new formulations', in Perelberg, R. (ed.), *Psychoanalytic Understanding of Violence and Suicide* (London: Routledge).

Perelberg, R. (1999b) 'The interplay between identification and identity in the analysis of a violent young man: issues of technique', *International Journal of Psychoanalysis*, 80, 31–46.

Pinel, P. (1962) *A Treatise on Insanity* (Davis, D. trans.) (New York: Hafner. Original work published 1801).

Pines, D. (1972) 'Pregnancy and motherhood: interaction between fantasy and reality', *British Journal of Medical Psychology*, 45, 333–343.

Pines, D. (1993) *A Woman's Unconscious Use of Her Body* (London: Virago).

Post, G. (2001) 'The mind of the terrorist', paper presented to the Association for Psychoanalytic Medicine, New York, 30 October.

Prichard, J.C. (1835) *A Treatise on Insanity and Other Disorders Affecting the Mind* (London: Sherwood, Gilbert and Piper).

Reich, W. (1945) *Character Analysis* 2nd Edition (New York: Farrar, Strauss and Giroux).

Resnick, P.J. (1969) 'Child murder by parents. a psychiatric review of filicide', *American Journal of Psychiatry*, 126(3), 325–334.

Rice, A.K. (1965) *Learning for Leadership* (London: Tavistock).

Rice, A.K. (1969) 'Individual, group and intergroup processes', *Human Relations*, 22, 565–584.

Richards, H. (1998) 'Evil intent: violence and disorders of the will', in Millon, T., Simonson, E., Birket-Smith, M. and Davis, R.D. (eds), *Psychopathy: Antisocial, Criminal and Violent Behavior* (New York and London: Guildford Press).

Rosenberg, D.A. (1987) 'Web of deceit: a literature of Munchausen syndrome by proxy', *Child Abuse and Neglect*, 11(4), 547–563.

Royal College of Psychiatrists (RCPsych) (2006) *Good Psychiatric Practice: Confidentiality and Information Sharing Council Report CR133* (London: Royal College of Psychiatrists).

Royal College of Psychiatrists (RCPsych) (2008) *Rethinking Risk to Others in Mental Health Services: Final Report of a Scoping Group* (London: Royal College of Psychiatrists).

Ruszczynski, S. (2006) 'The problem of certain psychic realities: aggression and violence as perverse solutions', in Harding, C. (ed.), *Aggression and Destructiveness: Psychoanalytic Perspectives* (London and New York: Routledge).

Rutter, M. (1987) 'Temperament, personality and personality development', *British Journal of Psychiatry*, 150, 443–448.

Sandler, J. (1960) 'On the Concept of the Superego', *Psychoanalytic Study of the Child*, 15, 128–162.

Sandler, J. (1976) 'Countertransference and role-responsiveness', *International Review of Psycho-Analysis*, 3, 43–47.

Saville, E. and Rumney, D. (1992) *'Let Justice be Done!': A History of the ISTD* (London: Institute for the Study and Treatment of Delinquency).

Schafer, R. (1997) *Tradition and Change in Psychoanalysis* (London: Karnac Books).

Schlapobersky, J. (1996) 'A group-analytic perspective: from the speech of hands to the language of words', in Cordess, C. and Cox, M. (eds), *Forensic Psychotherapy: Crime, Psychodynamics and the Offender Patient* (London and Philadelphia: Jessica Kingsley).

Scott, P.D. (1973) 'Parents who kill their children', *Medicine, Science and the Law*, 13, 120–126.

Segal, H. (1957) 'Notes on Symbol Formation', *International Journal of Psychoanalysis*, 38, 391–397.

Segal, H. (1978) 'On symbolism', *International Journal of Psychoanalysis*, 59, 315–319.

Segal, H. (1997) *Psychoanalysis, Literature and War: Papers 1972–1995* (London: Routledge).

Seligman, M.E.P. (1975) *Helplessness: On Depression, Development and Death* (San Francisco: Freeman).

Shapiro, S. (1984) 'The initial assessment of the patient: a psychoanalytic approach', *International Review of Psycho-Analysis*, 11, 11–25.

Shengold, L. (1989) *Soul Murder: The Effects of Child Abuse and Deprivations* (New Haven, CT: Yale University Press).

Shengold, L. (1991) *Father, Don't You See I'm Burning?* (New Haven and London: Yale University Press).

Sofsky, W. (1997) *The Order of Terror: The Concentration Camp* (Princeton, NJ: Princeton University Press).

Sohn, L. (1995) 'Unprovoked assaults – making sense of apparently random violence', *International Journal of Psychoanalysis*, 76, 565–575.

Southall, D.P., Plunkett, M.C., Banks, M.W., Falcov, A.F., Samuels, M.P. (1997) 'Covert video recordings of life-threatening child abuse: lessons for child protection', *Pediatrics*, 100, 735–760.

Steiner, J. (1982) 'Perverse relationships between parts of the self: a clinical illustration', *International Journal of Psychoanalysis*, 63, 241–253.

Steiner, J. (1993) *Psychic Retreats: Pathological Organizations in Neurotic, Psychotic and Borderline Patients* (London: Routledge, New Library of Psychoanalysis).

Steiner, J. (1994) 'Patient-centred and analyst-centred interpretations: some implications of containment and countertransference', *Psychoanalytic Inquiry*, 14, 406–422.

Stoller, R.J. (1974) 'Hostility and mystery in perversion', *International Journal of Psycho-Analysis*, 55, 425–434.

Stoller, R.J. (1975) *Perversion* (New York: Pantheon).

Stoller, R.J. (1979) 'Fathers and transsexual children', *Journal of the American Psychoanalytic Association*, 27, 837–866.

Stone, A.A. (1994) 'Revisiting the parable: truth without consequences', *International Journal of Law and Psychiatry*, 17, 79–98.

Stone, J. (1997) 'Medico-legal ethics in forensic psychotherapy', in Welldon, E. and Van Velsen, C. (eds), *A Practical Guide to Forensic Psychotherapy* (London: Jessica Kingsley).

Stone, M.H. (1980) *The Borderline Syndromes: Constitution, Personality and Adaptation* (New York: McGraw Hill).

Svrakic, D., McCallum, K. and Milan, P. (1991) 'Developmental, structural and clinical approach to narcissistic and antisocial personalities', *American Journal of Psychoanalysis*, 51, 413–432.

Swanson, J., Borum, R., Swartz, M. and Monahan, J. (1996) 'Psychotic symptoms and disorders and the risk of violent behavior in the community', *Criminal Behavior and Mental Health*, 6, 309–329.

Symington, N. (1996) 'The origins of rage and aggression', in Cordess, C. and Cox, M. (eds), *Forensic Psychotherapy: Crime, Psychodynamics and the Offender Patient* (London and Philadelphia: Jessica Kingsley).

Tan, R. (1993) 'Racism and similarity: paranoid schizoid structures', *British Journal of Psychotherapy*, 10(1), 33–43.

Taylor, P.J., Garety, P., Buchanan, A., Reed, A., Wessely, S., Ray, K., Dunn, G. and Grubin, D. (1994) 'Delusions and violence', in Monahan, J. and Steadman, H. (eds), *Violence and Mental Disorder: Developments in Risk Assessment* (Chicago: University of Chicago Press).

Taylor, R. (2008) 'Psychiatric aspects of the war on terror', paper presented at the Annual Meeting of the American Academy of Psychiatry and the Law, Seattle, October 2008.

Turquet, P. (1975) 'Threats to identity in the large group', in Kreeger, L. (ed.), *The Large Group: Dynamics and Therapy* (London: Constable).

US Department of Justice (2007) *Crime in the United States 2007* (Washington, DC: US Department of Justice).

Volkan, V.D. (1988) *The Need to Have Enemies and Allies: From Clinical Practice to International Relationships* (Northvale, NJ: Jason Aronson).

Walker, L.E. (1984) *The Battered Woman Syndrome* (New York: Springer).

Wall, N. (2000) *Expert Witnesses in Children Act Cases* (Bristol: Family Law).

Webster, C.D., Douglas, K.S., Eaves, D. and Hart, S.T. (1997) *HCR-20: Assessing Risk for Violence*, Version 2 (Vancouver: Mental Health, Law and Policy Institute, Simon Fraser University).

Welldon, E. (1988) *Mother, Madonna, Whore: The Idealization and Denigration of Motherhood* (New York: Other Press).

Welldon, E. (1996) 'Group-analytic psychotherapy in an out-patient setting', in Cordess, C. and Cox, M. (eds), *Forensic Psychotherapy: Crime, Psychodynamics and the Offender Patient* (London and Philadelphia: Jessica Kingsley).

Welldon, E. and Van Velsen, C. (eds) (1997) *A Practical Guide to Forensic Psychotherapy* (London: Jessica Kingsley).

Winnicott, D.W. (1951) 'Transitional objects and transitional phenomena', in Winnicott, D.W. (ed.), *Collected Papers: Through Paediatrics to*

Psycho-Analysis (London: Tavistock, 1958. Reprinted London: Karnac Books, 1991).

Winnicott, D.W. (1954) 'Metapsychological and clinical aspects of regression within the psychoanalytic set-up', in Winnicott, D.W. (ed.), *Collected Papers: Through Paediatrics to Psycho-Analysis* (London: Tavistock, 1958. Reprinted London: Karnac Books, 1991).

Winnicott, D.W. (1956) 'The anti-social tendency', in Winnicott, D.W. (ed.), *Collected Papers: Through Paediatrics to Psycho-Analysis* (London: Hogarth Press, 1984).

Winnicott, D.W. (1960) 'Ego distortion in terms of true and false self', in Winnicott, D.W. (ed.), *The Maturational Processes and the Facilitating Environment* (London: Hogarth Press. Reprinted London: Karnac Books, 1990).

Winnicott, D.W. (1959–1964) 'Classification: is there a psychoanalytic contribution to psychiatric classification?', in Winnicott, D.W. (ed.), *The Maturational Processes and the Facilitating Environment* (London: Hogarth Press. Reprinted London: Karnac Books, 1990).

Winnicott, D.W. (1967) 'Mirror-role of the mother and family in child development', in Lomas, P. (ed.), *The Predicament of the Family: A Psycho-Analytical Symposium* (London: Hogarth Press).

Winnicott, D.W. (1971) *Playing and Reality* (London: Tavistock).

Winnicott, D.W. (1986) *Deprivation and Delinquency* (London: Tavistock).

World Health Organisation (WHO) (1992) *International Classification of Mental and Behavioural Disorders, Tenth Edition (ICD-10)* (Geneva: WHO).

Wykes, M. (1995) 'Passion, marriage and murder: analysing the press discourse', in Dobash, R.E., Dobash, R.P. and Noaks, L. (eds), *Gender and Crime* (Cardiff: University of Wales Press).

Yalom, I.B. (1970) *The Theory and Practice of Group Psychotherapy* (New York: Basic Books).

Zanarini, M.C. and Frankenberg, F.R. (1997) 'Pathways to the development of borderline personality disorder', *Journal of Personality Disorders*, 11(1), 93–104.

INDEX

acting out, 86, 101, 102, 107, 111, 133, 152, 159, 160
affective violence, *see* violence
aggression, psychoanalytic history of, 8–10
anal stage, 62
'anal universe', 94
analyst-centred interpretation, 138, 139, 149
antisocial personality disorder, *see* personality disorder
antisocial tendency, 42
assessment, *see* group-analytic, group therapy; psychotherapy; risk
attachment theory, 7, 13, 72
attachment
  and risk, 110
  and assessment, 13–14
  and perversion, 62–3
  and psychopathy, 41, 44–5, 48, 49–51, 52
'attacks on linking', 36
auxillary ego, *see* ego

Balint group, *see* group
basic assumption, *see* group
battered woman syndrome, 81
Bion, W.R., 15, 21, 36, 85, 86, 92, 115, 116, 125, 145, 154, 157, 158, 159
borderline personality disorder, *see* personality disorder
Bowlby, J., 9, 13, 20, 42
Britton, R., 17, 123, 138

Campbell, D., 10, 17, 19, 71, 128
cannabis, *see* drug abuse
Care Programme Approach (CPA), 98, 119

Cartwright, D., 8, 9, 18, 20, 22, 23, 24, 39, 111, 138, 139, 140, 142, 144, 146, 147
castration anxiety, 18, 60–1, 63, 65, 66, 67, 70
Chasseguet-Smirgel, J., 66, 92
Children Act, 74
Cleckley, H., 42, 44, 46
Cognitive Behavioural Therapy (CBT), 119, 134, 140, 178
confidentiality, 3, 5, 112, 113, 134, 152, 155, 163, 165–8, 169, 170, 172, 174, 177
containment, 15, 17, 21, 45, 46, 72, 79, 84, 109, 112, 114–16, 125, 143, 146, 149, 150, 151, 152, 155, 156, 157, 160, 161, 162, 163, 166, 167, 171, 177
countertransference, 50–1, 55, 90, 101, 102–6, 107, 109, 112, 113, 121, 122, 128, 140–4, 147, 149, 158
core complex, 16, 17, 19, 63, 64, 67, 89, 111, 141
courts, 5, 27, 78, 124, 164, 168, 169, 172–6, 177
criminal justice system, 5, 44, 106, 164, 169, 176
cults, 95

Davies, R., 117, 124, 136, 138
death instinct, 8, 9, 94
defence mechanisms
  denial, 47, 49, 51, 65, 67, 96, 109, 116
  disavowal, 46, 61, 65, 116
  group, 31, 86, 92
  identification, 20, 21, 25, 31
  imitation, 20, 146
  institutional, 116–18
  introjection, 38, 49

primitive, 9, 20, 21, 24, 25, 31, 34, 35, 37, 40, 45, 52, 55, 79, 86, 92, 103, 109, 110, 113, 140, 145
projection, 9, 21, 35, 37, 81–2, 92, 103, 110, 126, 140, 161
projective identification, 21, 25, 31, 35, 37, 40, 81–2, 92, 103, 117
reaction formation, 59, 60, 87
repression, 20, 35, 47, 60, 61, 67, 87, 101
sexualisation, 11, 17, 57, 58, 62, 63, 64, 65, 67, 161
simulation, 20, 48, 49, 146
social, 92, 116, 125
splitting, 9, 21, 25, 31, 35, 47, 55, 79, 92, 103, 110, 117, 140
sublimation, 47, 60, 87
defensive organisation, see pathological organisation
dehumanisation, 93–6
denial, see defence mechanisms
developmental stages, 17, 62, 63, 72
    see also anal stage; genital stage; oral stage; phallic stage
depressive position, 9, 145, 146
De Zulueta, F., 10, 13, 14
diagnosis, 28, 32, 33, 39, 52–4, 75, 76, 78, 115, 120, 129, 152, 175
disavowal, see defence mechanisms
disclosure, 113, 143, 165, 166, 167
domestic violence, see violence
drive, 8, 10, 26, 31, 47, 59, 60, 97, 124
drug abuse, 23, 54, 111
dual diagnosis, 33, 39, 52–4
'Duty to Co-operate', 169
Diagnostic and Statistical Manual of Mental Disorders, Fourth Edition (DSM-IV), 29, 30, 43, 57

ego
    auxiliary, 137, 151
    psychology, 85, 88
    strength, 110, 127, 129, 130, 132, 149
ego-ideal, 18, 85
engaging the patient, 135–40
erotogenic zone, 59
'erotic form of hatred', 62–5
ethnicity, 5, 84, 88, 90
exhibitionism, 57, 60, 152, 163
expert witness, 78, 164, 172, 175, 176, 177

Fabricated or Induced Illness (FII), see Munchhausen's Syndrome by Proxy (MSBP)
'facts of life', 65–7, 89
Fairbairn, W.R.D., 9
Fallon report, 117, 121
'false self', 22, 46, 48, 146
fantasy, 3, 19, 58, 163
    see also phantasy
father, role of, 8, 16–18, 24
fetishism, 57, 58, 60, 62–3
Fonagy, P., 8, 14–15, 17, 19, 73, 136, 137
forensic hospital, 114, 118
forensic psychiatry, 2
forensic psychotherapist, role of, 5, 11, 118, 120, 122–3, 126, 164, 175
forensic psychotherapy, 1, 5, 121, 128, 131, 166
Foulkes, S., 153, 156, 158
free association, 147, 153
Freud, A., 20, 109, 137–8, 139
Freud, S., 7, 8–9, 18–19, 34–5, 41, 58–62, 65, 67, 85, 88, 94, 101–2, 107, 113, 129, 142, 154
frotteurism, 60

Gaddini, E., 20, 48, 146
gangs, 53, 54, 84, 86, 95, 151, 154
genital stage, 59
genocide, 5, 84, 92, 93–6
Gilligan, J., 15–16, 18, 89
Glasser, M., 9, 10, 11–13, 16–20, 48, 52–3, 63, 65, 67, 89, 101, 111, 128, 141, 146–8
Glover, E., 62, 65, 127, 128, 129
grandiose self, 46–54
Greenacre, P., 42, 48
Greenson, R., 139
group
    basic assumption, 85–6, 92, 154, 157, 159
    conductor, see group-analytic therapy
    Balint group, 105
    defences, 116, 126, 159–60, 163
    dynamics, 85, 116, 150, 155
    leadership, 85
    therapy, 31, 150, 151–3, 155
    transference, 152, 157–63
    trauma, 93–4
violence, see violence

group – *continued*
  work discussion group, 105, 108, 113
  work group, 85, 154, 171
group-analytic therapy
  assessment for, 151–3
  conductor, 153
  curative factors, 154
  interpretations, 157, 158
  process of, 153–5
  rules, 155–7
  setting, 155–7

Hale, R., 39, 51, 52–3, 71, 111, 128
high secure hospital, 33, 117, 121, 148,
  150, 166
Hinshelwood, R.D., 116, 122, 123,
  129, 131
Historical Clinical Risk-20 (HCR-20),
  100–1, 129
holding, 9, 115, 125, 136, 139
holocaust, 92
homicide, 12, 27, 37, 38, 51, 68, 74, 97–8,
  108, 147
Hyatt-Williams, A., 19, 20, 21, 38, 125,
  128, 146
humiliation, 8, 11, 15, 16, 25, 89, 95,
  104, 111

International Classification of Mental
  and Behavioural Disorders, Tenth
  Edition (ICD-10), 29, 43, 57
id, 38, 88, 143
identification, *see* defence mechanisms
ideology, 92, 95
imitation, *see* defence mechanisms
incest, 57
index offence, 23, 33, 53, 106–9, 111, 113,
  119, 132, 146, 148
individuation, 8, 9, 26, 63
infanticide, 74–7, 83
Infanticide Act, 75
instinct, 8–9, 53, 59, 94
institutional dynamics, 116
interpretation, 102, 107, 115, 130, 135,
  136, 138–40, 141–3, 148, 149, 157,
  158, 160, 162, 165
introjection, *see* defence mechanisms

Kernberg, O.F., 9, 30, 42, 45, 46, 49, 85,
  86, 92, 93, 94

Klein, M., 9, 18, 19–20, 21, 35, 87, 88, 89,
  107, 115, 145
Kohut, H., 9, 13, 139

Lacan, J., 61
learned helplessness, 80–1
libido, 62
libidinization, 62
Limentani, A., 10, 17, 128, 129

malignant pseudoidentification, 50
maternal object, 16, 19, 38, 63–5, 67, 70–3,
  82, 88, 89, 133
McDougall, J., 66
medium secure hospital, 121
Meloy, J.R., 12–13, 14, 21, 23, 30, 43, 45–6,
  47, 49, 50, 51, 52, 133
mentalization, 14–16, 17, 19, 24, 25, 31,
  36, 38, 73, 110, 128, 133, 137, 151, 163
mentalization-based treatment
  (MBT), 128
Mental Health Act, 26, 27, 43, 108,
  160, 165
mental illness, 1, 3, 26–39, 53, 74, 95, 97,
  103, 104, 112, 160, 171, 175
Menzies-Lyth, I., 116
Minne, C., 116, 135, 145, 148–9, 176
Money-Kyrle, R., 65–6, 89
Motz, A., 70, 72, 74, 75, 76, 78, 79, 81
mourning, 89, 93, 145–9
Multi Agency Public Protection
  Arrangements (MAPPA), 168–72,
  177
Multi Agency Public Protection Panels
  (MAPPPs), 164, 169
Munchhausen's Syndrome by Proxy
  (MSBP), 77–80, 83
murder, 16, 20, 21, 22, 24, 38–9, 74, 75, 94,
  108, 111, 131, 140, 147, 152

narcissistic exoskeleton, 22
National Health Service (NHS), 10,
  123–4, 125, 169
neurosis, 60, 61

object, role of, 9–10, 11, 16–18, 46–8
object relations, 9, 13, 16, 21–2, 43, 46–8,
  58, 82, 101, 103, 104, 107, 109, 113,
  117, 123, 129, 131–2, 142, 143, 148
Oedipus complex, 19

Oedipal phantasy, 34, 56, 77, 86, 89
oral stage, 59

paedophilia, 57, 152
paranoid schizoid position, 9
'parental couple', 120, 123, 134, 167, 174, 177
pathological organisation, 25
Perelberg, R., 17, 18, 19, 56, 71, 140, 141
personality disorder
  antisocial, 7, 9, 21, 26, 27, 30, 33, 43
  borderline, 7, 21, 29–30, 31, 33, 39, 102–3, 128
  dissocial, 29, 43
  narcissistic, 8, 9, 15, 16–17, 22, 26, 29, 31, 34, 43, 45–7, 49–50, 59, 63, 67, 76, 85, 93, 94, 117
personality organisation, 30, 31, 42, 45, 46, 140
perversion, 5, 7, 11, 12, 56–67, 70, 78, 82, 89, 93, 152, 160
  definition, 57–9
  as a defence, 60–1
  polymorphous, 59–60
perverse motherhood, 72
perverse psychic mechanism, 58
phallic stage, 59
phantasy, 8, 19–20, 22, 23, 24, 38, 46–8, 51, 56, 62, 76, 89, 103, 122, 140, 141, 146
  see also fantasy
Pines, D., 69, 70
pleasure Principle, 49, 59
police, 1, 2, 5, 54, 87, 108, 164, 168, 169, 170, 171, 177
Portman Clinic, 10, 70, 127–8, 161
public protection, 98, 123, 124, 164, 166, 168–72, 177
predatory violence, see violence
pre-oedipal, 16, 19, 36, 43, 46, 47, 48, 49, 56, 63, 65, 67, 71, 121, 153
primal scene, 8, 19, 56
prisons, 2, 21, 26, 27, 32, 33, 36, 41, 47, 48, 50, 77, 79, 82, 90, 91, 99, 106, 108, 112, 114–15, 119, 123–5, 126, 131, 134, 136, 151, 155, 168, 169, 171, 177
privation, 42
probation, 1, 2, 5, 60, 75, 112, 128, 131, 133, 134, 149, 152, 155, 164, 167, 168–71, 173, 177

projection, see defence mechanisms
projective identification, see defence mechanisms
pseudo-mourning, 146
psychic retreat, 89
psychoanalysis, 1, 2, 7, 8, 19, 35, 88, 98, 100, 107, 115, 127, 129, 144
psychoanalytic psychotherapy, see Psychotherapy
psychoanalytic technique, 100, 128, 135, 139, 142, 147
psychological mindedness, 110, 129, 149, 151
psychopathic disorder, 26–7, 43, 53
psychopathy, 3, 13, 26, 39, 41–54
Psychopathy Checklist, Revised (PCL-R), 43–4, 129
psychopathic violence, see Violence
psychopathic breakdown, 52–3
psychotherapy
  assessment, 129–33
  group, 31, 148, 150, 152
  individual, 63, 154, 167, 173
  psychoanalytic, 107, 127–49, 172
psychosexual disorder, 56–7
psychosis, 7–8, 20, 26, 27, 33–9, 42, 46, 61, 62, 70, 75, 76, 97, 115, 135
psychotic (persecutory) anxiety, 9, 15, 21, 33, 37, 49, 52, 53, 55, 130, 133, 135, 137, 142, 143, 170

race, 3, 5, 24, 76, 84–96
racial violence, see violence
racism, 5, 87–96
rage, 9, 10, 15–16, 18, 20, 22, 23, 32, 39, 48, 64, 89, 104, 109, 111, 120, 124, 132, 139, 142, 143, 144, 167–8
reaction formation, see defence mechanisms
reconstruction (or construction), 147, 148
reflective practice, 113, 120, 121–3, 125, 126, 143, 171
reverie, 186
repetition compulsion, 9, 23, 113
repression, see defence mechanisms
risk
  actuarial approach, 99, 110, 113
  assessment, 97–113
  clinical approach, 100–1
  formulation, 110–13

risk – *continued*
    framework, 110–13
    management, 98, 110, 113
    models of, 98–100
    prediction, 98, 99, 110
role responsiveness, 103, 113, 144

sadism, 10, 17, 49, 59, 62, 63, 64, 67, 94
sado-masochistic violence, *see* violence
Sandler, J., 18, 103, 144
schizophrenia, 28, 33–4, 35, 36, 39, 53, 55,
    76, 119
Segal, H., 17, 93, 146
self-harm, 3, 11, 69, 71, 79, 160
self-preservative violence, *see* violence
self-psychology, 13
separation-individuation, 8, 36, 63, 73
setting, 1, 3, 5, 22–4, 30, 36, 60, 112,
    114–25, 128, 134–5, 139, 149, 150,
    152, 155–7, 166, 168, 177
    see also group-analytic therapy, setting
sexuality, 3–4, 24, 56–67, 69, 70, 71, 92,
    159, 163
sexualisation, *see* defence mechanisms
shame, 8, 9, 15, 16, 18, 23, 24, 25, 41, 42,
    48, 60, 68–9, 71, 89, 107, 111, 130,
    141, 165, 174
Shengold, L., 15, 16, 18, 20, 140
simulation, *see* defence mechanisms
socialised violence, *see* violence
Sohn, L., 37, 38, 68, 128
'soul murder', 16, 140
splitting, *see* defence mechanisms
Steiner, J., 21, 89, 138
structural model, 30, 34
Stoller, R.J., 17, 58, 62, 65
sublimation, *see* defence mechanisms
substance misuse, *see* drug abuse
suicide, 3, 11, 38, 94–5, 116, 124, 146,
    160, 161
superego, 9, 11, 16, 18, 24, 25, 36–7, 42,
    48–50, 54, 85, 93, 94, 110–11, 129,
    139, 143, 155

symbolic thinking, 38, 130, 136
symbolisation, 17, 36, 38

terrorism, 84, 92, 93–5, 96
threat/control-override symptoms, 28
treatment alliance, 139
torture, 5, 12, 74, 94
transference, 34–5, 50, 90, 101, 103,
    106–9, 112, 113, 128, 131–3, 136,
    138–44, 146–9, 152, 157–61
transference focused psychotherapy
    (TFP), 128
transitional space, 137
trauma, 7, 9, 13–14, 15–16, 20, 23, 24, 25,
    31, 32, 35, 39, 54, 58, 60, 62, 66, 92–6,
    110, 111, 145
triangulation or third space, 123,
    138, 140

violence
    affective, 12, 19–20
    as communication, 2, 29, 96, 101–2
    definition, 10–11
    domestic, 21, 32, 68, 80–2
    group, 5, 84–7
    psychopathic, 51–2
    racial, 87–93
    sado-masochistic, 11–12, 17, 25, 55, 57,
        63–5, 82, 104, 111, 143–4, 146–7
    self-preservative, 11–13, 17, 19, 29, 53,
        55, 64, 65, 111, 141, 144
    socialised, 92, 94
    voyeurism, 57, 58, 60, 152, 163

war, 18, 92, 96
Welldon, E., 59, 69–72, 82, 128, 151, 152,
    157, 159, 176
Winnicott, D.W., 9, 15, 22, 35, 48,
    115, 137
women
    violent, 68–82
    victims of abuse, 71–3, 80–1
working through, 101, 145–9